P 452

FRANKLYN W. KIRK, B.S.

Manufacturers' Representative
Lecturer in Basic Instrumentation
Technical Institute at
The Cleveland State University
Cleveland, Ohio

Senior Member, Instrument Society of America
Member, Institute of Electrical and Electronic Engineers

NICHOLAS R. RIMBOI, B.S. in E.E., M.A.

Director
Technical Institute at
The Cleveland State University
Cleveland, Ohio

Member, Institute of Electrical and Electronic Engineers
Vice President, American Society for Training and Development
Greater Cleveland Chapter

instrumentation

AMERICAN TECHNICAL SOCIETY

Chicago, Illinois • 60637

Preface

TECHNOLOGICAL progress in the area of scientific and industrial instrumentation has been one of extraordinary advances. The next decade will see an even greater expansion in the dynamic technology of instrumentation. This means an increasing need for trained men to design, make, engineer, and service the instruments that have become so vital a part of the country's industrial growth.

This practical introductory book on instrumentation has been designed to lead the student by carefully planned steps to a familiarity with the latest developments in measurement, control, and analysis instrumentation. The importance of first learning fundamentals, and then becoming familiar with the equipment employing these fundamentals is the basis of our presentation of the subject.

The design of the book follows a fundamental educational principle—that effective learning depends upon three levels of achievement: recognition, comprehension, application. Part One of this book enables the student to recognize the various instruments and the basic principles of how they work. A simple, non-mathematical presentation is given of the variables encountered in instrumentation, with diagrams and photographs to illustrate typical means for their measurement.

Part Two deals with operating principles. Fewer variables are discussed, but in greater detail for complete comprehension, including simple mathematics and circuitry where it is deemed necessary. Part Three acquaints the student with examples of the practical application of instrumentation in industry.

Many instrumentation instructors have at one time or another experienced a loss of general class enthusiasm as the course exhaustively treated each area of instrumentation before going on to the next. The reason for this decline of student interest can be readily explained. Many students are interested only in particular areas of the field. As they are required to first wade through, to them, less interesting areas, students' interests fall off accordingly. This text has been so designed that all of the areas of instrumentation are introduced in Part One, a modern approach which retains general class interest in the whole of the material. When each of the areas is reintroduced later, a review of the related fundamental material in Part One is usually required. These reviews reinforce knowledge gained earlier and are widely regarded as an excellent teaching method.

The organization of this book also permits classes to concentrate on a specific area of instrumentation. The other areas can be excluded with no loss of comprehension. Many classes will be interested in only one area, such as Flow or Pressure Measurement. This is often true of employees being trained by their companies for particular control or maintenance positions. For example, classes can go directly from the chapter on Temperature in Part One to the more advanced material on Temperature in Part Two, skipping the material in between. Thus, this text is adaptable to intensive, short-term courses in addition to being a modern approach to a more academic treatment of the field of instrumentation.

In revising this edition, care was taken to include the latest developments in the continuously expanding field of instrumentation. Part Two of this text has been greatly enlarged to accommodate wider varieties of instruments in use in the field at present. Comments and criticisms from instructors and students across the country were carefully considered and, in many cases, are reflected in the changes made for this, the Second Edition.

FRANKLYN W. KIRK
NICHOLAS R. RIMBOI

Acknowledgments

The authors, publishers, and editors wish to acknowledge their indebtedness to the following organizations that have supplied illustrations or information used in this book:

American Meter Company

Bailey Meter Company

Black, Sivalls, and Bryson, Inc.

The Bristol Company

Brookfield Engineering Laboratories, Inc.

Buffalo Meter Company, Inc.

A. W. Cash Company

Commonwealth Edison Company

Conoflow Corporation

Cox Instruments Company

Decker Corporation

DeVar-Kinetics Division, Consolidated Electrodynamics Corp.

Fischer & Porter Company

Fisher Governor Company

Flow Measurements Corporation

Ford Instrument Company

Ford Motor Company

The Foxboro Company

Gilmore Industries, Inc.

Hagan Controls Corporation

Hallikainen Instruments

Hastings-Raydist, Inc.

Industrial Instruments Corporation

Instruments, Inc.

Instrument Society of America

Leeds & Northrup Company

Mason-Neilan, Division of Worthington Corporation

The Meriam Instrument Company

Minneapolis-Honeywell Regulator Company

Moore Products Company

Norcross Corporation

Ohio Bell Telephone Company

Ohmart Corporation

Penn Instrument Division, Burgess-Manning Company

The Perkins-Elmer Corporation

Potter Aeronautical Company

Precision Scientific Company

Republic Flow Meters Company

Robertson Manufacturing Company

Seegers Manufacturing Company

Simpson Electric Company, Division of American Gage & Machine Co.

Surface Combustion Corporation

Taylor Instrument Companies

Toledo Scale Corporation

Weston Instruments, Inc.

Illustrations on the cover of this book (top to bottom) from: Simpson Electric Co., Div. of American Gage and Machine Co., Bailey Meter Co., Foxboro Co., Commonwealth Edison Co.

Contents

Part Two

Part Three

part one

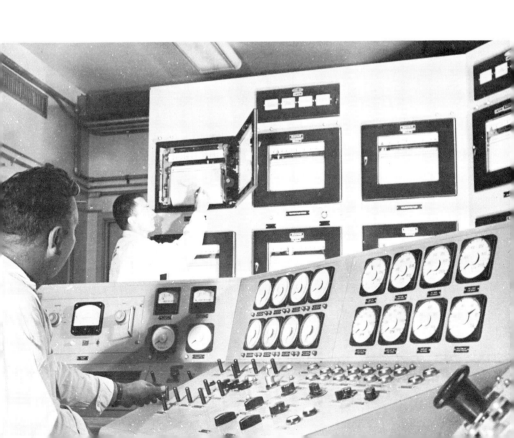

PART ONE deals with instruments for measurement, transmission and control. They are described with emphasis on their external appearance, and their operating principles are for the most part only briefly touched upon. The purpose of this section is to indicate in a general way the wide variety of instruments that are used in modern industrial processes, and to introduce the variables which are measured and controlled by these instruments.

Illustration on previous page: Sodium reactor experiment, an atomic energy power reactor project, is operated from the instrument console. Project, located near Los Angeles, was the first non-military atomic energy reactor to produce power for the generation of electricity by a private utility. (Minneapolis-Honeywell Reg. Co.)

Chapter 1

Introduction

THE advancement of science and technology has been accompanied by a continuous development of instruments for measurement and control. One could not have taken place without the other. Measuring instruments have enabled man to gather information about the world he lives in. Controlling instruments have provided the means to increase the quantity and improve the quality of the necessities of life, and to extend the number of luxuries as well as the time available for their enjoyment.

Measuring and controlling instruments are now in such widespread use in our modern world that we take them for granted. There are instruments to control the temperature in our homes, and instruments to assist in the preservation of our food. Our automobiles are provided with instruments that measure speed, the condition of the battery, the amount of fuel in the tank. Instruments guard our national security, and are used in the weapons systems with which we would defend it. Man-

made satellites are controlled in their flight by instruments, and contain other instruments for probing the mysteries of outer space and transmitting the information gathered.

The progress of industry has always depended on precise, effective and diversified instruments. This book will concentrate mainly on the instruments that serve industry and

Fig. 1. This familiar instrument, a heating control thermostat, includes an indoor thermometer and a regulator which can be set to maintain the room temperature you find comfortable. (Minneapolis-Honeywell Reg. Co.)

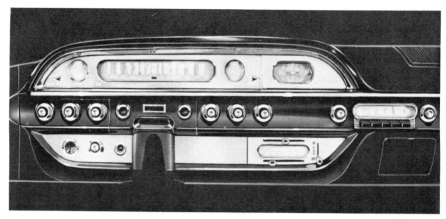

Fig. 2. Every driver knows and depends on these instruments and controls on the dashboard of his car. (Ford Motor Co.)

Fig. 3. A TIROS meteorological satellite launched by a three-stage Thor-Able rocket into a nearly perfect circular orbit to observe and photograph global weather conditions. A Command Guidance System, developed by Bell Telephone Laboratories and produced by Western Electric, was used to direct TIROS into orbit. (Ohio Bell Telephone Co.)

make possible the production miracles of modern manufacturing. It should be noted, however, that the principles of measurement and control do not vary whether the application be commonplace or exciting. Improvement in the methods of measurement in industry led to the development of equipment for making similar measurements in science. These improvements are as continuous as are the demands for them. A much wider use of instruments for measurement and control has become an essential feature of manufacturing process operations.

Industrial Instrumentation

The technology of using instruments to measure and control the physical and chemical properties of materials is called *instrumentation*. When the instruments are used for the measurement and control of industrial manufacturing, conversion, or treating processes, the term *process in-*

Fig. 4. Instrumentation is employed to produce good candy by modern process techniques, assuring uniform quality, reducing waste, and cutting operating costs. Temperature is automatically regulated by Recording Pneumatic Control Thermometers which operate diaphragm control valves in steam lines. (Minneapolis-Honeywell Reg. Co.)

strumentation is applied. And when the measuring and controlling instruments are combined so that measurements provide impulses for remote automatic action, the result is called a *control system*.

It isn't always possible to measure or control the properties of a material directly by instruments. This makes it necessary to deal with *variables* that affect these properties, such as temperature, pressure, flow, level, humidity, density, viscosity, and so on. The variable that is the object of measurement or control is called the *measured* or *controlled variable*. The variable that affects the

value of the measured or controlled variable is called the *manipulated variable*.

Some of the measured variables in a control system are not measurements of the physical or chemical properties of the material being processed. The measurement and control of such variables, however, is essential to the automatic process. Consider, for instance, flow measurement.

The rate at which a substance flows can be an indication of its temperature, density, or viscosity. More often, however, flow measurement and control are required to establish the rate

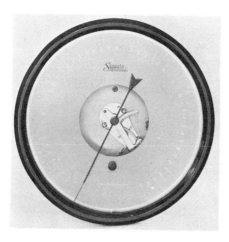

Fig. 5. A typical indicating instrument, in this case a pressure gage, with its scale calibrated in units of the variable which it is designed to measure. (Seegers Mfg. Co.)

at which a substance is subjected to the various process changes. And frequently it isn't the rate of flow of the process substance itself that is measured or controlled, but another substance that supplies or removes energy from the process. The control of the rate of flow of a substance used as a heating or cooling medium in a thermal process is a typical and common example.

Another example concerns level measurement and control. Measuring the level of a granular substance in a container can provide information about the size of the substance's particles; but more often the level of a substance is measured and controlled to insure the continuous nature of the process, since level is a measure of the amount available. And again it may not be the process substance itself that is measured, but another

substance that is necessary for the treatment of the process substance.

A control system, then, involves more than just the measurement and control of the characteristics of the substance being processed. The conditions embodied in the process must also be measured and controlled. In addition, the information about the measurements must be continuously available, and the performance of the control devices continuously monitored. The measurements can be observed on indicating instruments or recorded continuously. The performance of the control devices can be monitored through the use of visual and audible alarm signals.

Indicating instruments have one feature in common—a scale calibrated in units of the measured variable. The scale can be linear or circular, large or small; but the dermining factor is that it must be able to indicate the smallest detectable value of the measured variable. Usually a scale is laid out so that the final digit of the value of the measured variable is read by estimating the position of the indicator between two adjacent divisions.

Recorders and Monitors

Continuous recorders can have circular charts or strip charts (Fig. 6). They can be either entirely mechanical or entirely electrical, or a combination of both. There are two sets of units shown on most recording charts—one for the value of the measured variable, the other for time. This permits a study of the changes of

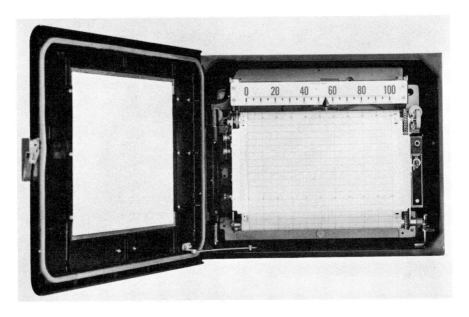

Fig. 6. A strip chart continuous recorder. (Bristol Co.)

the measured variable for any given period of time. Some recording instruments are limited to one measured variable; others accommodate many records. Instruments that trace the changes of one measured variable are called single point recorders. The trace on the charts of such instruments is usually in the form of a single continuous line (Fig. 7). On multiple point recorders there may be several continuous lines, especially when only a few variables are being recorded. Recording a greater number of variables on one chart requires a code of some sort (such as the use of colors or numbers) as shown in Fig. 8. The value of each variable is recorded at intervals. The interval between each record is dependent upon the operating speed of

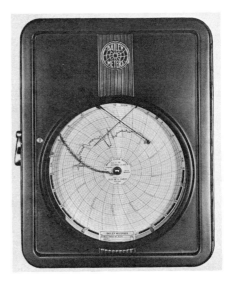

Fig. 7. In contrast to the strip chart recorder illustrated in Fig. 6, this single point recorder uses a circular chart, which has the advantage of being cheaper and easier to store. (Bailey Meter Co.)

Fig. 8. A multiple point recorder, which uses differently colored inks to trace the four variables that are being recorded on this chart. (Bailey Meter Co.)

the recorder. To obtain a trace of the changes of any one variable on this type of recording instrument, the coded marks for each variable must be checked.

Mechanical recorders most often draw continuous lines. The pen is positioned by a mechanical linkage, and the chart is driven by a spring wound clock. In a combination recorder the chart may be driven by an electric clock.

Electric recorders can draw continuous lines, or print coded marks. The continuous line can be drawn by a pen on paper, or by a stylus on carbon-coated film, or by a heated stylus on heat sensitive paper. The printed code type usually has an inked print wheel which makes a mark on a paper chart. The print wheel mechanism is positioned on the chart by an electric motor which receives its impulse from the measuring circuit. The chart is driven by a constant speed motor. Spring wound chart drives are also available for this kind of recorder.

The monitoring of control devices is accomplished through the use of alarm signals. These signals can be attached to the control device to monitor its action directly or attached to the measuring device to indicate when the controlling device has not had the desired effect on the controlled variable.

Panel Boards

Indicating and recording devices can be mounted on the plant equipment at the points of measurement and control. This is termed local mounting. They can also be centralized on a panel board. There are several kinds of panel boards in use —graphic, semi-graphic, and non-graphic. The graphic panel is a symbolic representation of the entire process system. The instruments are mounted on the panel in accordance with their locations in the system (Fig. 9). Special small size indicators and recorders have been developed for graphic panels.

On the semi-graphic panel, the process system layout is shown in miniature graphic form on a small section of the panel. The instruments are identified on this graphic section by code numbers (Fig. 10). Large size instruments, marked by the identifying code numbers, constitute the

Fig. 9. A graphic panel on which the instruments are mounted in accordance with their position in the system. (Tidewater Oil Co.)

remainder of the panel board.

On non-graphic panels no attempt is made to duplicate the process layout. Large size instruments are mounted on the board and their place in the process is described on nameplates.

Recently there has been a trend toward centralized recording of all variables on one information sheet

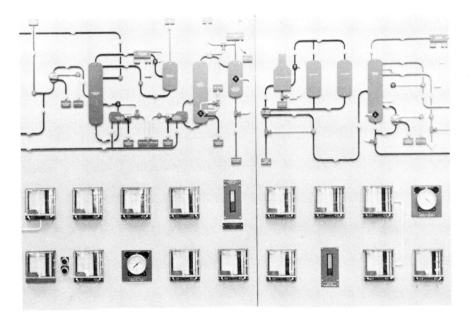

Fig. 10. A semi-graphic panel.

using digital printout. Digital printout simply means that the value of each variable appears on a chart in actual numbers instead of as a line or a coded symbol on a calibrated chart. Such a system makes it possible to combine the indicating, measuring, and control monitoring functions. It also permits the application of computers to the control system.

In actual industrial practice all types of indicating, recording, controlling, and monitoring devices are found singly or in combination. This variety does not affect the fundamentals of measurement and control. It is the primary task of the instrument technician to understand the fundamentals and to select the devices whose application is best adapted to the process.

General Characteristics of Instruments

Before proceeding to examine some of the variables encountered in industrial processes and some of the instruments used, the student should become acquainted with the general characteristics of instruments. These characteristics, which are the abilities an instrument must possess if it is to be useful, are divided into *static characteristics* and *dynamic characteristics*. The static characteristics occur in systems in which *the variables are not changing*. The dynamic characteristics occur in systems in which *the variables are changing*.

Static Characteristics

The static characteristics of instruments are:

Accuracy
Reproducibility
Sensitivity

Accuracy. In a measuring instrument, accuracy is the instrument's ability to indicate or record the true value of the variable being measured. The difference between the true value and the actual instrument reading is the *static error*. Accuracy is expressed as a percentage of the total amount of units on the instrument's scale.

In a controlling instrument, accuracy is the instrument's ability to establish the desired value of the variable being controlled. The difference between the desired value and the actual value established by the controlling instrument represents the static error of the instrument. Accuracy is expressed in terms of the limits within which the value of the variable will be held by the instrument.

Reproducibility. In a measuring instrument, reproducibility is the degree of closeness with which the instrument indicates or records identical values of the variable when the conditions are repeated. *Drift* is the gradual shift in the indication or record of the instrument over an extended period of time, during which the true value of the variable does not change.

In a controlling instrument, reproducibility is the ability of the instrument to repeat an output signal for the same input signal. Drift is the gradual shift in the value of the output signal over an extended period of time, during which the input signal remains unchanged.

Sensitivity. In a measuring instrument, sensitivity is the smallest change in the value of the variable being measured to which the instrument will respond. The *dead zone* is the range of values of the variable within which the measuring instrument does not respond.

In a controlling instrument, sensitivity is the smallest change in the input signal that will cause a change in the instrument's output signal. The dead zone is the range of changes of the input signal that does not result in a change in the instrument's output signal.

Dynamic Characteristics

The dynamic characteristics of instruments are:

Responsiveness
Fidelity

Responsiveness. In a measuring instrument, responsiveness is the instrument's ability to follow changes in the value of the variable being measured. *Measuring lag* is the instrument's slowness in response to a change in the variable. *Dead time* is the period during which the instrument does not respond to a change in the value of the variable.

In a controlling instrument, responsiveness is the instrument's ability to produce a changing output signal as the input signal changes. *Controller lag* is the slowness with which the instrument responds to a change in the input signal. Dead time is the period during which the instrument does not respond to a change in the input signal.

Fidelity. In a measuring instrument, fidelity is the degree of closeness with which the instrument indicates or records a changing value of the variable. The difference between the changing value and the actual instrument reading is the dynamic error.

In a controlling instrument, fidelity is the degree of correctness with which the instrument's output signal follows changes in the input signal. The difference between the instrument's changing output signal and the changing input signal is the dynamic error.

Chapter 2

Temperature

THE most important of the measured variables encountered in industrial processes is temperature. This is because there are changes in the physical or chemical state of most substances when they are heated or cooled.

Temperature is defined as "the degree of hotness or coldness measured on a definite scale." Hotness and coldness are the result of molecular activity—the faster the molecules of a substance move, the more heat it contains. Heat then, is a form of energy, and is measured in calories or BTU's (British Thermal Units). When two substances possessing different quantities of heat come into contact with one another, there is a flow of heat. This flow is away from the substance containing more heat and toward the one containing less.

Heat Transfer

There are three ways by which the flow of heat is transferred:

Conduction. Heat applied to one part of a substance is transferred to all parts of the substance. Conduction takes place only in solids. (Fig. 1)

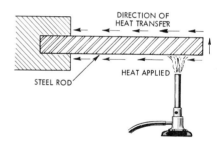

Fig. 1. In conduction, the heat is transferred through solids from molecule to molecule.

Radiation. Heat is transferred in the form of rays sent out by the molecules of a heated substance as they undergo internal change. Radiation takes place in any medium, or in a vacuum. (Fig. 2)

The direction of the flow of heat is determined by the heat level or temperature of the substance.

Convection. Heat is transferred by the movement of heated particles.

Fig. 2. In radiation, the heat is transferred by means of rays.

WATER HEATED BY CONVECTION CURRENTS

Fig. 3. In convection, the heat is transferred by moving particles of matter.

Convection takes place only in fluids, either liquid or gas. (Fig. 3)

Temperature Scales

The comparison of the heat content of one substance with another is made by reference to temperature scales. These scales also make it possible to measure and identify the heat level when there is a change in the state or condition of the substance, such as freezing, melting, or decomposition.

The instrument used to measure temperature is the *thermometer*. The temperature scales most commonly

used in calibrating thermometers are the Fahrenheit scale and the Centigrade scale. The difference between these two scales concerns their fixed points. On both scales the freezing temperature of water and the boiling temperature of water are used as fixed points. On the Fahrenheit scale the freezing temperature is set at 32°F and the boiling temperature at 212°F with 180 degrees between the fixed points. On the Centigrade scale the freezing temperature is set at 0°C and the boiling temperature at 100°C with 100 degrees between the fixed points. See Fig. 4.

Theoretically, there is a condition of no molecular motion, hence no heat. The temperature at this point is *absolute zero temperature*—the lowest temperature possible. There are two scales that have their zero points at this absolute zero level: the Kelvin scale and the Rankine scale. Fig. 5.

On the Kelvin scale the freezing point of water is at + 273°K and the boiling point at + 373°K with 100

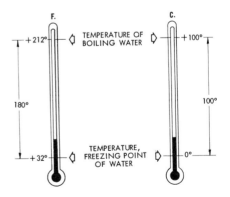

Fig. 4. On both the Fahrenheit and centigrade scales the boiling point and freezing point of water are used as fixed points.

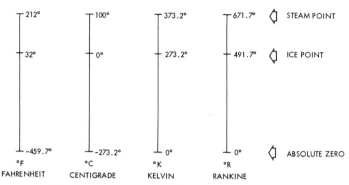

Fig. 5. Absolute zero is the temperature at which the particles whose motion constitutes heat cease to move and on the Kelvin and Rankine scales is hypothetically placed at —273.2°C or —459.7°F.

degrees between the fixed points, just as on the centigrade scale. The Kelvin scale is sometimes referred to as the *absolute centigrade scale.*

On the Rankine scale the freezing point of water is at + 491°R and the boiling point at + 671°R with 180 degrees between the fixed points, just as on the Fahrenheit scale. The Rankine scale is sometimes referred to as the *absolute Fahrenheit scale.*

The absolute scales are important because they are so often used in scientific and technical literature. The Kelvin scale is used in the study of physical chemistry. The Rankine scale is used in formulas for flow metering.

It is often necessary to convert temperature readings from one scale to another. Temperatures as read on the Fahrenheit thermometer can be converted to centigrade values by the following formula:

$$°C = \frac{100}{180} \, (°F - 32°), \text{ or}$$
$$°C = 5/9 \, (°F - 32°).$$

Centigrade readings can be converted to Fahrenheit thus:

$$°F = \left(\frac{180}{100}\right) °C + 32°, \text{ or}$$
$$°F = 9/5 \, °C + 32°$$

Examples:

Change 77°F to degrees centigrade
$$°C = 5/9 \, (77° - 32°)$$
$$°C = 5/9 \times 45°$$
$$°C = 25°C$$

Change 0°C to degrees Fahrenheit
$$°F = 9/5 \, °C + 32°$$
$$°F = 9/5 \times 0° + 32°$$
$$°F = 32°F$$

Centigrade readings can be converted to Kelvin by the formula:
$$°C = °K - 273°$$

Example:

Change 100°C to °K
$$100°C = °K - 273°$$
$$°K = 273° + 100°$$
$$°K = 373°K$$

Fahrenheit readings can be converted to Rankine by the formula:
$$°F = °R - 459.7$$

Example:
Change 212°F to °R
212°F = °R − 459.7°
°R = 459.7° + 212°
°R = 671.7°R

In industrial and scientific applications it is frequently necessary to measure and control temperatures much higher than the boiling point of water and lower than the freezing point of water. To calibrate thermometers for such temperatures other fixed points have been established. *Those recommended by the National Bureau of Standards, and known as the International Temperatures Scale, include:

Boiling Point of Oxygen −297°F
Solid-Vapor Point of
  Carbon Dioxide −109°F
Freezing Point of Mercury −38°F
Freezing Point of liquid
  Tin +449°F
Freezing Point of liquid
  Cadmium +610°F
Freezing Point of liquid
  Zinc +787°F
Boiling Point of liquid
  Sulfur +838°F
Freezing Point of liquid
  Antimony +1167°F

THERMOMETERS

Mercury-in-Glass Thermometers

The dimensions of all substances change a definite amount for every degree of temperature change. This

* The temperatures are measured with a standard platinum resistance thermometer. The apparatus and methods necessary for properly calibrating thermometers are completely described by the National Bureau of Standards in their Research Journal 42,209 of March, 1949.

is the principle of thermal expansion. In the mercury-in-glass thermometer the mercury expands more than the glass bulb containing it when heat is applied to the bulb. Because of this, the mercury is forced to rise up the small bore column of the tube, and thus indicates the temperature on the scale.

Mercury is not the only fluid used in glass thermometers; other fluids such as alcohol or toluol are also used, either to allow the thermometer to be used to measure temperatures below the freezing point of mercury (approximately −40°F), or to make the thermometer easier to read. With the right kind of fluid, glass thermometers can be used for measuring temperatures from −300°F to +1200°F.

The scale can be etched directly on the glass tube or it can be engraved on metal to which the glass tube is attached. Floating glass thermometers are also available — both the tube and the scale are enclosed in a glass envelope, which is formed and weighted so that the thermometer floats in an upright position. See Fig. 6.

Bimetallic Thermometers

The operation of bimetallic thermometers is based on the principle of the difference in the coefficients of thermal expansion of different metals. See Fig. 7. Two metallic alloys, having different physical characteristics, are fused together, and formed into a spiral or helix. When the bi-

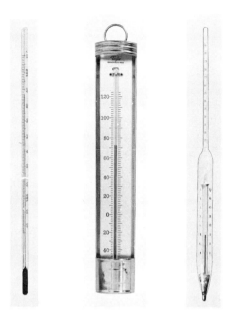

Fig. 6. Either Fahrenheit or centigrade scales can be etched directly on glass (left), engraved on metal to which the thermometer is attached (center), or both thermometer and scale can be enclosed in a glass envelope to form an instrument that will float (right). (Taylor Instrument Companies)

metallic helix is heated, the difference in the thermal expansion of the alloys causes it to unwind, moving the pointer attached to it. See Fig. 8.

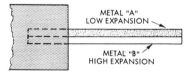

Bimetallic thermometers are available for industrial and laboratory use. The industrial type is somewhat heavier in construction, which entails a slight sacrifice in accuracy and speed of response. Temperatures from $-300°F$ to $+800°F$ can be measured by bimetallic thermometers. They can also be used to measure temperatures as high as $+1000°F$, but not continuously, since the helical element tends to overstretch at this temperature.

Pressure-Spring Thermometers

Both the mercury-in-glass and the

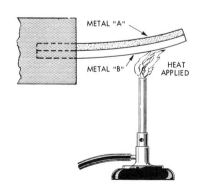

Fig. 7. The bimetallic strip depends on the different rates of expansion of metals on heating.

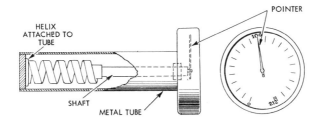

Fig. 8. When heated, this helical bimetallic strip unwinds and moves the pointer on the scale.

bimetallic thermometers provide local readings. But it is often necessary to detect a temperature at one point and read it at a remote point. For this reason the pressure-spring thermometer was developed. This kind of thermometer can be used for continuous recording of temperature and also as the measuring element in control instruments.

The principal component of pressure-spring thermometers is of course the pressure-spring itself. This is a hollow spring that can be made in the C-shape of the original Bourdon tube (Fig. 9), but is more often used in the form of a spiral (Fig. 10), or helix (Fig. 11).

One end of capillary (small bore) tubing is attached to the pressure spring. Joined to the other end of the tubing is a sensing bulb, which is the part of the thermometer that makes contact with the substance whose temperature is to be measured. When these three components—spring, tubing, and bulb—are filled with a suitable fluid, they form a measuring unit in just the same way as the glass tube, the mercury, and the bulb of the glass thermometer do.

The several types of pressure-

Fig. 9. C-shaped Bourdon tube. (Bailey Meter Co.)

Fig. 10. Spiral Bourdon tube. (Bailey Meter Co.)

Fig. 11. Helical Bourdon tube. (Bailey Meter Co.)

spring thermometers are classified by the kind of filling fluid used. Mercury is most often used in the liquid-filled types (Fig. 12), which are satisfactory for measuring temperatures from $-300°F$ to $+1000°F$. Nitrogen is most commonly used in the gas-filled types, which can measure temperatures from −450°F to +1000°F. A combination of liquid and vapor is also used as a filling fluid (Fig. 13). This type of pressure-spring thermometer differs from the liquid-filled and gas-filled types in that vapor does not expand uniformly as liquid and gas do. The result is that vapor-actuated thermometers do not satisfy a uniform scale. Instead, the divisions of the scale are spaced so that they are wider apart at the higher readings than at the lower

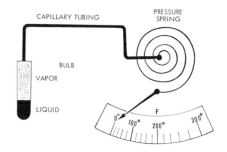

Fig. 13. When a liquid-vapor combination is used in a pressure-spring thermometer, the vapor does not expand uniformly as liquid and gas do.

may have a very short system, with the bulb attached to the recorder case (Fig. 15), or it may have long tube systems for remote readings (Fig. 16).

Thermocouples

The simplest electrical temperature-sensitive device is the *thermocouple*. It consists basically of a pair

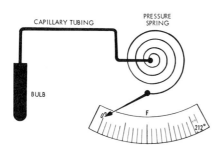

Fig. 12. As the temperature rises, the liquid in the bulb of the pressure-spring thermometer expands and increases the pressure in the spring, causing it to straighten somewhat and move the pointer on the scale.

readings. Vapor-filled thermometers can measure temperatures from −300°F to +600°F.

When the pressure-spring thermometer is used as an indicator, it may be of the simple dial type with a 270° scale (Fig. 14), or the rectangular case type with a 90° scale. Used as a recorder, the thermometer

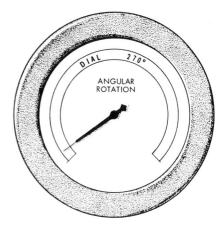

Fig. 14. Dials of pressure-spring thermometers can be graduated so that the pointer moves through 270 degrees.

Fig. 15. Pressure-spring thermometer used as a recorder with bulb attached to the recording case. (Bristol Co.)

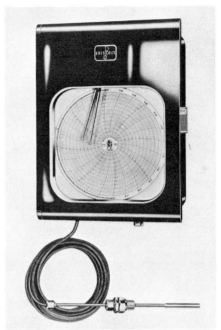

Fig. 16. Pressure-spring thermometer with long tube system for remote reading. (Bristol Co.)

of wires composed of different metals. These wires are joined at one end, and the other ends are connected to an appropriate *meter* or *circuit*. When the joined ends (the hot junction) are heated, a measurable voltage is generated across the other ends of the wires (the cold junction). With proper selection of the wires, the voltage varies in relation to the temperature being measured (Fig. 17).

The most common thermocouple wires are combinations of Iron-constantan, Copper-constantan, "Chromel"-"Alumel," and Platinum/rhodium-platinum. The characteristics and ranges of these wire combinations is shown in the Table.

TABLE OF THERMOCOUPLE RANGES

Type of Thermocouple	Useful Temperature Ranges (°F)
Iron-Constantan	0° to 1400°F
Chromel-Alumel	500° to 2300°F
Platinum/Rhodium-Platinum	1000° to 2700°F
Copper-Constantan	−300° to +700°F

The notation left of the hyphen in the nomenclatures of the types of thermocouples indicates the positive wire, right of the hyphen is the negative wire.

The *meter* used with the thermocouple is called a *millivoltmeter*—a

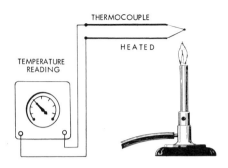

Fig. 18. The current indicated by the millivoltmeter is read in degrees of temperature. (Bristol Co.)

Fig. 17. When heat is applied to one junction of the thermocouple while the other junction is maintained at a constant known temperature, the difference in temperature of the two junctions causes the meter to indicate a very small current.

permanent-magnet moving-coil instrument that is sensitive to extremely small changes in electrical voltage (1 millivolt equals 1/1000th of a volt). For each voltage value, the moving coil takes a different position. A pointer is attached to the moving coil, and the position of the pointer is noted on a scale marked in voltage units. So when the millivoltmeter is connected to the thermocouple, it doesn't actually measure temperature — it measures voltage. But since there is a definite relationship between the voltage generated by the thermocouple and the amount of heat detected by it, the scale of the meter can be graduated in units of temperature. See Fig. 18.

The *circuit* used with the thermocouple is called a *potentiometer* circuit. At its simplest, it consists of a battery, a slidewire, the thermocouple, a standard cell, and a galvanometer. See Fig. 19. Part of the battery voltage is compared with the thermocouple voltage. Any difference in these voltages causes the galvanometer to deflect. The battery voltage is adjusted to a proper value by comparing it with a standard cell, which has a fixed voltage at all times. A sliding contact (or slider) moving along the slidewire can change the battery voltage to a value equal and opposite to that of the thermocouple, thus returning the galvanometer to its balance position. No current then flows through the galvanometer: this condition is called null balance. The

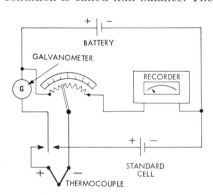

Fig. 19. Standard potentiometer circuit with battery, galvanometer, slidewire, standard cell, and thermocouple. The movement of the slider in the slidewire is used to adjust the working current from the battery so that the galvanometer reads zero.

indicating pointer is attached to the slider and its position is measured on a scale graduated in units of temperature.

Resistance Thermometers

The operation of the resistance thermometer also depends on an electrical circuit. In this instrument the heat-sensitive element consists of a carefully made electrical resistor. Platinum, nickel, or copper wire, wrapped around an insulator, are most often used for the resistance wire of the element. See Fig. 20. When subjected to heat, the resistance of the wire increases. The element is connected into a bridge circuit in which its resistance is compared with that of a fixed resistance. The resistance thermometer does not generate its own voltage. A battery must be incorporated into the circuit as a source of voltage.

A millivoltmeter can be used to measure change of value in one of the resistances in a Wheatstone bridge circuit. The Wheatstone bridge is often described schematically as a diamond shaped circuit (Fig. 21). The battery is connected to two opposite points of the diamond, the meter to the other opposite points. A rheostat regulates the overall bridge current.

The regulated current is divided between the branch containing the fixed resistor and range resistor No. 1, and the branch containing the resistance thermometer and range resistor No. 2. The millivoltmeter senses the difference in voltage caused by unequal division of current in the two branches. The range resistors establish the sensitivity of the bridge. The meter can be calibrated in temperature units because the only changing resistance value is that of the resistance thermometer due to temperature change.

Another arrangement (Fig. 22), has the resistance temperature detector in a bridge circuit and uses a galvanometer to compare the resistance of the detector with that of a fixed resistor. A slider-slidewire combination is used to balance the arms of the bridge. The circuit is in balance whenever the value of the slidewire resistance is such that no current flows through the galvanometer. For each temperature change detected by the resistance thermometer

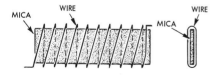

Fig. 20. Platinum, nickel, or copper wire is wrapped around the mica insulator of a resistance thermometer. As the temperature rises, the resistance of the wire increases, and this increased resistance is expressed in degrees of temperature.

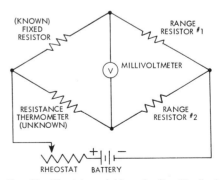

Fig. 21. Wheatstone bridge circuit with fixed resistors and millivoltmeter.

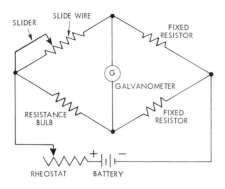

Fig. 22. Wheatstone bridge circuit with slidewire (variable resistor) and galvanometer.

there is a new value — and so the slider must take a new position to balance the circuit.

Recently the null-balance type of instrument has been modified to eliminate the galvanometer, which is somewhat slow and delicate. An electronic instrument has been developed in which the dc voltage of the potentiometer or the Wheatstone bridge is converted to an ac voltage by means of a chopper. The ac voltage is amplified in an electronic unit, and the stronger signal is then used to drive a two-directional motor that positions the slider on the slidewire to balance the circuit. See Fig. 23.

Pyrometers

Many special thermometers are required for industrial processes. The temperature of molten steel, for example, couldn't be measured by a mercury thermometer — the glass would melt and the mercury boil away. What is needed in such a case

is a thermometer whose sensing element does not make direct physical contact with the hot substance whose temperature is to be determined. When the temperatures being measured are higher than those which can be measured by a mercury thermometer the instrument used is called a *pyrometer*. The following

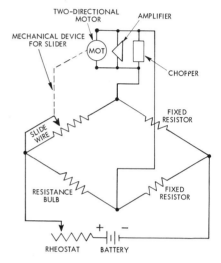

Fig. 23. Electronic automatic self-balancing Wheatstone bridge which eliminates the galvanometer.

instruments can be used only for higher temperatures, therefore they are exclusively pyrometers.

The radiation pyrometer (Fig. 24) "picks up" the radiant heat by means of a lens and focuses the heat waves on a vacuum tube containing a thermocouple. The potentiometer is most often used with the radiation pyrometer, and it operates just as it does when connected to a thermocouple that makes direct contact with a hot substance.

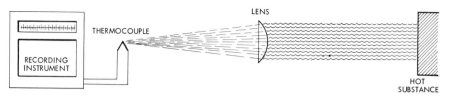

Fig. 24. In radiation pyrometry the radiant heat or energy from the hot substance is translated into emf by the thermocouple and indicated in degrees of temperature.

The optical pyrometer (Fig. 25) is another device for measuring high temperatures. It also uses a lens to pick up the radiant heat waves. The brightness of the hot substance is matched to the brightness of an in- resistor. The amount of adjustment needed to match the two sources of light is a measure of the tempera- ture. The position of the resistor is indicated on a dial graduated in units of temperature. When the re-

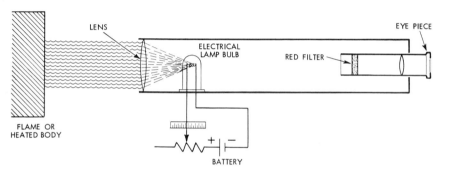

Fig. 25. In optical pyrometry the brightness of the lamp bulb is adjusted to match the brightness of the hot substance.

candescent lamp bulb. The compari- son is made by eye, and the bright- ness of the lamp bulb is manually adjusted by manipulating a variable sistor has been positioned so that the light sources are equal in bright- ness, the temperature can then be read directly on the dial.

Chapter 3 _____ Pressure

PROOF of the importance of this variable can be found in the great variety of instruments that are required to measure and control the exceedingly wide range of pressures encountered in industrial processes.

Pressure is defined as force divided by area. The force of the pull of gravity on an object resting on an area of the earth's surface is its weight. If an object weighs 100 pounds and rests on one square inch of the earth's surface, it is exerting a pressure of 100 pounds per square inch on the earth. See Fig. 1. All objects on earth have weight and therefore exert a pressure on the earth that can be expressed in a unit of weight per unit of area (pounds per square inch).

A column of liquid exerts a pressure on the earth just as a solid object does. For instance, a column of water 34½ feet high exerts a pressure of 15 pounds per square inch. See Fig. 2. It is possible, then, to express pressure in inches or feet of a particular liquid. Inches-of-mercury and inches-of-water are the common units of pressure measurement. One

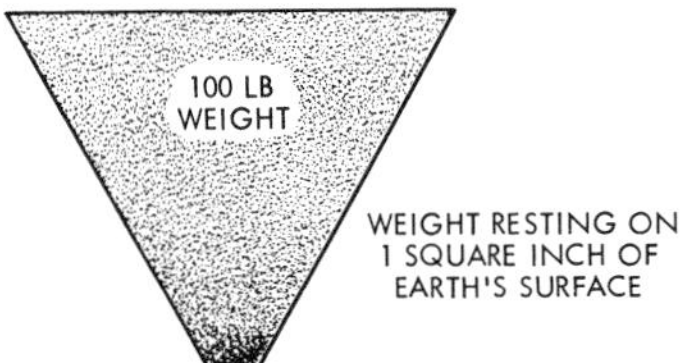

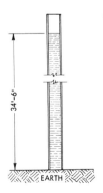

Fig. 1. An object weighing 100 pounds resting on one square inch of the earth's surface exerts a pressure of 100 pounds per square inch.

Fig. 2. A column of water 34½ feet high resting on one square inch of the earth's surface exerts a pressure of 15 pounds per square inch.

24

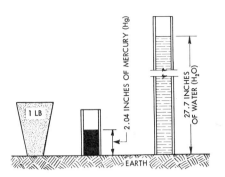

Fig. 3. The one pound weight, the 2.04 inches-of-mercury, and the 27.7 inches-of-water all exert a pressure of one pound per square inch.

mark appears in the center. See Fig. 5. The manometric fluid (water or mercury are the most widely used fluids) is poured into the tube until the level in both columns reaches the zero mark. With both columns open to the atmosphere the level of the fluid will remain at zero. When a pressure line

pound per square inch of pressure equals 2.04 inches-of-mercury or 27.7 inches-of-water. See Fig. 3.

Manometers

The simplest device for measuring pressure is the *manometer* (Fig. 4), and the simplest form of the manometer is the U-tube. This consists of a glass tube shaped like the letter U and a scale marked in inches and tenths of inches. On the scale the zero

Fig. 4. The scale of this simple U-tube manometer is marked in tenths of inches.

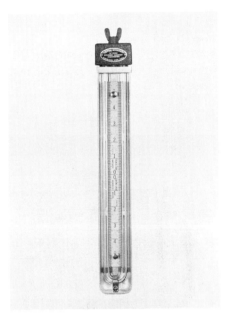

Fig. 5. Note that the zero mark of this typical industrial manometer is at the center of the scale. (Meriam Instrument Co.)

is connected to one column of the manometer, the fluid in that column will be forced down, while the fluid in the other column will rise. By measuring the difference in the height of the fluid in the two columns, the pressure of the inlet line can be expressed in inches of fluid. For example, say the manometric fluid is mercury (Fig. 6), and a pressure line is connected to the manom-

eter causing the mercury to be lowered one inch in one column and
raised one inch in the other. Then
the pressure in the inlet line is expressed as two inches-of-mercury, or
0.98 pounds per square inch.

With water as the manometric
fluid (Fig. 7), the same pressure
would cause the water to be lowered 13.58 inches in one column and
raised 13.58 inches in the other column. The pressure could then be
expressed as equal to 27.16 inches-
of-water.

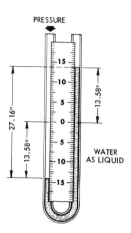

Fig. 7. The same inlet pressure as in Fig. 6 is
now expressed as 27.16 inches-of-water

voir. This design permits the pressure
to be measured by referring to the
rise of the fluid in the vertical tube.
See Fig. 9.

The manometer is termed a *primary standard* because it detects
pressure and indicates it directly on
a scale calibrated in actual units of
pressure.

Pressure Elements

There is a whole series of mechani-

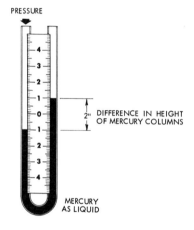

Fig. 6. Because the difference in height of the
mercury columns is two inches, the pressure at
the inlet is expressed as two inches-of-mercury.

Two other types of manometers
are:

1. The inclined-tube type, in which
the measuring column of the manometer is at an angle to the vertical
(Fig. 8). This serves to extend the
scale of the instrument.

2. The well type, in which one of
the columns is actually a large reser-

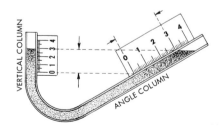

Fig. 8. Note how the scale of the inclined-tube
manometer is extended to conform with the scale
of the vertical column.

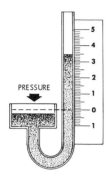

Fig. 9. A direct reading can be taken from the vertical scale of the well-type manometer.

cal devices that change shape when pressure is applied. These are called *elastic deformation pressure elements.* See Fig. 10. Each of them is adapted to a different range of pressures. The table on the following page lists these pressure elements, with their lower and upper limits

expressed in inches-of-water or in pounds per square inch.

Fig. 11 shows a typical industrial pressure gage with a Bourdon tube pressure element. The pressure enters the Bourdon tube, causing it to unwind. As the tip of the Bourdon tube unwinds, it moves a lever arm, which is connected by gears to the pointer. A spiral spring is connected to the pointer to eliminate any "play" in the linkage.

Recording pressure gages are frequently used in industry (Fig. 12). Generally, they use elastic deformation elements, with the spiral and helix being most common.

In recent years it has become necessary to develop pressure measuring instruments that provide an electrical output. In some of these, the

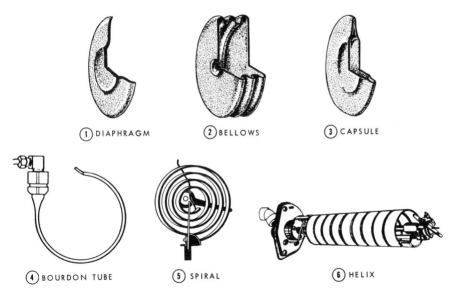

① DIAPHRAGM   ② BELLOWS   ③ CAPSULE

④ BOURDON TUBE   ⑤ SPIRAL   ⑥ HELIX

Fig. 10. Elastic deformation elements.

Table of Pressure Elements

	Minimum Range	Maximum Range
Diaphragm	0" to 2" H_2O	0 to 400 psi
Bellows	0" to 5" H_2O	0 to 800 psi
Capsule	0" to 1" H_2O	0 to 50 psi
Bourdon tube	0 to 12 psi	0 to 100,000 psi
Spiral	0 to 15 psi	0 to 4,000 psi
Helix	0 to 50 psi	0 to 10,000 psi

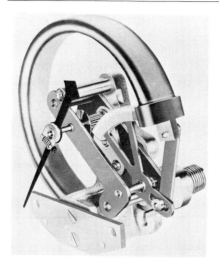

Fig. 11. This typical industrial pressure gage uses a Bourdon tube to actuate the pointer. (Bailey Meter Co.)

in bridge type circuits similar to those used for the resistance thermometer. Fig. 13 shows a typical electrical pressure measuring device.

Differential Pressure

Frequently, instead of measuring just one pressure, it is important to measure the difference between two pressures. This is called differential pressure measurement.

elastic deformation elements listed above are used, and electrical devices are attached to them. As the element expands or contracts, an electrical characteristic, such as resistance, is made to vary. For each unit of change in shape of the pressure element, there must be a unit change of the electrical variable. This conversion of one form of energy into another is produced by a device called a *transducer*. Most of these electrical transducers are used

Fig. 12. Pressure exerted on the elastic deformation element of this typical industrial recording pressure gage causes the pen to move. (Bailey Meter Co.)

Fig. 13. The Bourdon tube of this electrical pressure gage is attached to the transducer (upper right of instrument). (Bailey Meter Co.)

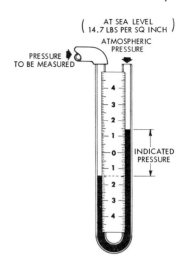

Fig. 14. In single pressure measurement, one column of the U-tube is open to atmospheric pressure.

Differential pressure measurement isn't unlike single pressure measurement. The same instruments are often used. The U-tube manometer is again the simplest. In single pressure measurement one column of the U-tube is left open to the atmosphere, with the result that the indicated pressure is the difference between the atmospheric and measured pressure (Fig. 14). If both columns of the manometer are connected to separate pressures, the indicated pressure is then the difference between them (Fig. 15).

The well-type manometer (Fig. 16) is used for differential pressure measurement, especially if recording is required. In this type of instrument the manometer is made of metal and is attached to, or enclosed in, the instrument case. Instead of reading the height of the liquid in

the column, the movement of a float in the well is used to drive the indicating pointer or recording pen. It's

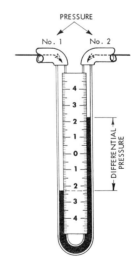

Fig. 15. In differential pressure measurement, the difference between two working pressures is indicated.

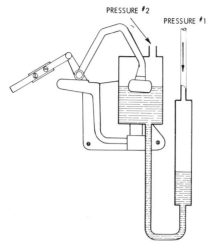

PRESSURE #2

PRESSURE #1

Fig. 16. The difference in pressures in the well-type manometer causes the float to move, and by means of linkage this movement drives the pointer or recording pen. (Bailey Meter Co.)

necessary, therefore, to transfer this float motion inside the manometer to linkage outside, without letting the manometric fluid leak out. The mechanism should be as friction free as possible. Manufacturers have developed several methods of doing this, involving special bearings, torque tubes, or magnetic followers. The float motion is slight so that, whatever the method used, precision manufacture is a necessity for accuracy and sensitivity.

Another kind of differential pressure measuring unit is the bellows type (Fig. 17). In this instrument a pair of matched bellows is used. Any pressure unbalance causes one bellows to become more deformed than the other, thus producing motion in the common shaft. The bellows may be liquid filled to permit hydraulic

damping and to prevent bellows damage if too much pressure is applied to one side.

As with the manometer float, a pressure bearing or torque tube is used to transfer the bellows motion from the inside to the outside of the meter body.

The bell manometer (Fig. 18) can be used to make differential pressure measurements. A bell (or inverted cup) is enclosed in a pressure housing. Two pressures are admitted to the bell, one to the under surface and the other to the outer surface. A sealing liquid is required to separate the two pressure fluids. A higher pressure on the under side causes the bell to rise; a higher pressure on the outer surface causes the bell to lower. This motion is transferred to the indicating or recording

Fig. 17. In the bellows-type differential pressure meter, a difference of pressure causes one of the bellows to be deformed more than the other. (Industrial Instruments Corp.)

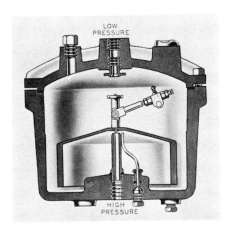

Fig. 18. Bell-type differential pressure meters are used when differences of pressure are very small. (American Meter Co.)

linkage through a pressure bearing, or other suitable device.

The weight-or-ring-balance meter (Fig. 19) measures differential pressure by allowing the liquid in the sensing device to be displaced, causing one side of the ring to become heavier than the other. The mechanism is mounted on a pivot, which permits it to move. The weight acts as a balance and the motion of the entire unit is connected to the indicating pointer or recording pen.

There are many kinds of differential pressure measuring instruments, but almost all of them use the ma-

Fig. 19. In the ring balance meter, the rotation of the hollow ring, caused by the pressure differential, is transmitted to the recorder or indicator. (Hagan Controls Corp.)

nometer, bellows, or bell as the actuating mechanism.

To obtain an electrical output from a differential pressure instrument, the motion of the float, bellows, or bell is used to position a mechanical element in an electrical bridge circuit, thus producing a unit change of electrical resistance, inductance, or capacitance for each unit change of differential pressure. This mechanical element may be the slider on a variable resistor, a transformer core, or a variable condenser plate.

In one interesting adaptation of the manometer principle the electrical conductivity of mercury is used. A spiral pack of resistance rods is enclosed in one column of a mercury manometer (Fig. 20). As the mercury rises in the column, it comes into contact with an increasing number of rods. Each rod adds to the electrical resistance, and this resistance is then connected into a bridge circuit. With a sufficient number of resistance rods, a very slight rise in the mercury column due to differen-

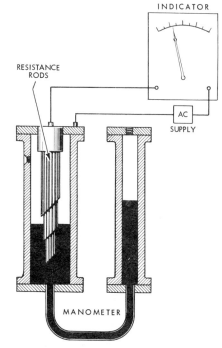

Fig. 20. Pressure differential in the resistance rod meter causes the mercury to rise and come increasingly in contact with the resistance rods.

tial pressure will cause a change in the bridge balance.

More will be written about these differential pressure instruments in the chapter on flow measurement.

Chapter 4 _____ Level

THE vast amount of water used by industry, let alone all the solvents, chemicals, and other liquids that are necessary for materials processing, makes the measurement of liquid level essential to modern manufacturing.

There are two ways of measuring level: *directly,* by using the varying level of the liquid as a means of obtaining the measurement; and *indirectly,* by using a variable, which changes with the liquid level, to actuate the measuring mechanism.

Direct Liquid Level Measurement

Bob and Tape. The simplest of the direct devices for liquid level measurement is the bob and tape (Fig. 1). All you need is a bob (or weight) suspended from a tape marked in feet and inches. The bob is lowered to the bottom of the vessel containing the liquid, and the level is determined by noting the point on the tape reached by the liquid. The actual reading is made after the tape is removed from the vessel. Ob-

viously this method isn't suited to continuous measurement.

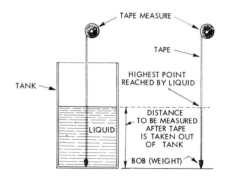

Fig. 1. A bob weight and measuring tape provide the most simple and direct method of measuring liquid level.

Sight Glass. Another direct means of liquid level measurement is the sight glass (Fig. 2). This consists of a graduated glass tube mounted on the side of the vessel. As the level of the liquid in the vessel changes, so does the level of the liquid in the glass tube. Measurement is a simple matter of reading the position of liquid level on the scale of the sight glass tube.

33

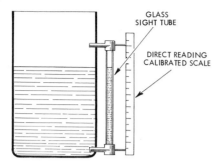

Fig. 2. As the level of the liquid in the vessel rises or falls, so does the level of liquid in the sight glass.

Floats. There are many kinds of float-operated mechanisms for continuous direct liquid level measurement. The primary device is a float that by reason of its buoyancy will follow the changing level of the liquid, and a mechanism that will transfer the float action to a pointer (Fig. 3). The float most familiar to

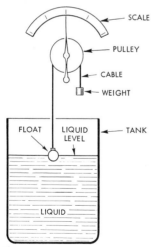

Fig. 3. The buoyancy of the float permits it to be immersed in the liquid, and its movement is transmitted to the indicator as it follows the changing liquid level.

you is the hollow metal sphere; but cylinder-shaped ceramic floats and disc-shaped floats of synthetic materials are also used.

The float is usually attached to a cable, which is wound around a pulley or drum to which the indicating pointer is attached. The movement of the float is thus transferred to the pointer, which indicates the liquid level on an appropriate scale.

In another kind of float-operated instrument, the float is attached to a shaft, which transfers the motion of the float to an indicator (Fig. 4).

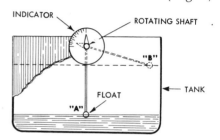

Fig. 4. When the level of the liquid is low, the ball float will be at position "A". As the tank fills, the float rises with the level of the liquid to position "B" and its movement rotates the shaft which operates the pointer.

This type doesn't permit a wide range of level measurement, but it does have mechanical advantages that make it excellent for control and transmitter applications. Another variation uses the float to move a magnet (Fig. 5). As this magnet moves, it attracts a follower magnet connected to the indicator, thus providing a reading of liquid level measurement.

The *displacer* (Fig. 6) is similar in action to the buoyant float described above, with the exception

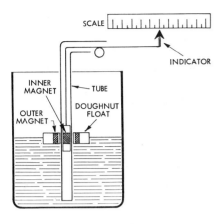

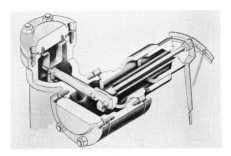

Fig. 5. The doughnut-shaped float with magnets in it rises and falls with the level of the liquid. The follower magnet, suspended by cable in the guide tube, rises and falls to maintain a corresponding position with the float, and thus moves the cable to the indicator.

that its movement is more restricted. With changes in liquid level, more or less of the displacer is covered by the liquid. The more the displacer is submerged, the greater is the *force* created by the displacer because of its buoyancy. This force is transferred through a twisting or bending shaft to a pneumatic system. For every new liquid level position, there is a new force on the shaft, causing it to assume a new position. The pneumatic system is so arranged that for each new shaft position there is a new air pressure to the indicator. The displacer float has the advantage of being more sensitive to small level changes than the buoyant float and less subject to mechanical friction.

Indirect Liquid Level Measurement

There are several types of indirect

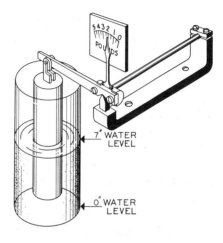

Fig. 6. In the lower drawing the displacer, which weighs 5 lbs., weighs only 2 lbs. when the water level is at 7 inches. The changes in weight are converted into torque (see upper illustration), which operates a pneumatic system to provide readings on the indicator. (Mason-Neilan Div. of Worthington Corp.)

level measuring devices that are operated by pressure. The simplest of these is the pressure gage located at the zero level of the liquid in a vessel (Fig. 7). Any rise in the level causes an increase of pressure, which can be measured by the gage. The gage scale is marked in units of level measurement (feet or inches).

If the nature of the liquid prevents its being allowed to enter the pressure gage, a transmitting fluid (such

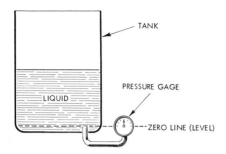

Fig. 7. As the tank fills, the pressure of the liquid naturally increases. This increase of pressure can be read on the gage in feet and inches of level.

as air, which is the cheapest and handiest) must be used between the liquid and the gage. The *air trap* and the *diaphragm box* provide a means of accomplishing this.

The air trap consists of a box, which is lowered into the liquid (Fig. 8). As the liquid rises, the pressure on the air trapped in the box increases. This air pressure is piped through a tubing to the pressure gage, which has a scale on which the level can be read.

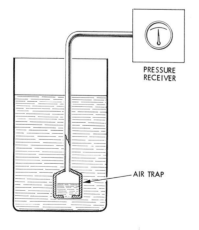

Fig. 8. The pressure of air in the air trap is expressed on the scale in units of level.

The diaphragm box (Fig. 9), like the air trap, transmits air pressure to a gage, but in this case the air is trapped inside it by a flexible diaphragm covering the bottom of the box. As the level of the liquid rises, the pressure on the diaphragm increases. This pressure acts on the air in the closed system and is piped to the pressure gage where a reading can be taken.

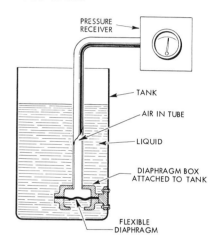

Fig. 9. Deflection of the flexible diaphragm by compression, as the liquid level rises, causes the gage to respond.

The pressure caused by the liquid column is used in the bubbler method of level measurement (Fig. 10). A pipe is installed vertically in the vessel with its open end at the zero level. The other end of the pipe is connected to a regulated air supply and to a pressure gage. To make a level measurement the air supply is adjusted so that the pressure is slightly higher than the pressure due to the height of the liquid. This is accomplished by regulating the air pressure until bubbles can be seen slowly leaving the open end of the pipe. The gage then measures the air pressure needed to overcome the pressure of the liquid. The gage is calibrated in feet or inches of level.

The methods described above can only be used when the vessel containing the liquid is open to the at-

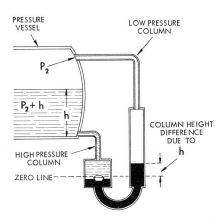

Fig. 11. When the liquid is in an enclosed vessel, level can be measured using a differential pressure manometer.

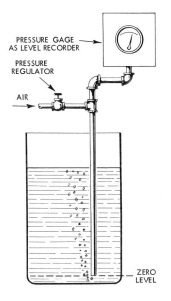

Fig. 10. The air pressure to the bubbler pipe is minutely in excess of the liquid pressure in the vessel, so that the air pressure indicated is a measure of the level in the tank.

mosphere. When the liquid is in a pressure vessel, the liquid column pressure can't be used unless the vessel pressure is balanced out. This is done through the use of differential pressure meters (Fig. 11). Connections are made to the vessel at top and bottom, and to the two columns of the differential pressure meter.

The top connection is made to the low pressure column of the meter, and the bottom connection to the high pressure column. In this way the pressure in the vessel is balanced out, since it is fed to both columns of the meter. The difference in pressure detected by the meter will be due then only to the changing level of the liquid. Most of the differential pressure devices described in Chapter 3 can be used for level measurement in this manner.

Liquid level can be measured using radioactivity or ultrasonics. For continuous level measurement by radioactivity, one or more radioactive sources are placed on one side of a vessel with a pick-up on the other side (Fig. 12). As the level of the liquid changes, it absorbs more or less of the radioactive energy received by the pick-up, which is a special electronic amplifier designed to produce enough electrical energy to actuate an electrical meter.

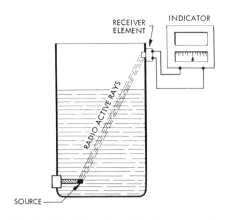

Fig. 12. Radioactive system of level measurement.

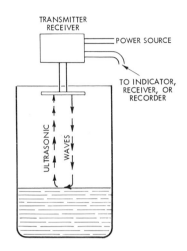

Fig. 13. Sound waves reflected back from the surface of the liquid to the receiving unit can provide an accurate measurement of liquid level.

The meter scale is marked in level units—inches or feet.

The ultrasonic method operates on the sonar principle (Fig. 13). Sound waves are sent to the surface of the liquid and are reflected back to the receiving unit. Changes in level are accurately measured by detecting the time it takes for the waves to

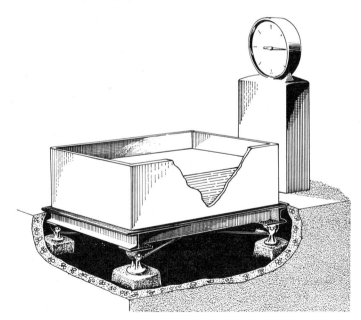

Fig. 14. Scale on which the vessel and its liquid content can be weighed mechanically.

travel to the surface and back to the receiver. The longer the time required, the further away is the liquid surface, providing a measurement of how much the level has changed.

These systems have been described very simply here. Actually they are highly complicated in both design and installation.

Another method of determining the level of liquid materials is to weigh the entire vessel, since the weight changes as the level of the material varies. The vessel may be weighed on mechanical scales (Fig. 14); or it may be weighed electrically using load cells (Fig. 15). *Load cells* are specially constructed mechanical units containing *strain gages*, which provide a measurable electrical output proportional to the stress applied by the weight of the vessel on the load cells. As the pressure on the cell due to the weight of the vessel changes, the electrical resistance of the strain gage changes. The strain gage is connected into a bridge circuit containing an electri-

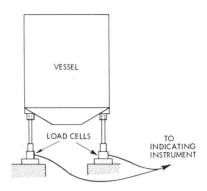

Fig. 15. Vessel weighed electrically using load cells.

cal meter graduated in units of level measurement. It should be noted that the weighing method is accurate only if the density and particle size of the substance being weighed are uniform and the moisture content remains constant. The change in weight must be due entirely to the change in level.

There are many other devices used for determining where the liquid level is at a particular point. In this chapter it has been possible to mention only some of them.

Chapter 5 _____ Flow

MANY different methods are used to measure flow in a wide variety of industrial applications. In this chapter, the fundamental differences between the methods will be outlined. In Part Two, particular instruments will be described, along with their principles of operation.

First, it should be noted that there are two kinds of flow measurement: *Rate of Flow*, which is the amount of fluid that flows past a given point at any given instant; and *Total Flow*, which is the amount of fluid that flows past a given point in a definite period of time.

Rate of Flow Meters

Meters designed to measure rate of flow include *differential-pressure meters, variable-area meters,* and *weir, flume, and open nozzle meters.*

Differential-Pressure Meters. In order to measure rate of flow by differential pressure there must be a method of creating two different pressures. This can be accomplished by placing a restriction in the pipe line that forces the fluid through a reduced area. The pressure on the entering side of the restriction is higher than the pressure on the exit side.

The simplest pipeline restriction for flowmetering is the *orifice plate,* which is a thin, circular metal plate with a hole in it. It is held in the pipeline between two flanges called orifice flanges. The shape and location of the hole is the distinguishing feature of the three kinds of orifice plate: The *concentric plate* has a circular hole located in its center (Fig. 1); the *eccentric plate* has a circular hole located below its center (Fig. 2); and the *segmental plate* has a hole that is only partly circular located below its center (Fig. 3). The kind of orifice plate used depends on the characteristics of the fluid that is to be measured.

Another pipeline restriction for flowmetering is the *Venturi tube,* which is a specially shaped length of

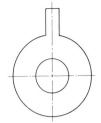

Fig. 1. Concentric orifice plate.

Fig. 2. Eccentric orifice plate.

Fig. 3. Segmental orifice plate.

pipe resembling two funnels joined at their smaller openings (Fig.4). The Venturi tube is used for large pipelines. It is more accurate than the orifice plate, but considerably more expensive, and more difficult to in-

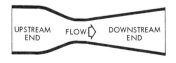

Fig. 4. Venturi tube.

stall. A compromise between the orifice plate and the Venturi tube is the *flow nozzle*, which resembles the entering half of the Venturi tube (Fig. 5). The flow nozzle is almost as accurate as the Venturi tube, and is not so expensive to buy or as difficult to install.

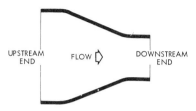

Fig. 5. Flow nozzle.

The orifice plate, the Venturi tube, and the flow nozzle (all primary flow elements) create a differential pressure. The differential pressure thus created varies with the rate of flow.

To obtain the pressure upstream of the primary element and the pressure downstream of the primary element requires taps on both sides of the restricted area. The location of these pressure taps varies. With the orifice plate three kinds of taps may be used: *flange taps*, located on the

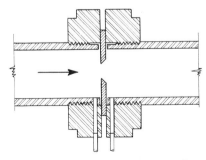

Fig. 6. Flange taps are located on the flanges that hold the orifice plate in position.

flanges that hold the orifice plate in the pipe (Fig. 6), *pipe taps*, located at fixed distances upstream and downstream of the orifice plate — the upstream tap is placed 2½ pipe diameters from the plate, and the downstream tap 8 pipe diameters

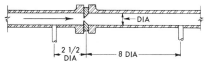

Fig. 7. The upstream pipe tap is located 2½ pipe diameters, and the downstream pipe tap 8 pipe diameters, from the orifice plate.

from the plate (Fig. 7); and *Vena Contracta taps* located 1 pipe diameter from the plate on the upstream side, and on the downstream side at the point of minimum pressure, which has to be determined by calculation (Fig. 8).

The pressure taps used with the Venturi tube are located at the points of maximum and minimum pipe diameter.

The pressure taps used with the flow nozzle are located at distances upstream and downstream of the

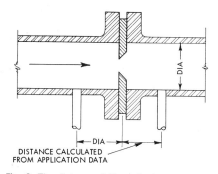

Fig. 8. The distance of Vena Contracta taps on the downstream side must be calculated from application data.

nozzle as designated by the manufacturer. This location is critical and the manufacturer's recommendations must be followed.

Any of the differential pressure instruments described in Chapter 3 can be used for rate of flow measurement with these primary flow elements. Since the desired measurement is rate of flow and not differential pressure, a conversion from differential pressure to rate of flow must be made. It is possible to make this conversion on the scale or chart of the instrument.

Variable-Area Meters. There are two types of variable-area meters: the *rotameter*, in which the area is

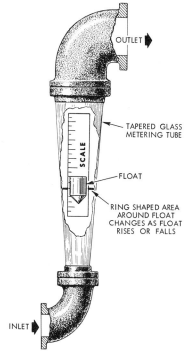

Fig. 9. In the rotameter, the flow rate varies directly as the float rises and falls in the tapered tube.

varied by a float in a tapered tube (Fig. 9); and the *valve-type area meter*, in which the movement of a self-positioning valve varies the area (Fig. 10).

If we compare the differential pressure instruments with the variable-area meters we find that the difference between them lies in the value they keep constant. In the differential pressure meter the *area is restricted to a fixed size* while the *differential pressure varies* with the rate of flow. In the variable-area meters, *the size of area is adjusted* by the amount necessary to keep the *pressure differential constant* when the rate of flow changes.

The float of the rotameter adjusts the size of the area by rising and falling in the tapered tube. Depending on the rate of flow, the float takes a position in the tube that increases or decreases the size of the area, and thus keeps the differential pressure constant. In the valve-type meter, a specially shaped plug or piston

moves to a new position to keep the differential pressure constant for each rate of flow.

The rotameter is chiefly used as an indicating device, although it is possible to obtain remote indication by attaching to the float different types of followers that will vary an electrical quantity such as resistance. The valve-type meter is used most often to provide remote indication. See Fig. 11.

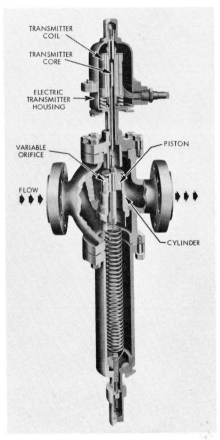

Fig. 10. In the area meter, the piston valve moves to a new position for each flow rate. (Bailey Meter Co.)

Fig. 11. Area meter with transmitter for use as a remote indicator. (Bailey Meter Co.)

Weirs, Flumes, and Open Nozzles.
The primary elements used for measuring rate of flow in open channels are weirs, flumes, and open nozzles.
A *weir* is a flat bulkhead with a specially shaped notch along its upper edge. It is placed across the open fluid stream, forcing the fluid to rise up the notch as the flow rate increases (Fig. 12). A *flume* is a formed

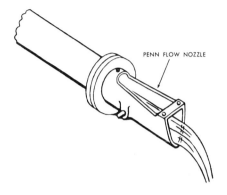

Fig. 14. In the open nozzle, the level of the fluid rises uniformly as flow rate increases. (Penn Meter Co.)

nozzle rises uniformly as the flow rate increases (Fig. 14).

The measurement of flow rate using these primary elements is accomplished by a float-actuated device located in a well adjoining the channel. The level in the well changes with each new rate of flow, due to the restriction caused by the primary element.

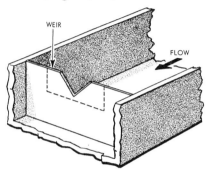

Fig. 12. The weir forces the fluid up the notch as flow rate increases.

structure that is placed in the open fluid stream, forcing the fluid to rise within it as the flow rate increases (Fig. 13). The *open nozzle* is shaped so that the level of the fluid in the

Total Flow Meters

Positive Displacement Meters. Meters operating by positive displacement admit a measured amount of fluid into a chamber of known volume and then discharge it. Each filling of the chamber and the number of fillings in a given time period is counted. Actually two chambers are used. They are arranged so that as one is being filled, the other is being emptied. This permits continuous flow, instead of "gulp by gulp" flow. By multiplying the number of fillings by the volume of the chambers, the total flow for a given time period can be determined. Di-

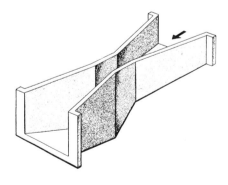

Fig. 13. The flume forces the fluid to rise within it as flow rate increases.

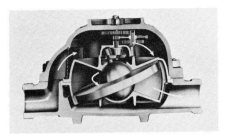

Fig. 15. Nutating-disc type of positive displacement flow meter. (Buffalo Meter Co.)

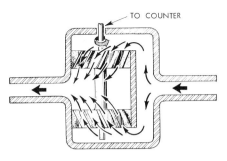

Fig. 16. In the velocity meter, the turbine wheel speed varies with the rate of flow.

vide this total flow by the total time units in the period, and the average flow rate can be obtained.

One type of positive displacement flow meter is shown in Fig. 15. The fluid moves through the rotating disc chambers, causing the disc to rotate and "wobble" as one chamber fills and the other empties. The movement resembles that of a slowly spinning top. The rotary motion is transferred to gearing, which drives a counter. As the disc rotates, the chambers change place, the inlet chamber becoming the outlet chamber, and vice versa.

Other positive displacement flow meters contain internal mechanisms similar to those found in pumps, such as oscillating pistons, rotary vanes, and oval gears. Though they all differ in details of design, their operation is similar in that they are driven by the rate of flow and measure the quantity of fluid flow.

Velocity Meters. This meter (Fig. 16) converts the velocity of a flowing liquid to a rotary spindle motion. The liquid enters the meter and drives a turbine wheel or propeller at a speed that varies with the rate of flow. The turbine wheel drives a gear train connected to a counter, which registers the total quantity of liquid passing through the meter. Some meters of this type contain secondary metering mechanisms and are called compound meters. For instance, a positive displacement mechanism might be included to provide better low flow measurement than would be possible with a simple velocity meter.

Integrators. Total flow can be measured with differential pressure meters that incorporate integrators. An integrator is a calculating device

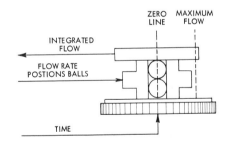

Fig. 17. The steel balls of this continuous mechanical integrator can be positioned by the carriage anywhere from the center of the disc to the outer edge. Their speed of rotation increases with their distance from the center. The balls are held against each other and against the disc by the pressure of two springs. (Ford Instrument Co.)

that combines multiplication and addition. The changing flow rate is multiplied continuously by the time elapsed, and the product is added continuously to the previous totals on the counter. A means of converting differential pressure to flow rate must be included.

Such integrators may be mechanical or electrical, continuous or intermittent. An example of a continuous mechanical integrator is the ball and disc type shown in Fig. 17. The disc is rotated at a constant speed to provide the time input. Two steel balls, one on top of the other, are held in position by a carriage which moves across the face of the disc. They are positioned on the disc by the flow rate. As the bottom ball moves from the center of the disc toward the outer edge its speed increases, so that the roller driven by the ball rotates

faster. The roller drives a counter, which totals the flow by continuously multiplying the flow rate by time.

Where the flow rate is not a rapidly changing value, the continuous mechanical integrator has been replaced in flowmetering by the intermittent type. In this device (Fig. 18) a constant speed motor drives a counter for a period of time dependent on the flow measurement. The greater the flow, the longer the period of time the motor operates, and the more counter movement there is. Generally, such an integrator includes a mechanism that converts the measured differential pressure to flow rate, so that the counter is then driven by the product of flow rate and time to indicate total flow.

Many types of continuous and intermittent electrical integrators for total flow measurement are available.

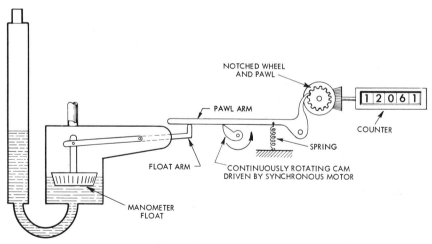

Fig. 18. In this intermittent mechanical integrator, the float arm positions the pawl arm. The continuously rotating cam moves the pawl arm for a part of each revolution. The pawl moves the notched wheel, which is directly connected to the counter. Since the float arm is positioned by the flow rate and the rotating cam represents time, the counter indicates the increment of flow per time increment.

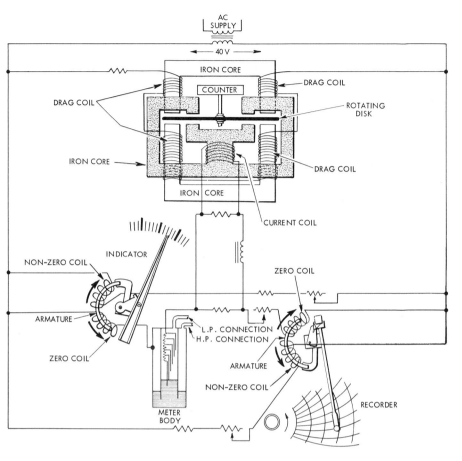

Fig. 19. In this differential pressure electric flow meter, the spiral ring of rods causes the resistance of the circuit to be changed in such a manner that the flowing current is directly proportional to flow, or the square root of the differential pressure. (Republic Flow Meter Co.)

With the resistance type differential pressure element illustrated in Fig. 20 (Chapter 3), it is possible to integrate the flow rate using a watt-hour meter. Fig. 19 shows such an arrangement. The current variation due to the changing resistance of the measuring element serves as an input to the watt-hour meter; the other input is a constant voltage from the supply transformer. The speed of the rotating disc of the watt-hour meter varies with the current through the resistance element. Since the current changes with resistance and because the resistance changes with the flow rate, the speed of the rotating disc changes with the flow rate. The disc is connected to a counter. The change in counter readings over a particular interval represents the total flow during that interval.

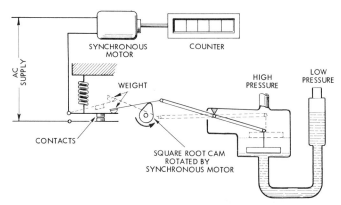

Fig. 20. In this intermittent electrical integrator, the motion of the counter is started and stopped by making or breaking the electrical circuit which operates the synchronous motor driving the counter. The square root extraction is achieved by having a square root cam, which is driven by another constant speed motor, perform the make and break function. The actual contact is made by linkage positioned by the differential pressure measuring element. (Foxboro Co.)

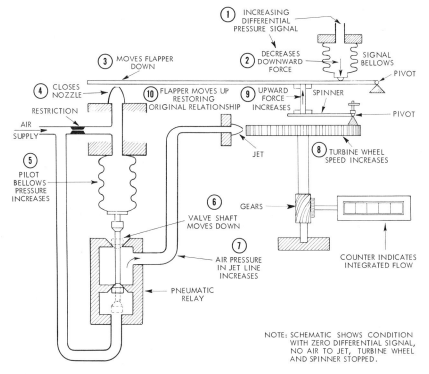

Fig. 21. This continuous pneumatic integrator operates on the force-balance principle. The rotation of the spinner is produced by an air or gas controlled turbine wheel controlled by a nozzle and flapper, whose relative position is controlled by the counteracting forces exerted by the spinner and the signal bellows. (Foxboro Co.)

There are other continuous electrical flow integrators that use electrically-operated mechanical devices to regulate the counter rotation. The intermittent electrical flow integrators also contain mechanically-operated contacts to control the number of impulses to the counting mechanism. See Fig. 20.

Recently pneumatically-driven integrators of the continuous and intermittent types have been developed to satisfy a demand for non-electrical operation in hazardous locations. The continuous pneumatic integrator (Fig. 21) operates on the force-balance principle. The force of the spinner, operating on the centrifugal governor principle, is balanced against a force produced by a bellows. The signal bellows may be subjected directly to the differential pressure, but it is usually actuated by the pressure signal from a differential pressure transmitter. Its force is imposed against the centrifugal force of the spinner. Since the force produced by a centrifugal element is directly proportional to the square of its speed of rotation, and the force produced by the differential element is directly proportional to the square of the rate of flow, a direct relationship results between the speed of the rotation of the spinner and the rate of flow of the fluid, as long as these forces are kept in balance.

Except for their source of power and the method of converting differential pressure measurement to flow rate, all integrators resemble one another and perform the same function. The principal requirements are an accurate measurement of the differential pressure, a near perfect conversion to flow rate, a constant time input, and an easy-to-read counter.

Chapter 6

Humidity

HUMIDITY refers to the water vapor content of the air (or other gas). There are two terms used for describing humidity: 1. *Absolute Humidity* is the amount of water vapor actually present in the air. It is usually expressed in grains per pound of air (1 grain is 1/7000 of a pound). 2. *Relative Humidity* is the ratio of the amount of water vapor actually present (absolute humidity) to the maximum amount of water vapor the air could hold at the same temperature. It is expressed as a percentage. 100% Relative Humidity means that air contains all the moisture it can hold. The higher the temperature of the air the more water it can hold, hence relative humidity measurement requires knowledge of the temperature and of the amount of water vapor air will hold at various temperatures.

The key to humidity measurement is the psychrometric chart, which graphically describes the properties of moist air. Fig. 1 shows how the variables for humidity measurement are laid out on a typical psychrometric chart.

The *dry bulb* temperature lines are vertical, and the dry bulb temperatures are read at the bottom of the chart. The *wet bulb* and *dew point* temperature lines run diagonally downward to the right, and their values are read at the left where the lines intersect with the 100 percent relative humidity line. The percent lines of relative humidity curve upwards to the right, with the percent values indicated on the lines themselves. The absolute humidity in grains per pound of air is read on the vertical scale at the right of the chart, where the value is indicated at the horizontal line that leads from the intersection of a wet bulb or dew point temperature line with a dry bulb line.

Measuring Relative Humidity

Relative humidity can be measured by either of two types of in-

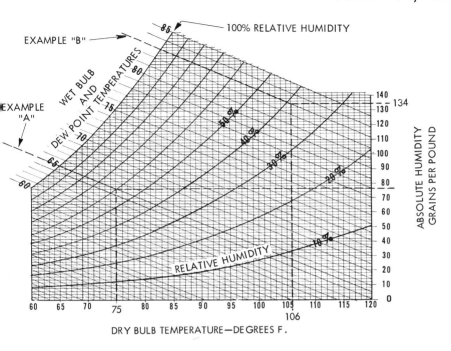

Fig. 1. A simplified psychrometric chart. Example "A": Find the relative humidity and absolute humidity, given a dry bulb temperature of 75°F and a wet bulb temperature of 65°F. First locate the 75°F dry bulb temperature at the bottom of the chart, then the 65°F wet bulb temperature along the 100 percent relative humidity line. Find the point where the lines drawn from these two locations intersect. The relative humidity is found to be approximately 60 percent; and following the horizontal line from the intersection to the right-hand scale, the absolute humidity is 76 grains per pound. Example "B": Find the relative humidity and absolute humidity, given a dry bulb temperature of 106°F and a dew point temperature of 83°F. Using the same procedure, the relative humidity is found to be 37 percent and the absolute humidity 134 grains per pound.

struments: 1) the *Hygrometer*, which utilizes the physical or electrical change of certain materials as they absorb moisture; and 2) the *Psychrometer*, which registers the temperature difference between two primary elements, one of which is kept wet so that water is continuously being evaporated from its surface.

Hygrometers that depend upon physical changes may employ human hair (for example, Fig. 2), animal membrane, or other materials that lengthen when they absorb water.

Fig. 2. This hygrometer employs human hair as the element that lengthens when it absorbs water. (Minneapolis-Honeywell Reg. Co.)

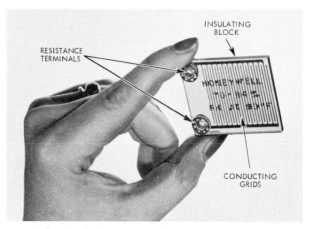

Fig. 3. Transducer used with electrical hygrometer. The amount of electrical current depends on the amount of moisture absorbed, and by connecting the transducer with a bridge circuit, the percent of relative humidity can be measured. (Minneapolis-Honeywell Reg. Co.)

Electrical hygrometers use transducers that convert humidity variations into electrical resistance changes. One type of transducer (Fig. 3) consists of an insulating plate bearing two grids of metal-coated hygroscopic material. (A hygroscopic material is one which tends to absorb moisture.) An electrical current is passed through the metal grids. As the amount of water absorbed from the air by the hygroscopic grids varies, so does the electrical resistance between them. This transducer may be used with a bridge type instrument, which will measure resistance changes and express them on a scale calibrated in percent of relative humidity.

The psychrometer or wet and dry bulb thermometer is available in several variations. The simple sling psychrometer (Fig. 4) consists of two glass thermometers attached to an assembly that permits the two thermometers to be rotated through the air. One thermometer has a moistened cloth cover (or wick) over its sensing bulb. After the thermometers have been rotated, the wet bulb will

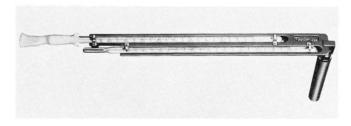

Fig. 4. After rotating this simple sling psychrometer through the air, the dry bulb and wet bulb readings are taken and from these, using a psychrometric chart, the relative humidity and absolute humidity can be ascertained. (Taylor Instrument Co.)

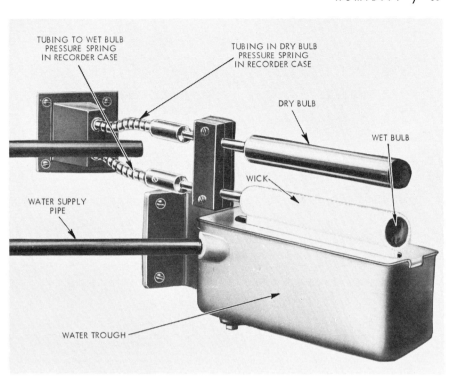

TUBING TO WET BULB
PRESSURE SPRING
IN RECORDER CASE

TUBING IN DRY BULB
PRESSURE SPRING
IN RECORDER CASE

DRY BULB

WET BULB

WICK

WATER SUPPLY
PIPE

WATER TROUGH

Fig. 5. Typical pressure spring psychrometer, showing the installation of the wet bulb and dry bulb elements. The instrument is used for the continuous recording of humidity.

indicate a lower temperature than the dry bulb, because of the effect of the evaporation of water on the wick. Using these two temperatures and the psychrometric chart, the relative humidity or absolute humidity can be determined.

Recording psychrometers use the same principle. Two separate pressure spring thermal systems or two separate resistance thermometer bulbs can be used. Fig. 5 shows a typical pressure spring psychrometer. Generally, psychrometers are used for determining the humidity of air at temperatures between 32°F. and 212°F.

Measuring Dew Point

For many processes dew point is probably a more significant measurement than relative humidity. Dew point is the temperature at which a given sample of moist air will become saturated and deposit dew.

A typical instrument (Fig. 6) for measuring dew point employs a mirror against which a jet of the air (or gas), whose humidity is to be measured, is directed. A light beam is aimed at the mirror and reflected by the mirror to a photo-electric (light sensitive) tube. The mirror is enclosed in a chamber which may be

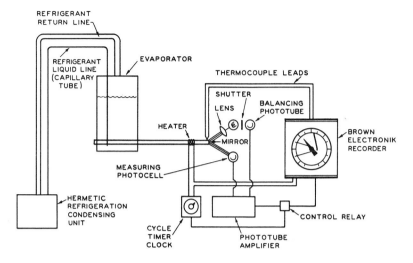

Fig. 6. This schematic of a continuous dew point recorder shows the optical system, which is enclosed in a dew chamber, the refrigerator system, photoelectric cell, amplifier, and cycle control system. (Surface Combustion Corp.)

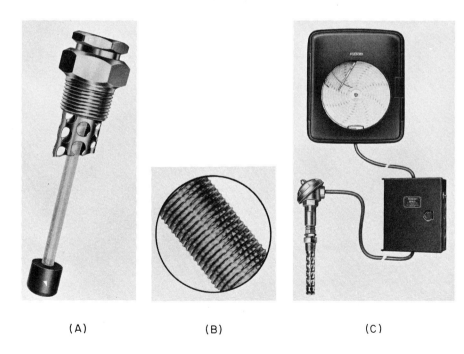

(A)   (B)   (C)

Fig. 7. Continuous dew point recorder. (A) The hygroscopic element. (B) Close-up of wire. (C) The complete unit. (Foxboro Co.)

heated or cooled, and a thermo-couple is attached to the mirror to measure its temperature. When the mirror is cooled the water vapor in the air causes the mirror to fog. When the mirror is heated the fog disappears.

The temperature of the mirror is controlled to maintain an equilibrium between the two conditions. This temperature is the dew point.

Another instrument for measuring dew point (Fig. 7) uses a specially constructed sensing element consisting of a thin-walled metal tube coated with insulating varnish and wrapped with glass fibre cloth. This assembly is then covered with a double winding of gold wire. A temperature bulb is placed inside the metal tube. A solution of lithium chloride is used to saturate the glass cloth. Lithium chloride is a hygroscopic chemical salt, so that it absorbs moisture from the air surrounding it. As the moisture absorbed by the lithium chloride increases, the current passing through the gold wire increases. This increase in current through the wire creates heat which passes through the tube wall to the temperature sensing bulb. The sensing bulb may be a resistance thermometer type or a filled system type. The temperature of the cell is the dew point.

Measuring Moisture

The measurement of the moisture content of solid materials is important in some industries, particularly the paper and textile industries. As

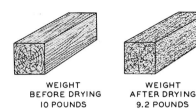

WEIGHT BEFORE DRYING 10 POUNDS   WEIGHT AFTER DRYING 9.2 POUNDS

Fig. 8. The loss of weight of the block of wood after drying is .8 pounds, all of which was moisture. A loss of .8 pounds in 10 pounds equals a loss of 8 percent moisture.

moisture is absorbed the weight of the material increases, so one method of determining the moisture content is by measuring the loss of weight of the material after it has been dried. The moisture content of lumber can be determined in this manner (Fig. 8). A piece of the lumber is weighed, then baked in an oven and weighed again. There will be an evident loss of weight. This loss is noted, and from this the amount of moisture per pound of lumber can be calculated as a percentage. This, of course, is a slow method and not suited to continuous processing.

More rapid, and in some cases continuous, moisture measurement can be made by electrical methods using the variation of the electrical resistance or capacitance of the materials due to moisture changes.

Typical of the resistance type is the moisture meter used for measuring the moisture of paper (Fig. 9). The electrical resistance of paper varies with its moisture content. Using the resistance of the paper as the unknown resistance in a bridge circuit, it is possible to measure this resistance, and from tabulated data determine its moisture content. The

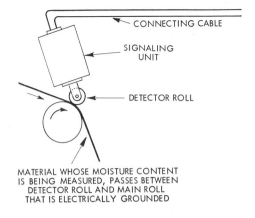

CONNECTING CABLE

SIGNALING UNIT

DETECTOR ROLL

MATERIAL WHOSE MOISTURE CONTENT
IS BEING MEASURED, PASSES BETWEEN
DETECTOR ROLL AND MAIN ROLL
THAT IS ELECTRICALLY GROUNDED

Fig. 9. A small electric current passes from the detector roll through the material being measured to the grounded main roll. The resistance of the material is used as the unknown resistance in a Wheatstone bridge circuit and the potentiometer measurements are calibrated so that they can be recorded by the instrument on the right. (Minneapolis-Honeywell Reg. Co.)

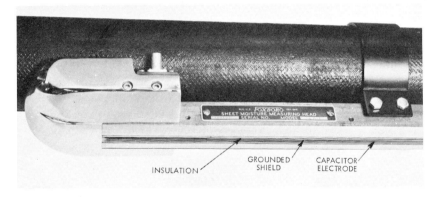

INSULATION

GROUNDED
SHIELD

CAPACITOR
ELECTRODE

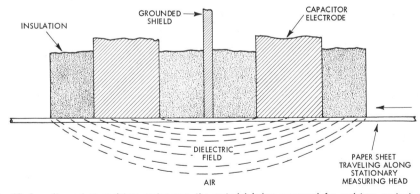

INSULATION

GROUNDED
SHIELD

CAPACITOR
ELECTRODE

DIELECTRIC
FIELD

AIR

PAPER SHEET
TRAVELING ALONG
STATIONARY
MEASURING HEAD

Fig. 10. Capacitance type moisture meter uses the material being measured for moisture content as the dielectric between the plates. (Foxboro Co.)

bridge instrument can be calibrated in percent of moisture, but it must be understood that the resistance of one paper at a particular content might be quite different from that of another paper.

Capacitance type moisture meters depend for their operation on the change in dielectric quality of the material concerned. To determine this change an electrical capacitor is formed using the material as the non-conductive medium (dielectric) between the plates. The resultant capacitor (Fig. 10) is then connected in a bridge circuit to determine its value in microfarads. To be able to convert this value into a moisture reading it is necessary to calibrate the capacitor element using samples of the material with known moisture content.

Chapter 7   Transmission

THE transmission of the measured value of a variable from the point of measurement to a remote point has become an important function in process instrumentation because of the size and complexity of modern industrial plants. Temperature, pressure, level, and flow are the values usually transmitted. The measuring elements may be any of those we have discussed in previous chapters, such as pressure springs, thermocouples, bellows, floats, and so on. (See Fig. 1.)

Transmitting transducers are devices that convert the measured variable into a transmittable signal, either pneumatic or electrical, so that it can be received by a remote indicating, recording, or controlling device. In process instrumentation the selection of either a pneumatic or electrical transmitter depends upon the nature of the variable and the distance the signal must be sent. When the signal reaches the receiver, it is converted back to a measurement, which may be indicated on a

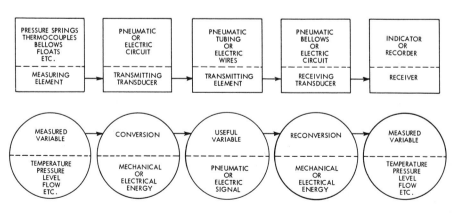

Fig. 1. Transmission of process variables shown graphically.

58

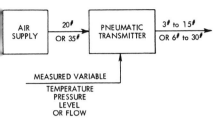

Fig. 2. Constant air supply pressures, usually of 20 psi or 35 psi, are an absolute necessity for pneumatic transmission.

gage or recorded on a chart. An electrical signal, for example, may be converted to mechanical energy, which will position a pointer or recording pen.

Pneumatic Transmission

A constant air supply is the first requirement for pneumatic transmission. Supply pressures of 20 psi or 35 psi are most common. There must also be a means of varying the supply so that for each value of the measured variable a definite pneumatic pressure signal is produced. With an air pressure supply of 20 psi, the signal pressure will vary between 3 psi and 15 psi. With 35 psi, the signal pressure will vary between 6 psi and 30 psi (Fig. 2). The signal pressure is converted by the receiver into a value of the measured variable. Essentially, the receiver is an indicating or recording pressure gage with its scale or chart graduated in units of the measured variable. Pneumatic transmission is limited to distances up to 600 feet.

There are many makes of pneumatic transmitters. Even though they may vary in details, the basic principle used in almost every pneumatic transmission system is the flapper-nozzle mechanism illustrated in Fig. 3. This consists of an open nozzle supplied with air through a restriction, and a flapper positioned by the measuring element.

When the flapper is moved against the nozzle, air cannot escape and maximum air pressure passes to the amplifier. When the flapper is moved away from the nozzle, air can escape, thus reducing the amount of air pressure to the amplifier. As the flapper moves from one extreme position to another, it serves to control the amplifier, which produces an air pressure proportional to the measured variable and of sufficient signal strength for transmission over the required distance.

Electrical Transmission

The useful characteristics of elec-

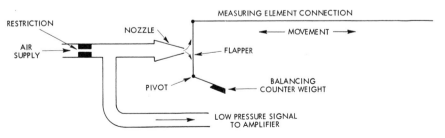

Fig. 3. Almost every pneumatic transmission system uses the flapper-nozzle mechanism.

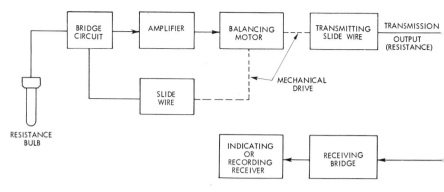

Fig. 4. Typical temperature transmitter.

trical transmitters include *resistance, inductance,* and *time impulse.* Although there are electrical transmitting systems that use other useful characteristics, those mentioned represent the most common ones, particularly for such process variables as temperature, pressure, level, and flow.

A resistance bulb for temperature measurement, although it qualifies as a transducer, is not generally regarded as a transmitter. When, however, the measuring instrument used with a resistance bulb produces a signal of sufficient strength, the combination is called a transmitter. For example, a resistance thermometer of the self-balancing Wheatstone bridge type will often be equipped with a transmitting slidewire in addition to the measuring slidewire. This additional slidewire, which is in a separate electrical circuit, provides a resistance signal that varies with the measured temperature. This arrangement is illustrated diagrammatically in Fig. 4.

In the same manner other meas-

ured variables may be converted to resistance values suitable for transmission. Because of the resistance of the wires connecting the transmitter and receiver, the transmission distance of such systems is limited. For this reason, care must be taken in the installation of the transmitting wires to make sure that the current passing through them does not leak to ground, or become affected by outside influences such as nearby power lines.

Inductance Transmission

Inductance transmitters consist of a metal rod inside an electrical coil (Fig. 5). The position of the rod in the coil depends on the degree of

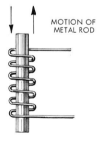

Fig. 5. Inductance transmitter device.

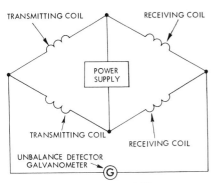

Fig. 6. Inductance bridge.

a system. The unbalance is fed into the amplifier, which provides a strong enough electrical impulse to cause the motor to run. The motor then moves the metal rod in the receiving coil to a position which restores bridge balance.

The inductance bridge (Fig. 7) is generally supplied for use with alternating current power supply.

Time Impulse Transmission

movement of the measuring element. As the metal rod moves, it changes the current passing through the coil. The transmitting coil and rod can be duplicated in the receiving instrument and combined with the receiving coil into an inductance bridge circuit. See Fig. 6.

When the measuring element moves the metal rod in the transmitting coil, the bridge balance is upset. This unbalance is then corrected by a movement of the metal rod in the receiver coil. Usually there is an amplifier and a motor in such

The time impulse system of transmission is used for long distances. The transmitter consists of a cam which is driven at a constant speed by an electric motor (see Fig. 8). The cam follower is positioned by the measuring element. As the cam rotates, the follower opens and closes an electric circuit. The position of the follower determines how long the circuit is open or closed. Since there is a follower position for each value of the measured variable there is a different "time open", "time closed" ratio of the electrical circuit.

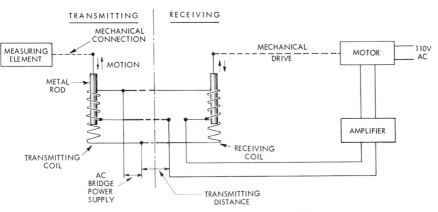

Fig. 7. Inductance bridge as used for transmission.

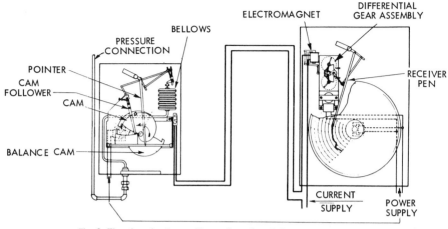

Fig. 8. Time impulse transmitter and receiver (telemeter). (Bristol Co.)

Through a combination electrical and mechanical arrangement, the receiver pointer or pen is positioned to indicate the value of the measured variable. Time-impulse transmission requires only two wires for its voltage signal. Frequently telephone wires are rented for such use.

Chapter 8 — Control

THE automatic control of measured variables is one of the principal objectives of process instrumentation. Reduced to simple diagrammatic form, an automatic control system is shown in Fig. 1.

Control Elements

The **Primary Element** is the name given in control study to the device that senses changes in the value of the measured variable. It may be a thermocouple, an orifice plate, a float, or other element.

The **Measuring Element** is the device (or apparatus) that receives the output of the primary element. It may include indicating or recording devices—when it does not it is termed "blind."

The **Controlling Element** (controller) uses the changes in the value of the measured variable as sensed by the primary element and measured by the measuring element to regulate a source of power in accordance with these changes. The power may be mechanical, pneumatic or electrical.

The **Final Element** is the device that actually varies the input to the process so that the value of the measured

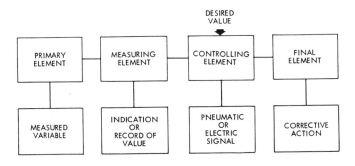

Fig. 1. Block diagram of an automatic control system.

63

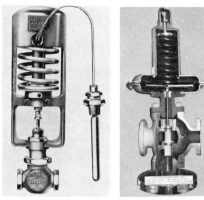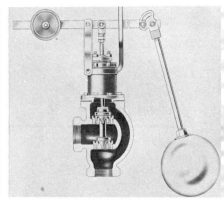

Fig. 2. Left: self-operating temperature controller (Taylor Instrument Co.). Center: self-operating pressure controller (A. W. Cash Co.). Right: self-operating level controller (Fisher Governor Co.).

variable remains within the desired range.

When the three elements are combined into one unit which requires no outside power source, the result is the self-operating controller. Fig. 2 shows three such units.

Most of these self-operating controllers are blind and require the use of a separate measuring device for installation or for changing the desired value of the measured variable. The power source in such devices is principally mechanical.

Control Actions

Of the types of automatic controller actions available, the following four are most common:

1. ON-OFF controller action
2. Proportional controller action
3. Proportional + Reset controller action
4. Proportional + Reset + Rate controller action

The names of these actions describe the response of the final element as the value of the measured variable moves above or below the desired value (set point).

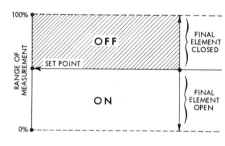

Fig. 3. On-off action.

On-Off Action (Fig. 3) means that the final element has only two positions—one for the occasion when the value of the measured variable is above the set point, and the other for the occasion when the value is below the set point.

Proportional Action (Fig. 4) allows the final element to take intermediate positions between ON and OFF. This permits the final element to vary the amount of energy to the process, depending upon how much

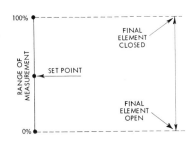

Fig. 4. Proportional action.

relationship between final element position and measured variable value. This lets the controller make up for changes in the process characteristics, which proportional action alone could not do. With the addition of reset action, the controller can continue the corrective positioning of the final element until the measured variable returns to the desired value.

Proportional + Reset + Rate Action (Fig. 6) adds still more flexibility to the movement of the final element. In a process that responds very slowly (one in which it takes a long time to detect or to correct changes), a change in the measured variable rate action provides corrective positioning of the final element related to the *rate* at which the value of the measured variable is changing.

Note that reset and rate actions do not exist separately. They are refinements of proportional action.

The means by which the controller learns that the corrective action of the final element has been taken, and that this action has had the desired effect on the value of the measured

the value of the measured variable has shifted from the desired value. It is important to note that in proportional action there is a particular position of the final element for each unit of departure of the measured variable from the set point. Although it is possible to limit the range of values of the measured variable in which the final element will move from one extreme position to another, it is not possible to move the final element to a new position unless the value of the measured variable changes.

Proportional + Reset Action (Fig. 5), in addition to allowing the final element to take intermediate positions, makes it possible to shift the

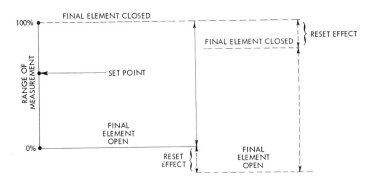

Fig. 5. Proportional + Reset action.

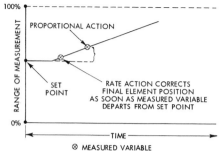

Fig. 6. Proportional + Reset + Rate action.

variable, is called *feedback*. A control system that possesses feedback is termed a *closed loop* (Fig. 7).

Pneumatic Control Systems

In a pneumatic control system, compressed air is supplied to the controlling element. As the value of the measured variable changes, the pneumatic output of the controlling

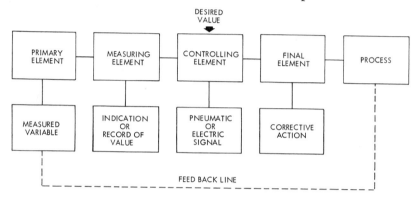

Fig. 7. Block diagram of automatic control system with feedback line.

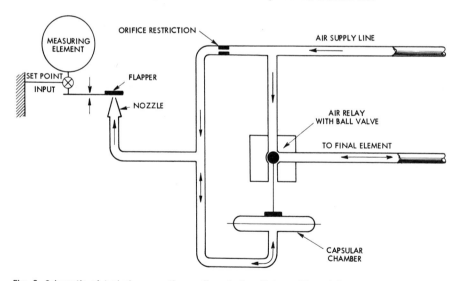

Fig. 8. Schematic of typical pneumatic on-off controller. Note position of flapper-nozzle mechanism and air relay valve.

element changes with it. A flapper-nozzle mechanism provides the means of controlling the pneumatic output.

On-Off Action. In Fig. 8 is a simple diagram of a typical pneumatic ON-OFF controller. When the measuring element senses that the measured variable has departed from the set point, the flapper-nozzle relationship

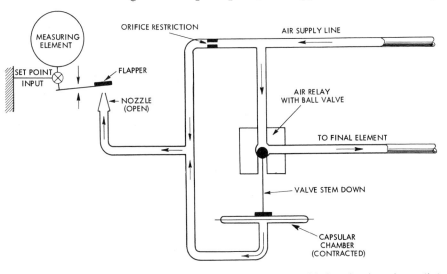

Fig. 9. Flapper-nozzle mechanism in pneumatic controller is open, positioning air relay valve so that maximum signal is sent to final element.

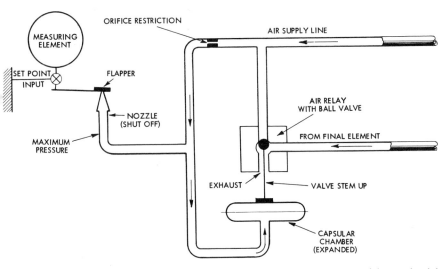

Fig. 10. Flapper-nozzle mechanism is closed, positioning air relay valve so that minimum signal is sent to final element.

changes. When the flapper is moved away from the nozzle, a minimum signal is sent to the air relay, which in turn sends a maximum signal to

the final element, causing it to move to one extreme position (Fig. 9). When the flapper is moved against the nozzle a minimum signal results

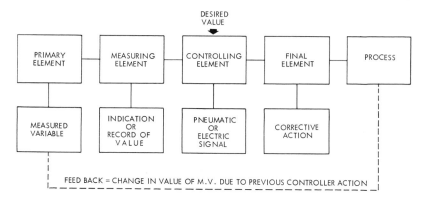

Fig. 11. On-off control system in which feedback is provided by the process. Feedback equals change in value of measured variable due to previous controller action.

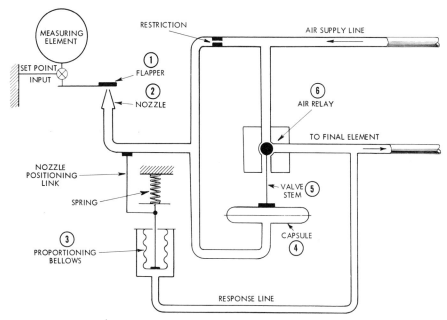

Fig. 12. Flapper-nozzle mechanism in pneumatic control system. (1) Flapper, positioned by measuring element. (2) Moveable nozzle positioned by (3) proportioning bellows which expands or contracts as pressure in the response line changes. (4) Capsule which expands or contracts as pressure in nozzle line changes. (5) Valve stem, positioned by capsule. (6) Air relay valve which regulates pressure to final element and response line.

and the final element moves to its other extreme position (Fig. 10). There is no in-between signal. The only feedback in this system is provided by the process itself (Fig. 11). When the final element moves to an extreme position it causes a maximum change in the energy to the process. This leads to a change in the value of the measured variable. This change is sensed by the measuring element and a new signal goes to the controlling element, closing the loop.

Proportional Action. To achieve proportional action in a pneumatic control system, the flapper-nozzle relationship is modified to permit the use of more than just two positions. Using the same schematic as for the ON-OFF controller, all that needs to be added is a response line to carry the output signal from the air relay to a mechanism that accurately positions the flapper or nozzle. If the measuring element positions the flapper, this added mechanism positions the nozzle, and vice versa. In Fig. 12 the flapper is positioned by the measuring element; hence the nozzle is positioned by the added mechanism.

The action of such a pneumatic proportional action controller, using

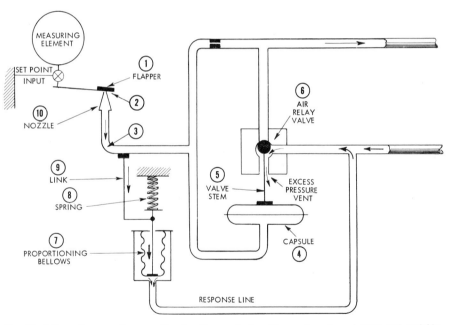

Fig. 13. Action of pneumatic proportional action controller. Change in value of measured variable causes measuring element to move flapper down (1), reducing passage of escaping air (2) and increasing air pressure in nozzle line (3). Capsule (4) expands due to increased pressure and raises valve stem (5). Air relay valve (6) reduces air pressure to final element and to response line, causing proportioning bellows (7) to expand, which causes spring (8) to expand and move the nozzle positioning link (9) downward so that the nozzle (10) is also moved downward, re-establishing its original relationship with the flapper but at a new position.

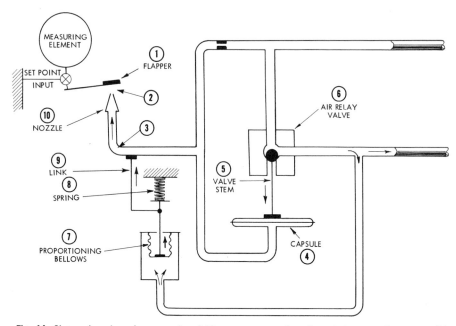

Fig. 14. Change in value of measured variable causes measuring element to move flapper up (1), increasing passage of escaping air (2) and reducing air pressure and lowers valve stem (5). Air relay valve (6) increases air pressure to final element and to response line, causing proportioning bellows (7) to contract, which compresses spring (8) and moves nozzle positioning link (9) upward so that nozzle (10) is moved upward, re-establishing original relationship but at a new position.

a bellows-actuated linkage to position the nozzle, can be seen in Fig. 13, which shows the direction of motion of the nozzle and bellows linkage when the flapper moves in a downward direction. Fig. 14 shows the direction of motion for the opposite condition. The addition of the response line provides many positions of flapper and nozzle. Each position of the measuring element calls for a new flapper-nozzle position and therefore a new controlled air pressure output signal.

Proportional Band. Deviation of the measured variable from the set point will cause a change in the controlled air output. It is often neces-

sary to regulate the amount of deviation which will cause a maximum change of the controlled air output. The proportional band of a controller is the range of values of the measured variable through which the measuring element moves as the controlled air output changes from mini-

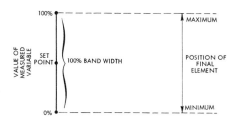

Fig. 15. Effect of 100% proportional band on final element.

mum to maximum. The adjustment of this range is termed proportional band adjustment. The proportional band is expressed in percentage of total range of the measured variable. Thus, in the instrument described above, the proportional band is 100% since the measured variable must change from its maximum to its minimum value for the controlled air pressure to do likewise (Fig. 15). In some processes it may be necessary to reduce the proportional band, and in others it may be necessary to expand it. There are pneumatic controllers available with proportional band adjustment from 5% to 400%.

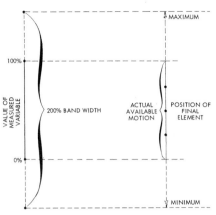

Fig. 17. Effect of 200% proportional band on final element.

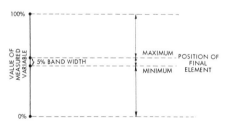

Fig. 16. Effect of 5% proportional band on final element.

Assuming that the measuring range of the instrument is 0 to 100, a 5% proportional band means that the control signal changes from minimum to maximum for a change of 5 in the measured variable (Fig. 16). This change of 5 could occur between 20 and 25, 45 and 50, 73 and 78, etc., depending upon the location of the set point. If the set point were at 50, the 5% would be between 47½ and 52½.

A proportional band of 200% does not permit the controller to reach its minimum or maximum signal (Fig. 17). Again, assuming the measuring range of the instrument to be 0 to 100, the 200% proportional band requires the value of the measured variable to change from 0 to 200, −50 to +150, or 50 to 250, and so on. This is impossible since the range of the instrument is only 0 to 100. The effect of such a wide proportional band is to provide finer control, since for a change of 100% of the range of the measured variable, the controlled air pressure changes only 50%.

This proportional band adjustment is made by regulating the amount of motion of the nozzle for each unit of air pressure from the air relay (Fig. 18).

Automatic Reset. Automatic Reset is added to the pneumatic controller by modifying the output signal from the air relay as it passes to the flapper-nozzle mechanism. Using the same schematic as for proportional control, reset action requires the ad-

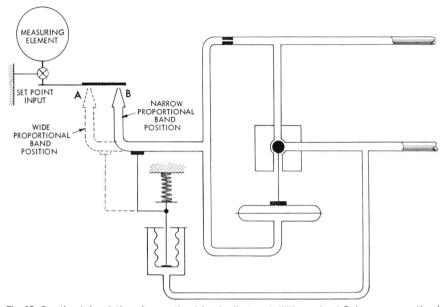

Fig. 18. Functional description of proportional band adjustment. With nozzle at B (narrow proportional band position), less movement of flapper is required to cause change in pressure in line to capsule than with nozzle at A (wide proportional band position). This means that a smaller change in response line pressure is required with nozzle at B to restore original relationship of flapper and nozzle.

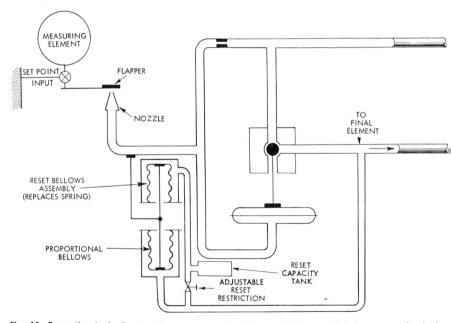

Fig. 19. Proportional + Reset action requires adjustable restriction, reset bellows, capacity tank.

dition of an adjustable restriction, a capacity tank and a reset bellows (Fig. 19). The air signal from the air relay, in addition to entering the proportional bellows, passes through the adjustable restriction and the tank to the reset bellows. The motion of the reset bellows opposes the motion of the proportional bellows.

The proportional and reset bellows are in balance only when the signal to the final element positions it so that the energy supplied to the process is correct to maintain the set point (Fig. 20). When this is not true, and the measuring element continues to move the flapper because of the error between set point and control point, the proportional and reset bellows are not in balance. As long as these bellows are not in balance the air pressure signal to the final element continues to change. This permits the final element to provide more or less energy to the process as required. The actual adjustment is measured in the number of times per minute the proportional and reset bellows are allowed to balance when there is an error. This is called reset time. Such action may be necessary to take care of changes in the energy requirements of a process. These changes are called load changes.

Rate Response. Rate response—

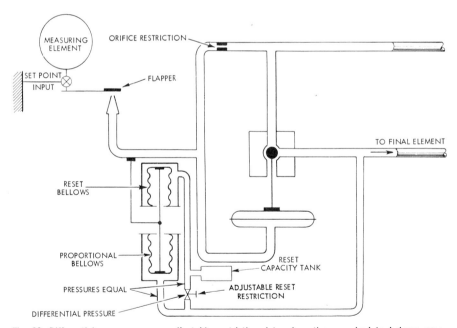

Fig. 20. Differential pressure across adjustable restriction determines time required to balance pressures between proportional bellows and reset bellows. As long as unbalance exists, air flows through restriction. During reset action pressures are unbalanced, causing nozzle motion and therefore change in signal to final element. Only when control is at set point are pressures in lines to proportional and reset bellows equal and nozzle and flapper maintained in original relationship.

sometimes called derivative action —is added to a pneumatic controller by further modifying the output signal from the air relay.

In the schematic of a pneumatic controller with proportional + reset + rate action (Fig. 21), note addition of another restriction and tank. The restriction and the capacity tank delay the corrective motion of the proportional bellows. The amount of delay varies with the rate at which the difference between set point and control point is increasing or decreasing. The actual adjustment is in terms of *rate time*. This action is required for controlling processes where there is very slow response to energy changes. Such a process is said to possess lags. The lags may be due to slow measurement or slow control.

With the four controller actions available, the decision about the proper application of each type must be made.

ON-OFF control is best when the process reacts immediately after an energy change, and when the energy change itself is not too rapid. There should be little or no load change in the process.

Proportional control is best when the process reacts almost at once after an energy change, and when the energy change is quite slow. There may be load changes, but they should not be large or rapid or of long duration.

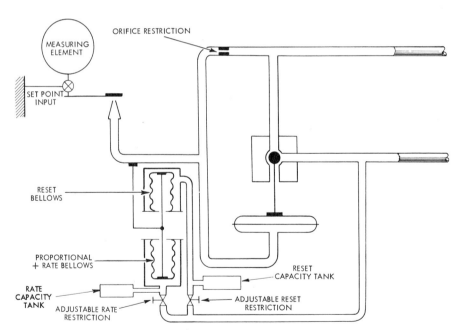

Fig. 21. Proportional + Reset + Rate action requires addition of another adjustable restriction and capacity tank which delays change of pressure acting on proportional + rate bellows. This permits pressure to final element to continue to change as flapper nozzle relationship changes.

Proportional + Reset control is best when the process reacts moderately soon after an energy change. The energy change itself may be fast or slow. There may be load changes, but they should not be too rapid, although they may be greater and of longer duration than can be handled by proportional action alone.

Proportional + Reset + Rate control should be able to handle any process regardless of its characteristics. It should be noted that the adjustment of proportional band, reset time, and rate time are interdependent. If a change is made in one adjustment it will not benefit the control unless changes in the other adjustments are also made. Ideally, there is a given setting for each of the control actions for each process condition. Although there are mathematical methods by which approximation of the proper settings may be made, study of the control achieved and an understanding of the effects of each control action adjustment generally provide better results. A proper understanding of the four controller actions is essential to the study of control.

Electrical Control Systems

There are electrical controllers available that will provide all the control actions previously mentioned.

ON-OFF Control can be accomplished by any device which will open or close an electrical circuit when the measured variable departs from the set point. Thermostats, float switches, and pressure switches are typical of these.

Proportional Control in an electrical controller requires an arrangement that will provide an electrical output that changes as the measured variable departs from the set point. There are many such arrangements. A typical electrical proportional controller is shown in block diagram form in Fig. 22.

Note that there are two slidewires — one for measurement and one for control. The unbalance detector senses the difference between the value of the measured variable and the desired value (set point). This difference is transmitted to the amplifier, which in turn sends it to the control motor. The control motor responds by driving to the new posi-

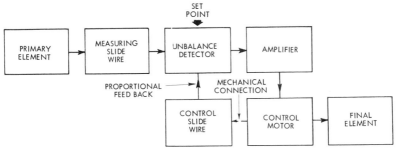

Fig. 22. Block diagram of electrical proportional controller.

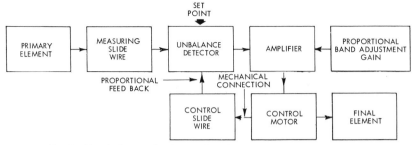

Fig. 23. Electrical proportional controller with proportional band adjustment.

tion called for. At the same time the control motor positions the final element and the control slidewire, which transmits a signal to the unbalance detector, nullifying the original unbalance. The unbalance detector then produces no output signal, hence the control motor receives no signal and its movement stops, leaving the control slidewire and final element at their new position. Thus the position of the final element changes with each departure from the desired value of the measured variable.

To achieve proportional band adjustment in this proportional controller, a means must be provided that will permit a variation in the magnitude of the unbalance signal from the balance detector for each unit of departure of the measured variable from the set point (Fig. 23). In an electric controller this is frequently called a gain adjustment. For a narrow proportional band the adjustment is set so that a small departure from set point creates considerable unbalance, causing the control motor to drive a large amount

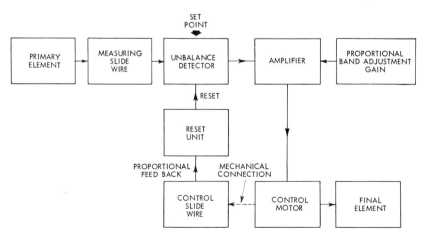

Fig. 24. Electrical proportional controller with reset.

to restore balance. Likewise in a wide proportional band the adjustment is set so that a large departure from set point creates little unbalance, causing the control motor to drive only a small amount to restore balance.

Automatic Reset. Automatic reset may be added to such an electric controller by modifying the feedback signal from the control slidewire as shown in Fig. 24. The reset unit allows a shift in the relationship of the control slidewire position and the measuring slidewire position, as long as an unbalance between measured value and set point exists. Thus if the position of the control motor called for with proportional controller action does not restore balance, the automatic reset unit continues to send a signal to the unbalance detector until a position is reached that restores balance to the system.

Rate Response. Rate response requires further modification of the proportional feedback signal from the control slidewire as shown in Fig. 25. The rate unit receives the proportional feedback signal from the control slidewire and introduces a delay in the signal to the unbalance detector. The delay varies with the rate at which the unbalance occurs. The more rapid the unbalance, the longer the delay, and vice versa. As a result, the unbalance signal to the control motor is greater than if feedback were to restore balance immediately, thus allowing the control motor to move more than with proportional action alone.

The foregoing description of an electric controller refers to a system in which the final element may take many positions. There are electric control systems in which the final element may be either ON or OFF, but throttling control is still required. A heating process that uses electric heating elements is typical. The heaters can only be turned ON or OFF.

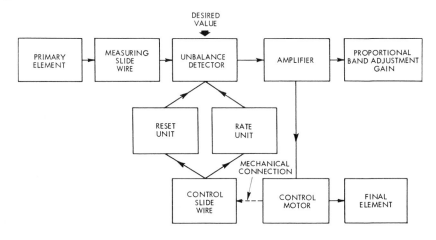

Fig. 25. Electrical proportional controller with reset and rate.

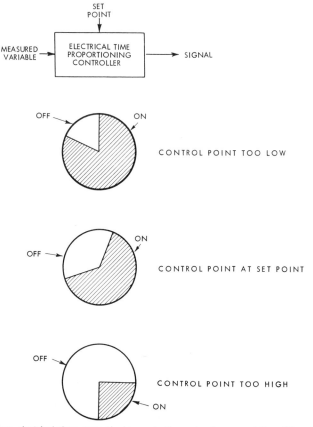

Fig. 26. Signal from electrical time proportioning controller varies the percent time ON and the percent time OFF as measured variable departs from set point.

There is no intermediate position. In such a system, throttling is accomplished by proportioning the TIME-ON TIME-OFF cycles (Fig. 26). Thus, for each particular set point there is a particular % time ON, % time OFF ratio. As the measured variable departs from the set point this ratio changes. This arrangement is equivalent to proportional action.

Automatic Reset may be added to such a system (Fig. 27). This allows the ratio to be changed as long as the measured variable is not at the set point.

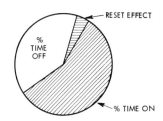

Fig. 27. Reset effect permits the ratio of percent time ON to percent time OFF to be changed if ratio called for by proportional control does not maintain set point.

Rate response is generally not offered in such systems, hence the installation requires that lags be kept to a minimum. Though schematically such a system resembles the control motor type system, the electrical circuitry and components are quite different. Time proportioning cannot be performed with the same equipment as position proportioning.

Final Elements

Final elements are those devices which actually regulate the level of energy of a process. These include valves, dampers, louvres, pumps, heating elements, etc.

All of these require operators that will provide precise regulation. These operators must be compatible with the control system used, whether pneumatic, electric, or hydraulic.

Typical of the pneumatic final elements is the diaphragm operated valve (Fig. 28). The diaphragm operator receives the pneumatic signal from the controller and moves the valve stem up or down as the signal varies. The force on the diaphragm is balanced by the force of the spring. The body contains the throttling mechanism, which consists of a plug attached to the valve stem, and the valve seat, which is built into the body.

Some valves have an air-to-close diaphragm operator and a globe body. See Fig. 29. Air-to-open dia-

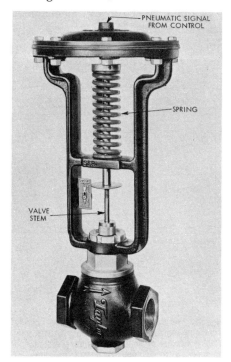

Fig. 28. Pneumatic diaphragm motor valve. (Taylor Instrument Co.)

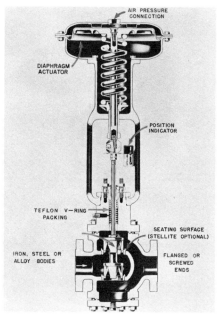

Fig. 29. Air to close operator. (Bailey Meter Co.)

phragm operators are also available as are many other types of bodies.

In addition to diaphragm operators there are also pneumatic piston and cylinder types.

The positioning of dampers and louvres may also be accomplished using such pneumatic operators. In addition to the variations mentioned here many others are available.

Electrical positioners may be solenoid- or motor-operated. Solenoids permit only two positions, whereas motors can provide continuous positioning. The solenoids and motors may be ac or dc operated.

It is also possible to combine electrical and pneumatic operations. For instance, a solenoid operated valve may be used to regulate the flow of air to a pneumatic final element or a pneumatic operator may be used to control the position of a rheostat which regulates the movement of an electric motor-operated final element.

There are also electro-hydraulic actuators in which an electric motor drives a pump in a hydraulic system. The pump in turn forces oil into an actuating cylinder. The cylinder moves the positioning shaft. Fig. 30 is an example of such an operator.

Pneumatic valve operators are sometimes affected by mechanical difficulties that make it extremely difficult to achieve accurate positioning of the valve stem. To overcome

Fig. 30. Globe valve with electro-hydraulic actuator. (Minneapolis-Honeywell Regulator Co.)

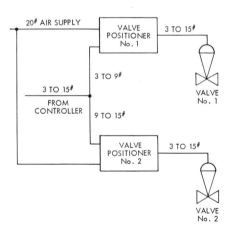

Fig. 31. Two valves with positioners can operate from one controller. Valve positioner 1 uses only 3 to 9 pounds of controller signal pressure and produces 3 to 15 pounds output pressure for valve 1. Valve positioner 2 uses only 9 to 15 pounds of controller signal pressure and produces 3 to 15 pounds output pressure for valve 2.

such difficulties auxiliary valve positioners are frequently used. These are combination balance and power amplifiers. The pneumatic signal from the controller enters the valve positioner which passes it to the valve operator. By means of a link attached to the stem, the positioner receives a mechanical signal, which indicates the stem position. If the stem does not stop at the correct position called for by the controller, the valve positioner senses this and makes the necessary correction. It is also possible to use a valve positioner to permit total valve motion for a limited pneumatic signal from the controller. By this means (Fig. 31), two valves—with positioners— can be operated from only one controller, with a portion of the controller signal operating one valve and the remaining portion operating the other. This is sometimes required when the control of two separate fluids is required to produce the desired value of the measured variable. Steam and cold water are sometimes controlled by one temperature controller in this manner.

part two

PART TWO discusses some of the same instruments that were examined in Part One, but in greater detail, and includes a chapter on electricity and electronics. Level measurement is not repeated since the principles involved are not sufficiently distinctive to warrant extensive discussion. For the most part, the devices used for level measurement are adaptations of those used for other measurements such as pressure or differential pressure. And although the transmission of process information is a valuable function of instrumentation, transmission is not repeated because the methods used are adaptations or complications of mechanical or electrical systems used in measurement and control.

Chapter 9 _____ Electricity

ELECTRICAL energy is produced by chemical cells (batteries), light sensitive cells (photocells and solar batteries), temperature sensitive elements (thermocouples), pressure sensitive elements (crystals), and magnetic devices (rotating generators).

Voltage is the measure of the potential energy difference between two points in an electrical circuit. The unit of voltage is the volt. Current is the measure of the flow of electrical

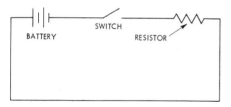

Fig. 1. Battery, resistor, and switch comprise a simple electrical circuit.

energy between two points at different potential levels. The unit of current is the ampere. Resistance in an electrical circuit refers to the resistance to current flow. The unit of resistance is the ohm.

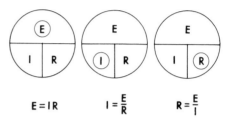

$$E = IR \qquad I = \frac{E}{R} \qquad R = \frac{E}{I}$$

Fig. 2. An easy way to remember Ohm's law.

Direct Current

The simplest direct current (dc) electrical circuit consists of a battery, a resistor, and a switch (Fig. 1). When the voltage at the battery is equal to 1 volt, and the resistance is equal to 1 ohm, the current is equal to 1 ampere. This relationship follows Ohm's law, which can be expressed mathematically as E (voltage) = I (current) × R (resistance). Fig. 2 shows a simple way to remember Ohm's law.

Circuits in Series. There are frequently several resistances in an electrical circuit. When these resistances are joined like the links of a chain, they are said to be in series. In this arrangement (see Fig. 3), the resistances are additive: the total

85

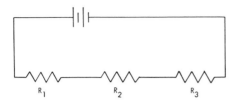

Fig. 3. Resistances joined like the links of a chain are said to be in series.

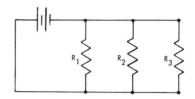

Fig. 4. Resistances joined like the rungs of a ladder are said to be in parallel.

resistance is equal to the sum of the separate resistances: R total $= R_1 + R_2 + R_3$ and so on.

As the current passes through each resistance, there is a loss of voltage in accordance with Ohm's law: voltage loss through R_1 is equal to IR_1; voltage loss through R_2 is equal to IR_2; therefore, the total voltage loss through several resistances in series equals IR_T. ($_T =$ total.)

The sum of the voltage drops in a circuit is equal to the sum of the supply voltages. This is called Kirchoff's law of voltage.

The characteristics of series circuits can be summarized as follows:

1. The total resistance is equal to the sum of the individual resistances.

2. The current through all the resistances is the same.

3. The sum of the voltage drops across the individual resistances is equal to the applied voltage.

Circuits in Parallel. When resistances in an electrical circuit are joined like the rungs of a ladder, they are said to be in parallel. In this arrangement (see Fig. 4), the reciprocal of the total resistance equals the sum of the reciprocals of the individual resistances:

$$\frac{1}{R_T} = \frac{1}{R_1} + \frac{1}{R_2} + \frac{1}{R_3}$$ and so on.

Since each individual resistance is connected to the applied voltage terminals, the voltage across each resistor is equal to the applied voltage. The current through each resistor varies with the value of the resistor. The battery current is equal to the sum of the currents through the parallel resistances. According to Kirchoff's law of current, the sum of the currents entering a junction point in an electrical circuit is equal to the sum of the currents leaving the junction point (Fig. 5).

The characteristics of parallel resistance circuits can be summarized as follows:

1. The reciprocal of the total resistance is equal to the sum of the

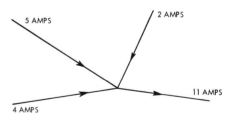

Fig. 5. The sum of the currents leaving a point in a circuit must always be equal to the sum of the currents entering that point (Kirchoff's law of current).

reciprocals of the individual resistances in the circuit.

2. The total current is equal to the sum of all the branch currents.

3. The ratio of the branch currents is the inverse of the resistance ratio:

$$\frac{I_1}{I_2} = \frac{R_2}{R_1} \text{ and } \frac{I_1}{I_3} = \frac{R_3}{R_1},$$

and so on.

Networks. Resistances in a circuit may be arranged in combination series-parallel arrangements. When two or more components of an electrical network are in series, all the characteristics of series circuits must apply to these components. In the same way, when two or more components of an electrical network are in parallel, all the characteristics of parallel circuits must apply to these components. Electrical circuits may have several sources of voltage in addition to several series-parallel resistances. These are termed resistance networks.

The Wheatstone bridge, which is frequently used in instrumentation for measurement and control, is a special type of resistance network. To determine the voltages and currents, the Wheatstone bridge must be considered as three separate current loops. See Fig. 6.

$$I_T = I_1 + I_2 + I_3$$

$I_1 = $ current through R_3

$I_2 = $ current through R_2

$I_3 = $ current through the galvanometer

$I_1 + I_3 = $ current through R_1

$I_2 + I_3 = $ current through R_4

When the meter is a deflection type and R_4 is the unknown resistance, the scale of the meter may be calibrated in units of resistance since any change in R_4 causes a proportional change in I_3 (the current through the meter). Because it is the current through the meter which causes its deflection, there is a position of the pointer for each value of R_4.

In the null-balance Wheatstone bridge the meter is used to detect the condition when there is no current

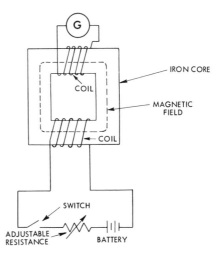

Fig. 7. Circuit showing mutual inductance in which the flux from one inductance links the turns of another inductance.

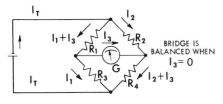

Fig. 6. Diagram of the Wheatstone bridge network.

through it. In this type of bridge circuit, R_3 is an adjustable resistance and R_4 is the resistance being measured. R_1 and R_2 are the fixed resistors. The scale is located at R_3 in such a position that the slider, in addition to establishing the value of R_3, also indicates the value of R_4.

Since there is no current through the galvanometer when the null-balance Wheatstone bridge is in balanced condition,

$$I_1R_1 = I_2R_2, \text{ or } I_1 = \frac{R_2I_2}{R_1},$$

and

$$I_1R_3 = I_3R_4, \text{ or } I_1 = \frac{R_4I_2}{R_3}.$$

Eliminating I_1,

$$\frac{R_2I_2}{R_1} = \frac{R_4I_2}{R_3}$$

and solving R_4,

$$R_4 = \frac{R_2R_3}{R_1}.$$

From this relationship it can be seen that for each value of R_4 there is a balancing value of R_3, making it possible to determine the value of R_4 by adjusting R_3.

Inductance. In addition to the components of an electrical circuit which resist the flow of current, there are those which resist a *change* in the current. This property of an electric component is called *inductance*. Fig. 7 is a simple circuit which demonstrates inductance.

When the switch is closed, a current flows in the primary circuit. Magnetic lines of force are produced by the coil wrapped around the iron core. As the adjustable resistance is changed, the number of lines of force changes. This change causes a current to flow in the secondary circuit. The current in the secondary circuit flows in the direction which counteracts the effect of a change of current in the primary circuit. The voltage in the secondary circuit is called the induced electromotive force (emf).The magnitude of the voltage in the secondary circuit depends upon the rate of change of the primary circuit. This type of inductance involving a primary and a secondary winding is called *mutual inductance*.

The symbol for inductance is L, and the basic unit is the henry. When a current in the primary, which is changing at the rate of 1 ampere per second, induces an emf of 1 volt in the secondary, the circuit has a mutual inductance of 1 henry.

In addition to mutual inductance involving primary and secondary windings, there is also *self inductance*, which describes the property of a circuit to oppose any change in the current through it. See Fig. 8. Although even a straight wire has self-inductance, a coil is the most

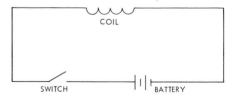

Fig. 8. Circuit showing self inductance which produces an electromotive force in the circuit tending to oppose the flow of the current producing the magnetic field.

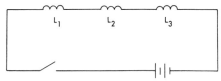

Fig. 9. Inductance in series.

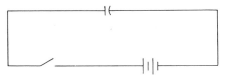

Fig. 11. Capacitor in circuit.

common inductor, since the magnitude of the self-inductance is great enough to be of importance. When a current changing at the rate of 1 ampere per second induces a counter emf of 1 volt in a coil, the value of the inductance is 1 henry.

Inductances may be joined in series or in parallel. When in series (Fig. 9), the total inductance equals the sum of the individual inductances: $L_T = L_1 + L_2 + L_3$, and so on.

When in parallel (Fig. 10), the reciprocal of the total inductance equals the sum of the reciprocals of the individual inductances:

$$\frac{1}{L_T} = \frac{1}{L_1} + \frac{1}{L_2} + \frac{1}{L_3},\text{ and so on.}$$

Capacitance. Inductance is the property of an electric circuit that resists a change in current; *capacitance* is the property which resists a change in voltage. The circuit component which possesses capacitance is called a *capacitor*. A simple capacitor consists of two parallel metal plates separated by air or other nonconductive material called the *dielec-*

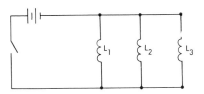

Fig. 10. Inductance in parallel.

tric. Fig. 11 illustrates a simple circuit containing a capacitor.

When the switch is closed, current begins to flow in the circuit. It continues to flow until the voltage across the plates of the capacitor equals the battery voltage. The current flow stops when capacitor voltage reaches this magnitude. The capacitor stores this voltage. The symbol for capacitance is the letter C. The unit of capacitance is the *farad*. A circuit has a capacitance of one farad when a charge of one coulomb is required to raise the circuit voltage by one volt:

$$C = \frac{Q}{V}.$$

A coulomb (Q) is a unit of quantity of electrical charge—it refers to the number of charged particles (electrons) and is a calculated unit. Another definition of the farad is: When a voltage changing at the rate of one volt per second causes a current of one ampere to flow into a capacitor, the capacitance is one farad. The farad is too large a unit for most electrical circuitry, hence the microfarad is used; 1 microfarad equals one millionth of a farad. To express even smaller units of capacitance, the picofarad is used. One picofarad equals one millionth of a microfarad.

Capacitors may be connected in series or in parallel.

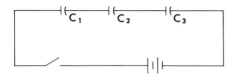

Fig. 12. Capacitors in series.

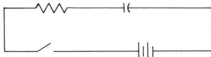

Fig. 14. The resistor is in the circuit to protect the battery.

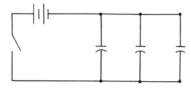

Fig. 13. Capacitors in parallel.

When in series (Fig. 12), the reciprocal of the total capacitance equals the sum of the reciprocals of the individual capacitances:

$$\frac{1}{C_T} = \frac{1}{C_1} + \frac{1}{C_2} + \frac{1}{C_3}, \text{ and so on.}$$

When in parallel (Fig. 13), the total capacitance equals the sum of the individual capacitances:

$$C_T = C_1 + C_2 + C_3, \text{ and so on.}$$

The build-up of voltage in a capacitor is called "charging," and the dis-

sipation of the voltage "discharging." In actual circuits, a resistor is added to the circuit to limit the charging current as shown in the resistor-capacitor network in Fig. 14.

The effect of this current limiting resistor is to increase the time required to charge the capacitor. Fig. 15 is a graph of the rise of voltage in a capacitor being charged through a resistor. The curve starts the instant the switch is closed.

The time required for the capacitor voltage to reach 63.2% of its final value is termed the *time constant*. The time constant (t, in seconds) equals Resistance (in ohms) times Capacitance (in farads), or t = RC.

Fig. 16 is a graph of the discharge of the *same* capacitor in the *same* circuit.

Note that the capacitor discharge

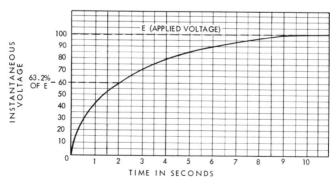

Fig. 15. Graph showing the rise of voltage in a capacitor that is being charged through a resistor.

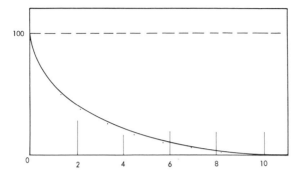

Fig. 16. Graph showing the discharge of the same capacitor in the same circuit.

curve has the same shape as the charge curve — in fact is almost the mirror image of it. The time constant of discharge is the same as that for the charge t = RC.

Resistance-capacitor networks have many applications in instrumentation. For example:

1. Reset action in an electrical controller which is accomplished in an R-C network as shown in Fig. 17.
2. Rate action in an electrical controller which is accomplished in an R-C network as shown in Fig. 18.
3. Precise timers for short intervals can be made using these R-C networks.

In conclusion: *Resistance* is the property of an electrical device in a circuit, which opposes the flow of current in the circuit. *Inductance*

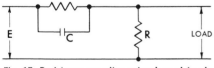

Fig. 17. Resistance-capacitor network used to obtain reset action.

is the property of an electrical device in a circuit which opposes a *change* in the flow of current in the circuit. *Capacitance* is the property of an electrical circuit which opposes a change in voltage in the circuit.

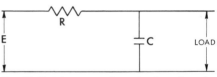

Fig. 18. Resistance-capacitor network used to obtain rate action.

Alternating Current

All the preceding information pertains to direct current which may be defined as having a steady rate of current flow in one direction. Since the resistance of the circuit is of a fixed value, the voltage will also maintain a steady value.

In an alternating current (ac) circuit the voltage and current vary continuously between zero and maximum values. A comparison of ac and dc currents is illustrated in Fig. 19. In the diagram, the horizontal line represents a zero value of current. The portion of the drawing above the line

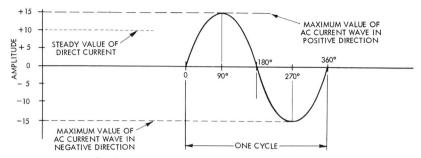

Fig. 19. A comparison of alternating and direct currents.

represents current values in a positive direction; the portion below the line, negative current values. The dotted line beginning at 10 amps in the left of the figure represents a direct current of 10 amps. The curved lines illustrate an ac wave passing from zero value to maximum in a positive direction, back to zero, and then to maximum value in a negative direction, returning to zero value. Each complete set of positive and negative changes of current is called a full wave or cycle.

The number of complete cycles occurring in one second is referred to as the frequency of the circuit. Alternating current is usually supplied at 60 cycles per second, although frequencies may vary with individual countries.

In the diagram the points of the ac wave are marked in angular degrees because of the angular rotation of the generator that produces alternating current. The amplitude of the curve at any point indicates the value of the current at that instant. The number of degrees in a complete cycle is always 360 even though its frequency may change. In the

diagram, if the time required for one cycle is 1/60 of a second, the frequency is 60 cycles per second.

Fig. 20 shows the curves of the voltage and current in an alternating current resistance circuit. Note that both reach their peak value at the same instant.

Inductive Reactance. Consider now an inductor in an alternating current circuit. It should be remembered that an inductor opposes a change in current through it by creating a voltage which opposes the supply voltage. The voltage across an inductor must always equal the supply voltage. Since in an alternating current circuit

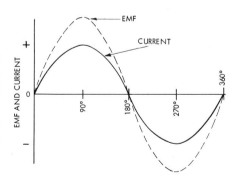

Fig. 20. Emf and current reach peak value at the same instant.

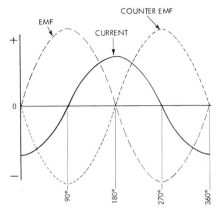

Fig. 21. Applied voltage and induced voltage in a single inductor circuit.

the supply voltage is changing continuously, the opposing voltage also changes continuously. The value of the opposing voltage is proportional to the rate at which the current through the inductor is changing. Fig. 21 is a graph of the applied voltage and the induced voltage in a single inductor circuit. Note that when the applied voltage is at its maximum value, the opposing voltage is at its minimum value. When the opposing voltage is at its maximum value, the current must be changing at a maximum rate. When the opposing voltage is at the zero level, the current is not changing.

It is now possible to draw a curve of the current on the graph (Fig. 22). It will be seen that the current lags the applied and opposing voltage by 90° or 1/4 of a cycle. Since the curves of voltage and current both follow fixed patterns, for a particular inductance and applied voltage there is a constant voltage to current ratio.

Since, according to Ohm's law, the ratio E/I represents resistance it can be said that in an ac circuit inductance is similar to but not the same as resistance. A special term is applied to the resistive effect of inductance. In an alternating current circuit this term is *inductive reactance*. The unit of inductive reactance is the ohm and the symbol is X. A subscript $_L$ may be used to indicate inductance:

$$X_L = \frac{E_L}{I_L} \text{ or}$$

1 ohm inductive reactance

$$= \frac{1 \text{ volt across inductor}}{1 \text{ amp through inductor}}.$$

The magnitude of inductive reactance is directly proportional to the frequency. The inductive reactance is expressed by the formula:

$$X_L = 2\pi fL$$

where

L = inductance in Henrys

X_L = inductive reactance in ohms

f = frequency in cycles per second.

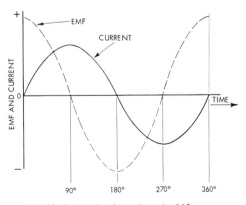

Fig. 22. Current lagging voltage by 90°.

Changing only the magnitude of the applied voltage does not change the inductive reactance. This is true because the E/I ratio remains constant for a particular inductance.

Capacitive Reactance. Capacitance, it should be recalled, is the property of a circuit which resists a change in voltage. In a single capacitance alternating circuit the supply voltage is changing continuously, therefore the voltage across the capacitor must change continuously. This means that the capacitor must be continuously charging and discharging, thus causing a current to flow through it. The current is proportional to the rate at which the voltage across the capacitor is changing. When the voltage is changing at its maximum rate the current is at its maximum value. When the voltage is not changing the current is zero. From the graph (Fig. 23) it can be seen that the current leads the voltage by 90° or ¼ cycle. The curves of voltage and current maintain a fixed pattern, therefore a constant ratio exists.

As has been pointed out under inductance the ratio E/I represents resistance, therefore capacitance in an ac circuit behaves like resistance. The term for this resistance to the flow of alternating current is *capacitive reactance*. The unit of capacitive reactance is the ohm and the symbol is X. A subscript $_c$ may be used to indicate capacitance:

$$X_c = \frac{E_c}{I_c} \text{ or}$$

1 ohm capacitive reactance

$$= \frac{1 \text{ volt across capacitor}}{1 \text{ amp through capacitor}}$$

The magnitude of capacitive reactance (X_c) is inversely proportional to frequency, expressed by the formula:

$$X_c = \frac{1}{2\pi fC}$$

where

X_c = capacitive reactance in ohms

C = capacitance in farads

Changing the magnitude of the applied voltage does not change the capacitive reactance.

Impedance. The total resistance to current flow in an alternating current circuit is called *impedance*. The symbol for impedance is Z:

$$Z = \frac{E \text{ (applied voltage)}}{I \text{ (circuit current)}}.$$

The value of impedance is obtained by diagramming, using a right triangle with θ being the angle be-

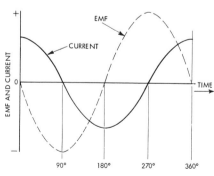

Fig. 23. Current leading voltage by 90°.

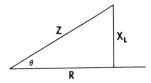

Fig. 24. Inductive reactance.

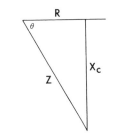

Fig. 25. Capacitive reactance.

In this discussion of reactance and impedance the mathematical relationships have been reduced to a minimum. The purpose of the discussion was to introduce the student to the terms and explain them as simply as possible.

ELECTRONICS

Vacuum Tube Fundamentals

The vacuum tube operates on the principle known as *thermionic emission,* which refers to the freeing of electrons electrically heated in a vacuum. The heat is supplied by a wire filament heated to incandescence. The higher the temperature, the more electrons emitted (Fig. 26). Another electrical conductor *(plate),* located in the vacuum and supplied with a positive electric charge from outside the vacuum, gathers the electrons which are negatively charged. This directional flow of electrons constitutes an electric current. The higher the positive charge on the plate, the higher the plate current. A simple two element vacuum tube is called a *diode* (Fig. 27).

tween the applied voltage and the resulting current.

For a circuit containing a resistance and an inductance in series the value of $Z = \sqrt{R^2 + X_L^2}$. (See Fig. 24.)

For a circuit containing a resistance and a capacitance in series the value of $Z = \sqrt{R^2 + X_C^2}$. (See Fig. 25.)

For a circuit containing a resistance, an inductance and a capacitance in series the value of

$$Z = \sqrt{R^2 + (X_L - X_C)^2}.$$

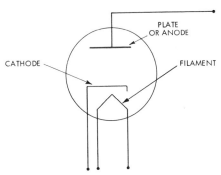

Fig. 27. The elements of a diode.

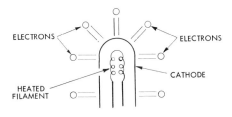

Fig. 26. Thermionic emission.

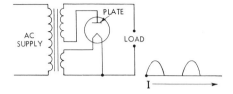

Fig. 28. Half-wave rectification.

Rectification. Since the current flow in a vacuum tube is always in one direction (from negative to positive) a two element tube (diode) can be used to change alternating current to direct current. This is known as *rectification*. Since the plate is positive with respect to the *cathode* (the element which emits electrons) only during each half cycle of the alternating current, the resulting direct current occurs only during this half cycle, and hence is not continuous, nor is it of constant magnitude. This is known as *half-wave rectification* (Fig. 28). It is possible to make the direct current continuous by adding a second plate which is positive with respect to the cathode during the other half cycle of the alternating current. This is termed *full-wave rectification* (Fig. 29).

Amplification. A third element called a *grid*, when inserted between the cathode and the plate, permits

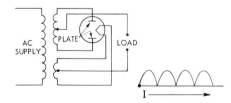

Fig. 29. Full-wave rectification.

regulation of the number of electrons reaching the plate. Such a tube is called a *triode* (Fig. 30). When the grid is positive with respect to the cathode, more electrons pass to the plate. When the grid is negative with respect to the cathode, few electrons reach the plate. A small change in the voltage of the grid has the same effect as a large change in the plate voltage. This is what is meant by *amplification*, and the ratio of grid voltage and plate voltage which produces equal results is called the amplification

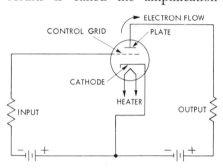

Fig. 30. The elements of a triode.

factor of the tube. An amplification factor of 20 (Fig. 31) means that if the grid voltage is changed by 1 volt, the effect on the plate current is the same as if the plate voltage were changed by 20 volts.

The symbol for the amplification factor is the Greek letter μ (pronounced mu). The amplification factors of vacuum tubes range from about 3 to 100. When the amplification factor is less than 8 the tube is said to have a low μ. Medium μ tubes are those whose amplification factor is between 8 and 30. Above 30 the tube has a high μ.

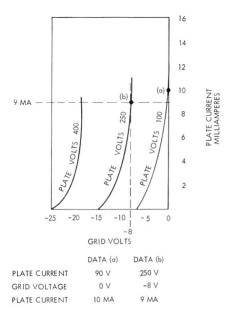

DATA (a)	DATA (b)	
PLATE CURRENT	90 V	250 V
GRID VOLTAGE	0 V	-8 V
PLATE CURRENT	10 MA	9 MA

Fig. 31. Characteristics of a tube with an amplification factor of 20.

The amplification characteristics of a tube are generally described in graphic form. The curves describe tube performance when the plate current is made to flow through resistances of various magnitudes.

Oscillation. The amplification can be modified by adding or subtracting some of the plate voltage and the grid voltage. This arrangement is called *feedback.* When a part of the plate voltage is added to the grid voltage, the feedback is positive; when it is subtracted, the feedback is negative. Positive feedback increases the amplification; when all the grid voltage is supplied by positive feedback and the magnitude of the feedback is great enough, the tube becomes an oscillator.

Negative feedback decreases the amplification. The more the negative feedback, the less the tube performs according to the characteristic curve. Negative feedback also tends to eliminate distortion of the plate current.

The three elements of the vacuum tube form three small capacitors. The capacitances are those between:

1. cathode and plate
2. cathode and grid
3. grid and plate

They are called interelectrode capacitances and may cause instability. The capacitance between the grid and plate, which is the most disturbing, may be reduced by the addition of a fourth element—a *screen.* The four element tube is called a *tetrode* (Fig. 32). The screen is placed between the grid and the plate, and is positive with respect to the cathode. It attracts electrons from the cathode, but most of these pass through the screen to the plate. Thus, the screen reduces the capacitance between grid and plate. In addition, because the plate current is more dependent on the screen voltage than on the plate voltage, it is possible to obtain higher amplification with a tetrode.

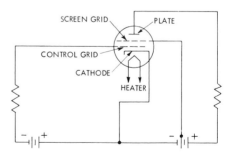

Fig. 32. The elements of a tetrode.

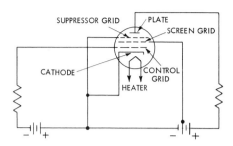

Fig. 33. The elements of a pentode

Because of the closeness of the screen to the plate, it is possible for the electrons which pass to the plate at very high speed to dislodge electrons already there and cause them to be attracted to the screen. This would lower the plate current. To eliminate this possibility, a fifth element—a *suppressor*—is added between the screen and the plate. The five element tube is called a *pentode* (Fig. 33). The suppressor is generally connected to the cathode and is negative with respect to the plate. Because of its negative charge, the suppressor repels the dislodged electrons back to the plate. Thus, the pentode is more efficient than the tetrode or triode and permits greater amplification.

In instrumentation, electronic circuits employing vacuum tubes are in extensive use: the electrical primary elements may provide variable voltages (thermocouples), and resistances (resistance bulbs); the measuring elements may use resistances, voltages, inductances, or capacitances in balancing circuits. Control elements may be electrical, with voltage or resistance as the output.

Amplification is the most common application of vacuum tube circuits in instrumentation. For instance the voltage output of a thermocouple requires amplification, enabling it to operate a motor. As has been stated, the dc thermocouple voltage is converted to an ac voltage before amplification. A simple electronic amplifier (Fig. 34) uses a single triode with appropriate resistors to establish the voltage levels on filament, grid and plate. The plate resistor is large, making the voltage variations across it considerably greater than the variations of the input voltage. The plate voltage establishes the output voltage.

The addition of a second tube

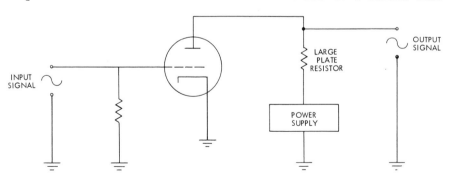

Fig. 34. A triode voltage amplifier.

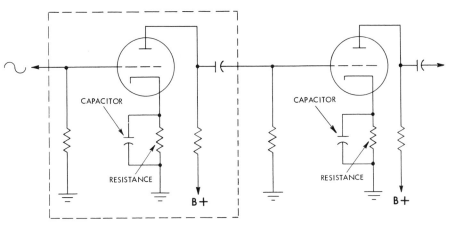

Fig. 35. A two-stage amplifier circuit. Within the dotted lines is one stage.

(Fig. 35) and associated resistors results in a total amplification equal to the product of the amplification of each section. The result is a two-stage amplifier. Note that a capacitor is connected across the resistance to the filament of each tube.

These capacitors maintain a constant voltage across the resistors. There is also a capacitor between the output of the first stage and the second. This capacitor blocks the dc potential of the plate of the first tube from entering the second stage. Other methods for joining the two stages are also used. An inductor or transformer may be substituted for the capacitor. This is the arrangement on which all amplifiers are based. Although multi-stage amplifier circuits are considerably more complicated, close examination will reveal the presence of several fundamental circuits.

Transistor Fundamentals

Recently transistors have replaced vacuum tubes in many electronic circuits because of their small size, low operating voltage, stability and long life. Transistors are made of materials called semiconductors, such as silicon and germanium. These materials have greater resistance to the flow of current than conductive metals, but not as great a resistance as insulators.

Semiconductor crystals used in the manufacture of transistors may be either of two types—N-type or P-type. The N-type is one which, by the addition of a "donor" impurity, possesses a quantity of free electrons. Therefore the N-type is a conductor which depends upon the flow of free electrons for its conductivity.

The P-type is one, which, by the addition of an "acceptor" impurity, is left with a quantity of "holes".

These holes are electrical charge carriers similar to electrons but possessing instead a positive charge. Therefore the P-type is also a conductor which depends upon the flow of positively charged holes for its conductivity.

There are three principal classifications of semiconductors:

1. the diode
2. the bipolar or junction transistor

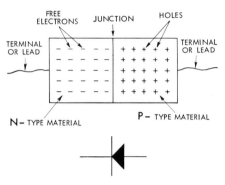

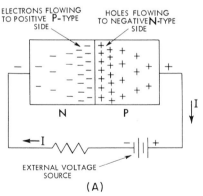

Fig. 36. A semiconductor diode and its schematic symbol.

3. the unipolar or field effect transistor.

Semiconductor Diodes. A semiconductor diode is usually a single crystal of semiconductor material which is artificially created. One half of the crystal is made N-type and the other made P-type by the addition, during processing, of the appropriate impurities. See Fig. 36.

If an external voltage source is applied to a diode so that the negative lead is attached to the N-type half and the positive lead attached to the P-type half, current will flow through the diode. The negatively charged electrons are attracted to the positive P-type side, and the positive holes are attracted to the negative N-type side (Fig. 37A). However, if the externally applied voltage is reversed, making the lead to the N-type side positive and the lead to the P-type side negative, no current will flow through

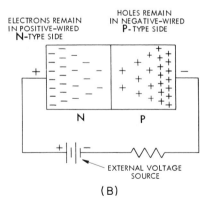

(A)

CURRENT FLOWS THROUGH DIODE AND IN THE EXTERNAL CIRCUIT WHEN THE EXTERNALLY APPLIED VOLTAGE MAKES THE N-TYPE SIDE NEGATIVE AND THE P-TYPE SIDE POSITIVE.

(B)

NO CURRENT FLOWS IN THE DIODE WHEN THE EXTERNALLY APPLIED VOLTAGE MAKES THE N-TYPE SIDE POSITIVE AND THE P-TYPE SIDE NEGATIVE.

Fig. 37. Unidirectional current flow in a semiconductor diode. To pass through the diode, current must be of the correct polarity.

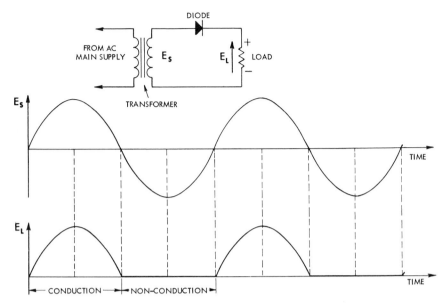

Fig. 38. Only one half of the wave form, representing AC current phase of the acceptable polarity, passes through the half-wave rectifier.

the diode. The electrons are repelled from the negative P-type side and the positive holes are repelled by the positive N-type side. See Fig. 37B.

The practical value of the semiconductor diode lies in its ability to conduct electricity when the N side is wired negative and the P side positive, and to stop conducting when the N side is wired positive and the P side negative. The most common use of this selective conduction is the process known as rectification.

Rectification. The process known as rectification, as we have seen in the section on vacuum tubes, involves converting alternating current (ac) into direct current (dc). The simplest form of rectifier circuit is the half-wave circuit (Fig. 38). In this circuit an ac voltage E_s is applied to

the series combination of the load and the diode. During one half of the input cycle the P region of the diode is positive and the N region negative, and current flows through the diode giving an output voltage E_L across the load. During the other half of the input cycle the N region of the diode is positive and the P region is negative. The diode will not conduct, resulting in no output voltage.

A better, more common form of rectifier circuit uses four diodes in a bridge circuit. It is known as a full-wave bridge rectifier circuit (Fig. 39). During the first half-cycle when the top lead of the transformer is positive and the bottom lead negative, diodes 1 and 3 will not conduct but diodes 2 and 4 will conduct, resulting in a voltage across the load. During the

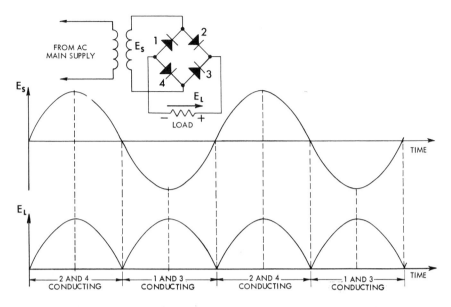

Fig. 39. Using this circuit arrangement, all AC current will be passed by the alternating pairs of diodes. The effect is full-wave rectification.

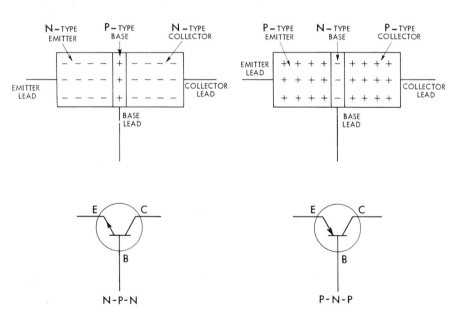

Fig. 40. The construction and the schematic symbols for NPN and PNP transistors.

next half-cycle when the voltage from the transformer has reversed, diodes 2 and 4 will not conduct but diodes 1 and 3 will, again giving an output voltage. In both cases, the output voltage is of the same polarity.

The output voltage from the rectifier circuits is not steady dc. The "dips" in the output voltage can be filled in by placing a capacitor across the load. A capacitor so used is called a filter capacitor. Usually several capacitors are used in conjunction with resistors or inductors.

Junction Transistors. A bipolar transistor is a single crystal of silicon or germanium containing three dissimilar sections: N-type, P-type, and N-type; or P-type, N-type, and P-type. See Fig. 40. The three sections are referred to as the emitter, base, and collector. The base is always the center region. In both types there are two separate N-P junctions, hence the term "bipolar."

NPN Transistors. Fig. 41 shows an NPN transistor connected to the external power source necessary to provide a current flow through the transistor. Disregarding the N-type collector for a moment, we see that the negative lead of one battery is connected to the N-type emitter. The positive lead is connected to the P-type base. The negative terminal connection has the effect of repulsing the negatively charged free electrons in the N-type emitter to the emitter-base junction. At the same time, the positive terminal connection to the base repulses the positive holes to the emitter-base junction where the electrons and holes readily combine.

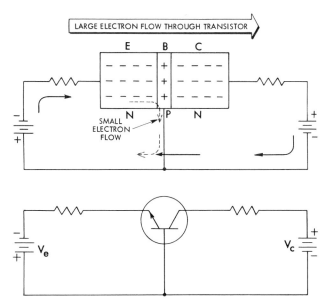

Fig. 41. A complete biasing circuit for an NPN transistor, connected in a common base configuration.

The net effect is an electron flow across the junction, sustained as long as the battery is connected.

If the battery leads are reversed, the positive battery lead attracts the free electrons of the N-type emitter away from the junction. The negative battery lead similarly attracts the holes away from the junction. The net effect is to prevent electrons from flowing across the junction.

We see then that the emitter-base connection resembles the simple diode. When the battery leads are connected as shown in Fig. 41, current crosses the emitter-base junction. The emitter and base are said to be forward biased. When the battery leads are reversed, no current flow is possible. The emitter and base are then said to be reverse biased.

Checking the base-collector connections, it would seem that there can be no current flow through the base-collector junction. The base and collector are reverse biased. It would seem that since there can be no current flow from the base to the collector, then there can be no current flow through the transistor. However, the transistor is so constructed that the base is made extremely thin. Electrons readily cross the emitter-base junction. The extreme thinness of the base means that relatively few electrons crossing the emitter-base junction combine with holes of the P-type base material. The positive connection at the N-type collector terminal attracts most of the electrons *through* the base region, across the base-col-

lector junction, and to the collector. Enough electrons do combine with holes, however, to create a small emitter-base current. This completes the emitter-collector circuit and establishes a current flow through the transistor.

PNP Transistors. PNP transistors are normally connected so that for the emitter-to-base junction, the N-type region is wired negative and the P-type region positive. See Fig. 42. For the base-collector junction the N-type region is wired positive and the P-type region negative.

One would again expect from diode theory that a current would flow from the emitter to the base, but that no current would flow from the base to the collector. This, however, is not correct. In the case of a PNP transistor, holes are attracted from the emitter to the base because the base has been biased negative by the external voltage source. The collector is, in turn, negative with respect to the base. Since the base is thin, most of the holes attracted to it from the emitter flow through it into the collector. In a given transistor, the percentage of holes leaving the emitter that get into the collector is relatively constant for a wide range of applied bias voltages. This value is usually about 98%. The remaining 2% of the holes are conducted out of the base lead.

The NPN transistor shown in Fig. 41 operates primarily by establishing a large electron flow through the

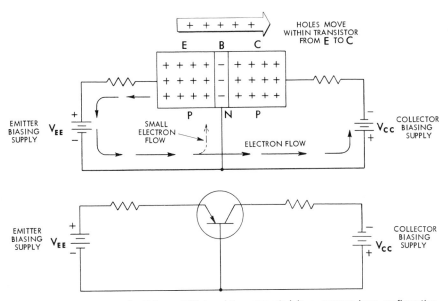

Fig. 42. The basic biasing circuit for a PNP transistor, connected in a common-base configuration.

transistor from the emitter to the collector. The PNP transistor, however, depends for its operation on the flow of *holes* from emitter to collector. Although there is a flow of electrons through the transistor circuit in a direction opposite to that of the flow of holes within the transistor, the main current-carrying activity *within the PNP transistor itself* (not the entire circuit) is the flow of positively charged holes.

Transistor Amplification. The function of the transistor, when used as an amplifier, is simply to use a small current flow between base and emitter to control a larger current flow between emitter and collector. The ability of a transistor to increase (or amplify) a signal current depends upon the fixed percentage of current which

flows from the emitter to the collector. When a voltage is applied to the base in such a manner as to increase the forward biasing, or voltage, the emitter and collector currents are increased. The percentage of amplification is a fixed characteristic of the particular transistor.

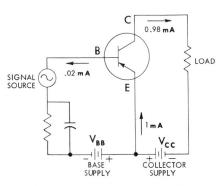

Fig. 43. A transistor used as an amplifier, connected in a common-emitter configuration.

For example, assume that a transistor has an emitter current of 1 milliampere (Fig. 43). Using the 98% and 2% values mentioned above, the collector current would be 0.98 ma and the base current 0.02 ma. If a voltage of 4 millivolts is applied to the base, the base current and the collector current would both be increased by 10%. Thus by merely applying the voltage to the base, the transistor has amplified the current.

Junction transistors can be used as amplifiers in several different circuit arrangements. One possibility is the common-base amplifier arrangement, in which the base is common to both the input and the output. See Fig. 42. This type is used infrequently. Its current gain factor is always less than one, which does not mean that this particular transistor arrangement is useless in amplifier design. While current output may be less than input, output voltage may be greatly increased.

Another amplifier circuit is the common-emitter circuit shown in Fig. 43, in which the emitter is common to the input and output. The common-emitter amplifier is the most widely used circuit configuration. Collector current (output) can be as high as 25 times greater than base current (input).

Feedback in Amplifiers. As with vacuum tubes, when some of the signal coming out of a transistor amplifier is fed back to the input, the process is called feedback. Negative feedback results when the output signal being fed back decreases the input signal. This results in a lower gain for the amplifier but it makes the amplifier more linear and more stable against temperature and power supply voltage variations. If enough negative feedback is employed, the gain of the amplifier becomes almost independent of the transistor. This type of amplifier is usually referred to as an operational amplifier.

If the voltage being fed back into the input tends to increase the input signal, the result is positive feedback. Positive feedback will increase the gain of an amplifier but will reduce its temperature and voltage supply stability. If too much positive feedback is used, the output of the amplifier becomes independent of the input signal and oscillation results.

Transistor Oscillators. An oscillator is a circuit that is used to generate a constantly varying ac voltage from a dc voltage source. There are two general types of oscillators: (1) Sinusoidal oscillators, and (2) Non-sinusoidal. Sinusoidal oscillators generate a sinusoidal (appears as a sine wave on an oscilloscope or when graphed) voltage. This is done by applying just enough positive feedback to start and maintain oscillation. Fig. 38 illustrates an ac sinusoidal pattern. Non-sinusoidal oscillators generate a voltage that is of a "square" or "sawtooth" shape. This is done by applying many times the amount of positive feedback that would be re-

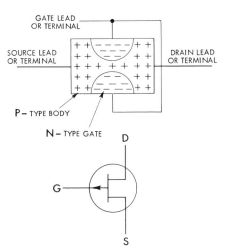

Fig. 44. The construction and schematic symbol for a Field Effect transistor.

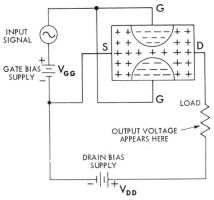

Fig. 45. A Field Effect transistor wired for use as an amplifier.

quired for oscillation. Oscillators are used to generate audio frequency voltages for telemetering and remote control applications.

Field Effect Transistors. Recently field effect, or unipolar, transistors

have been introduced into electronics. They are made from a single crystal of silicon which is completely P-type except in two small regions on opposite sides of the crystal which are N-type. The two N-type regions are usually electrically connected and are called the gate. One end of the main body is called the source and the other end the drain (Fig. 44).

A dc voltage source, in series with a load resistor, is placed between the source and drain leads (Fig. 45). The controlling signal or input voltage is placed in series with the source and gate leads. The polarity of the dc source is such that the N-type gate is made positive with respect to the P-type body of the transistor. This causes a reverse bias on the gate-body junction and no current flows from the gate or control circuit.

The operation of this transistor is based upon a phenomenon called conductivity modulation. As the signal voltage applied to the gate lead increases, the reverse bias on the gate-body junction increases, causing the holes in the body in the region of the junction to move away. This causes the effective cross-sectional area of the body to decrease and the current flowing from the source to drain to decrease. Since this current is large compared to the nearly zero current in the gate circuit, the amplification of the device is extremely high.

Almost any circuit that can be built around vacuum tubes can be duplicated with transistors. Transistors offer many advantages over tubes, including small size, stability, remarkable linearity, and longevity. Transistors are at present being used in many control and reset applications. In the near future, increased use of transistorized circuits in the various fields of electronics will require that technicians, including those in instrumentation, be familiar with the application of transistors.

Chapter 10

Temperature

HEAT is a form of energy. When heat is applied to a substance, the activity of the molecules of that substance is increased. The amount of heat required to raise the temperature of one pound of water one degree Fahrenheit is called a British Thermal Unit (BTU). The amount of heat required to raise the temperature of one pound of any substance one degree Fahrenheit is called the *thermal capacity* of that substance.

The ratio of the thermal capacity of a substance to the thermal capacity of water is called the *specific heat* of that substance. Specific heats of some solids and liquids are given in the table below. Specific heat has no unit of measurement, but is the same numerically as the thermal capacity.

The amount of heat (Q) required to raise the temperature of a mass (M) of a substance having a thermal capacity of (C) from temperature t_1 to t_2 is expressed:

$$Q \overset{BTU}{=} \overset{lbs}{M} \times C \overset{deg.\,F}{(t_2 - t_1)}$$

Temperature measurements determine the amount of heat possessed by a body at a particular instant. Temperature scales provide a means to express this in numbers.

All solids expand when heat is applied to them. When a metal rod is heated uniformly along its entire length, each unit of its length gets longer. This increase in length per unit of length per degree of temperature rise is termed the *coefficient of linear expansion*. This coefficient has different values for different materials. A table of typical coefficients of linear expansion (α) is shown. From the table it can be learned that each

Table of Specific Heats

MATERIAL	SPECIFIC HEAT (C)
ALCOHOL	0.59
COPPER	0.093
GLASS	0.14
MERCURY	0.033
PLATINUM	0.032

Table of Coefficients of Expansion

MATERIAL	α/F°	β/F°
ALCOHOL		0.00061
WATER		0.000115
MERCURY		0.0001
GLASS	0.000005	0.000015
COPPER	0.000009	0.000039
PLATINUM	0.000005	0.000016
INVAR	0.0000008	0.0000027

inch of a copper strip becomes 1.000009 inches long when heated 1°F. This is expressed:

$$L_{t2} = L_{t1} \left[1 + \alpha \left(t_2 - t_1 \right) \right].$$

The expansion of a solid due to heat affects not only its length, but all its dimensions. The thermal expansion of the volume of substance can be expressed:

$$V_{t2} = V_{t1} \left[1 + \beta \left(t_2 - t_1 \right) \right].$$

β is the coefficient of *volumetric* expansion and is approximately equal to 3α. Liquids also expand, when heated, according to the same equation. Coefficients of volumetric expansion of various materials are also listed in the table.

TEMPERATURE MEASUREMENT — MECHANICAL

Mercury-in-Glass Thermometers

From the above table it can be seen that the volumetric expansion of mercury is over six times greater than that of glass. The mercury-in-glass thermometer (Fig. 1) depends on this inequality for its operation. Such a thermometer consists of a glass tube of very fine bore joined to a reservoir at the bottom and sealed at the top. A measured quantity of mercury is enclosed.

When the thermometer is heated, the mercury expands much more than the glass and therefore is forced to rise up the tubing. For each particular temperature, the mercury rises to a certain point. Using a regulated bath which can establish and maintain temperatures very closely, reference marks can be made on the thermometer. The spaces between these marks are evenly divided. The more reference marks, the more accurately can the thermometer be read.

Some mercury-in-glass thermometers are calibrated for complete immersion and others for partial immersion. For accurate readings, the thermometer should be immersed as recommended by the manufacturer.

The most common type of mercury-in-glass thermometer used for process measurements is the industrial thermometer. See Fig. 2. In this type, the glass tube is unmarked; the graduations are engraved on metal scales. Both the tube and scales are enclosed in a metal case. The lower portion of the glass tube extends out of the bottom of the case, into a metal bulb chamber with an external pipe thread permitting it to be screwed into a pipe line.

The industrial thermometer is available in vertical, horizontal, or

Fig. 1. Heat causes the expansion of the mercury within the glass envelope, forcing the mercury up the fine-bore tube.

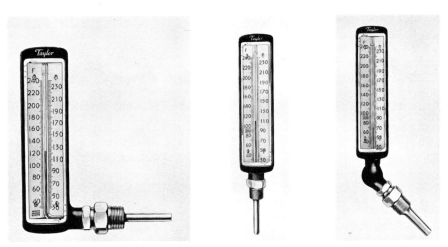

Fig. 2. Industrial thermometers are available in many styles. All have threaded bases which allow direct mounting on pipes or containers which contain the process substance to be measured. (Taylor Instrument Co.)

oblique angle types (Fig. 2). For better thermal conductivity between the metal bulb chamber and the glass thermometer, the chamber contains a liquid with excellent heat transfer characteristics. To prevent damage to the thermometer, and to permit replacement without draining the process pipe line, the chamber may be screwed into a secondary chamber called a separable socket. This however slows down the response of the thermometer to temperature changes.

Fig. 3 shows the response characteristics of industrial thermometers. The points marked on these curves indicate the time required for the

thermometer to reach 63.2% of its final value. This is referred to as the *time constant* of the thermometer. Because it is usually of more value

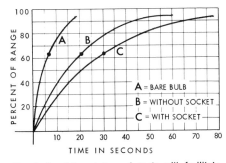

Fig. 3. Special sockets and seats will facilitate handling and changing of the theromometers without disturbing the process. Sockets will however, affect the response speed of the thermometer.

to know the time required to reach 90, 95, or 99% of final value, manufacturers frequently use these values when stating the response speed of their thermometers.

Bimetal Thermometers

With the development of alloys whose coefficients of thermal expansion can be closely controlled, the bimetal thermometer has become a most dependable temperature measuring device. One of these is a nickel alloy named Invar, which hardly expands at all when heated. Another nickel alloy is available which expands considerably when heated. Welded together and rolled to the desired thickness, these alloys provide the bimetallic material used in the modern thermometer. Alloys of widely differing rates of thermal expansion are used for short temperature ranges; those of less differing expansion for longer ranges.

The term used to describe the ther-

Fig. 5. Bimetal thermometers are made for precision laboratory work as well as for a variety of industrial purposes. (Weston Instruments, Inc.)

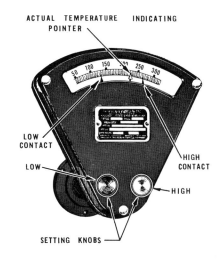

Fig. 6. Bimetal thermometers are available to suit a wide range of needs. Many feature secondary pointers and alarm contacts. (The Bristol Co.)

Fig. 4. A multiple helix device offers the advantage of being able to use long bimetallic elements within a relatively compact space. (Weston Instruments, Inc.)

mal activity of a bimetal is *flexivity*. The actual movement of a bimetal strip is proportional to its flexivity. With one end fixed, a straight bimetal strip deflects in proportion to its temperature, to the square of its length, and inversely with its thickness. The angular deflection of a pointer attached to a helical bimetal is determined by the same factors.

The modern bimetal thermometer (Fig. 4) employs a multiple helix arrangement, or coils within coils. This construction permits the use of a long bimetallic element in a small space. One end of the bimetal is usually fixed to the bottom of the stem and the other end to a shaft to which the pointer is attached.

Bimetal thermometers are available with slender stems for laboratory use and thicker stems for industrial use. See Fig. 5. Special thermometers with alarm contacts and with secondary pointers for indicating maximum or minimum temperatures are also available. See Fig. 6.

Pressure Spring Thermometers

There are four classes of pressure spring thermometers, as listed by the Instrument Society of America Standards:

Class 1. Liquid-filled (except mercury)
Class 2. Vapor-pressure
Class 3. Gas-filled
Class 4. Mercury-filled.

Liquid-Filled and Mercury-Filled Thermometers. Both types operate on the principle of thermal expansion, just as the mercury-in-glass thermometer does. When the bulb is immersed in a heated substance, the liquid expands causing the pressure spring to unwind. See Fig. 7. The indicating, recording, or controlling mechanisms are attached to the pressure spring. It should be noted that the liquid or mercury is put into the system under pressure and completely fills it.

The measuring range of the system is determined by the volume of liquid in the bulb. The wider the range, the greater the required volume. The bulb expands with temperature, but since this expansion is small compared to the expansion of the liquid, the effect is negligible. If the coefficients of volumetric expansion of the metal and the liquid vary similarly, the overall effect is to reduce the net expansion for a given range. Slight variations in the coefficients can be

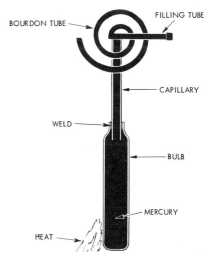

Fig. 7. In a totally-filled system, pressure develops when the bulb is heated since the fluid has no room for expansion.

accommodated in the calibration of the thermometer.

Compensated Thermometer Systems. The object of the thermometer is to detect changes of temperature *at the bulb*. There is, however, the possibility of error caused by variation of temperature along the tubing or at the pressure spring itself. The bulb of the liquid-filled system is designed to contain most of the liquid. In long systems, however, the volume of the tubing may be great enough to allow temperature changes along the tubing. Several methods have been devised to eliminate such error. Systems employing these modifications are termed *compensated systems*.

Fully compensated systems (Fig. 8) employ a second pressure spring and tubing. This tubing is not con-

nected to the bulb but instead is terminated at that point. By means of linkage, the motion of the compensating pressure spring is made equal and opposite to the motion of the primary pressure spring. If temperature along the primary tubing varies, causing expansion of the primary spring, the expansion of the compensating spring due to the same variation acts to cancel out the resulting motion of the

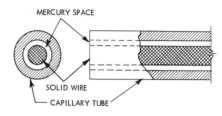

Fig. 9. Self-compensating capillary tubing encloses a solid wire, expansion and contraction of which compensates for changes of temperature along the tubing.

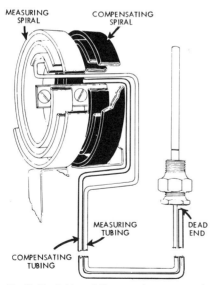

Fig. 8. The tubing of the second pressure spring (compensating spiral) in series with the first does not enter the bulb.

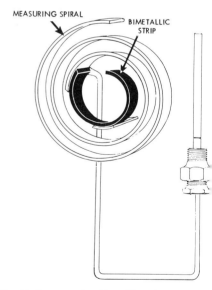

Fig. 10. Compensating bimetallic strip overcomes error caused by temperature change of the pressure spring. (Minneapolis-Honeywell Reg. Co.)

indicating mechanism. The only motion remaining is caused by expansion of the fluid in the bulb.

Another method of compensation involves the use of a special type of tubing containing a solid wire (Fig. 9). As the tubing expands due to temperature variations, the wire expands so that the effective volume of the system remains constant.

Variations in the temperature surrounding the pressure spring require correction. The thermometer must be compensated to nullify these variations which will affect correct readings of process temperature. This can be accomplished by including a bimetal strip (Fig. 10) in the mechanism joining the pressure spring to the indicator. This bimetal acts to move the indicator in a direction op-

posite to that caused by the expansion of the pressure spring, but only enough to eliminate the small amount of movement due to temperature changes at the spring.

Another method employs a secondary pressure spring but without tubing (Fig. 11). This secondary spring is part of the primary system, but the linkage connecting them is arranged so that the movement of the secondary spring cancels out the movement of the primary spring caused by changes of temperature at the springs.

Gas-Filled Pressure Spring Thermometers. This type (Fig. 12) depends upon the increase in pressure of a confined gas (constant volume) due to temperature increase. The relationship between temperature and

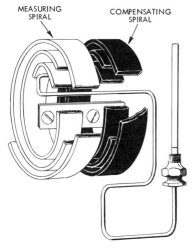

Fig. 11. A secondary spring, identical with and linked to the primary spring, is used to cancel out any movement of the primary due to temperature change at the spring which is not related to process temperature. (Minneapolis-Honeywell Reg. Co.)

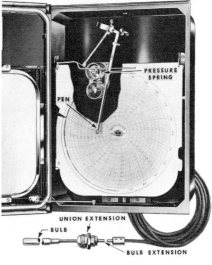

Fig. 12. In gas-filled pressure spring thermometers, the gas is inserted at high pressure. This makes the thermometer more sensitive to temperature change. (The Bristol Co.)

pressure in this kind of system follows Charles Law and may be expressed:

$$\frac{T_1}{T_2} = \frac{P_1}{P_2}$$

where

T_1 = initial temperature

T_2 = increased temperature

P_1 = initial pressure

P_2 = increased pressure

The system is filled under high pressure. The increase in pressure for each degree of temperature rise is therefore greater than if the filling pressure were low. Nitrogen is the gas most often used for such systems, because it is chemically inert and possesses a favorable coefficient of thermal expansion.

Except for the size of the bulb, the gas-filled system is identical to the liquid-filled types. The gas-filled bulb must be larger and its volume must be considerably greater than that of the rest of the system. Special bulbs consisting of a length of small diameter tubing may be used to measure the average temperature along the bulb; these may be as much as 200 feet long.

Gas-filled systems are subject to the same errors as liquid-filled systems, and the same methods may be used to compensate for them.

Vapor-Pressure Thermometers. Unlike the liquid-filled and gas-filled systems which depend upon volumetric expansion for their operation, vapor-pressure thermometers depend upon the vapor pressure of a liquid which only partially fills the system. In this type of system the liquid can expand, but as it is heated its vapor

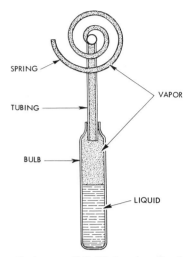

Fig. 13. In a partially-filled system the liquid expands when the bulb is heated and the vapor pressure increases.

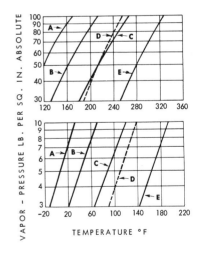

TEMPERATURE °F

LEGEND:

A — ETHYL CHLORIDE
B — ETHYL ETHER
C — CHLOROFORM
D — METHYL ALCOHOL
E — DISTILLED WATER

Fig. 14. The unit vapor pressure change increases logarithmically with the temperature.

pressure increases (Fig. 13). Water in a pressure cooker behaves in the same manner—as the water is heated and changes to steam (water vapor), the pressure builds up. Vapor pressure does not increase according to a linear proportion (a unit increase in pressure for each unit of temperature rise). At lower temperatures, the vapor pressure increase for each unit of temperature change is small; at higher temperatures the vapor pressure change is much greater. Fig. 14 shows some typical vapor pressure vs. temperature curves which illustrate this non-uniform characteristic.

Another characteristic of the partially-filled vapor pressure thermometer is the shift of the vapor and the liquid when the temperature of the sensitive bulb changes from a value lower than the temperature of the pressure spring to a value higher.

When the temperature of the bulb is lower, the liquid remains in the bulb and the vapor occupies the tubing and spring (Fig. 15). When the bulb temperature is higher than that of the rest of the system, the liquid and vapor change places, with the bulb now containing the vapor and the pressure spring the liquid (Fig. 16). Therefore, with the simple partially-filled vapor pressure thermometer, the temperature of the bulb should always remain *lower than* or *higher than* the temperature of the remainder of the system.

Manufacturers have developed a method of filling the vapor pressure thermometer that overcomes this limitation. This is the dual-filled system in which two different liquids, a vaporizing and a non-vaporizing type, are used (Fig. 17). The temperature sensitive fluid which vaporizes is

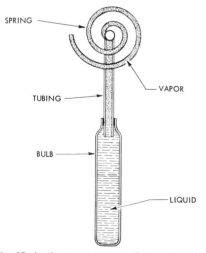

Fig. 15. In the vapor pressure thermometer the liquid remains in the bulb when the bulb temperature is lower than the rest of the system. Vapor occupies tubing and spring.

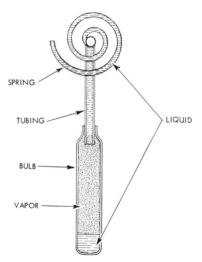

Fig. 16. When the bulb temperature is higher than the rest of the system, the vapor stays in the bulb. The liquid occupies tubing and spring.

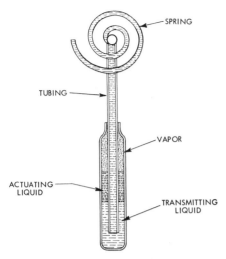

Fig. 17. In the dual-filled system there is no transfer of liquid and vapor as there is in the partially-filled system.

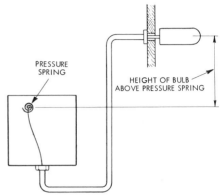

Fig. 18. With the bulb located above the pressure spring of a partially-filled vapor pressure system, the column might create sufficient pressure to cause an error in the reading.

called the "actuating liquid." The vapor pressure acts on a second liquid which does not vaporize. This second liquid is called the "transmitting liquid," since it transmits the vapor pressure of the first liquid to the pressure spring much as any hydraulic fluid does. In this dual-filled system, there is no transfer of vapor and liquid; the actuating liquid and its vapor remain in the bulb at all times.

Location of bulb. The difference in height between the bulb and the pressure spring may also introduce errors, especially in the partially-filled vapor pressure system. Since this system is not filled under pressure as are the totally-filled systems, any column of fluid could create a pressure sufficient to cause an error in the reading. It is important, therefore, to inform the manufacturer about the height of the bulb if it is to be located above the pressure spring, and to maintain that dimension when installing the thermometer (Fig. 18).

Because totally-filled systems are filled under high pressure, the pressure due to the height of the bulb has little effect and little or no error is involved.

Response to change in temperature. The next important considera-

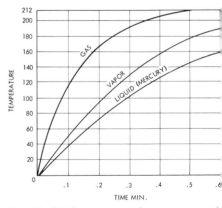

Fig. 19. Relative response of gas, vapor, and mercury thermometers.

tion in the study of pressure spring thermometers is their response to change in temperature. The installation, of course, influences the speed of response. It should be noted however, that the gas-filled system has the fastest response, the vapor-pressure system the next fastest, and the liquid-filled has the slowest (Fig. 19).

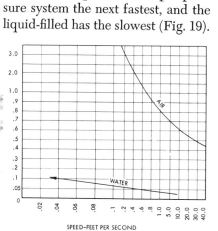

SPEED—FEET PER SECOND

Fig. 20. The response of pressure spring thermometers is faster in moving liquid than in moving air.

The response of all three is faster in a moving air or gas; and the faster the liquid moves the faster will be the response (Fig. 20). A faster response will be obtained if more bulb area is exposed to the fluid. Manufacturers have designed many special bulbs to improve the response, especially for measuring air or gas temperatures (Fig. 21). For liquid temperature measurement, the bulb should be large enough to provide sufficient area to sense temperature changes, but not so large that its mass slows its response.

For every application there is a "best selection." A complete description of the operating conditions will permit the manufacturer to supply this.

In conclusion, the characteristics of the types of tube systems are shown in the table below.

Fig. 21. Specially designed bulb for measuring air or gas temperatures. (Bristol Co.)

Table of Characteristics of Classes of Tube Systems

	Filling Fluid	Low Limit	High Limit	Shortest Span	Longest Span
Class 1	liquids other than Mercury	−300°F	600°F	25°F	300°F
Class 2	Vapor	−300°F	600°F	40°F	300°F
Class 3	Gas	−450°F	1000°F	100°F	1000°F
Class 4	Mercury	−48°F	1000°F	40°F	1000°F

TEMPERATURE MEASUREMENT— ELECTRICAL

Thermocouples

A device which converts one form of energy into another is called a *transducer*. A thermocouple is a transducer which converts thermal energy into electrical energy. It is a simple device consisting of two dissimilar wires joined at their ends. When an end of each wire is connected to a measuring instrument (as in Fig. 25), the thermocouple becomes an accurate and sensitive temperature measuring device. Three phenomena govern the behavior of a thermocouple: the Seebeck, Peltier, and Thompson Effects.

The Seebeck Effect. The joined ends of a thermocouple form a junction called the hot junction, or measuring junction. The other ends of the wires which are connected to a measuring instrument form the cold junction, or reference junction. Simply stated, the voltage produced by heating the measuring junction varies with the difference in temperature between the measuring junction and the reference junction.

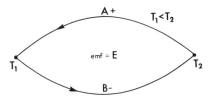

Fig. 22. If A and B are dissimilar metals, current will flow through the junctions which are at temperatures T_1 and T_2, provided T_1 and T_2 are different temperatures.

The Seebeck effect describes the result of heating one junction of a circuit formed of two dissimilar metal conductors. In such a circuit, electric current flows as long as the two junctions are at different temperatures. See Fig. 22.

The Peltier Effect. When a current flows across the junction of two dissimilar metal conductors, it has been noticed that heat is either liberated or absorbed, depending upon the direction of current flow (Fig. 23). If the current flow is in the same direction as the current produced by the Seebeck Effect, heat is liberated at the hot junction and absorbed at the cold junction.

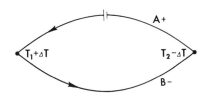

Fig. 23. The arrows show the direction of current. Heat is lost at the hot junction (T_2) since the direction of the current is the same as that produced by the Seebeck effect.

The Reversible Heat Effect. The *Thompson Effect* concerns the reversible heat effects resulting from the passage of an electric current through a conductor in which there is a temperature gradient. The temperature of a current-carrying copper wire may vary along its length. Heat is liberated at any point where the current at that point flows in the same direction as the heat. See Fig. 24. With an iron wire however, heat is absorbed at any point where the cur-

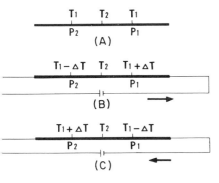

Fig. 24. The Thompson (Reversible Heat) Effect. (A) A bar of metal is heated at its midpoint to a temperature of T_2. (B) A current from an external source is passed through it. Points P_1 and P_2 which were at equal temperature T_1 (lower than T_2) when no current was flowing have their temperature changed to $T_1 + \Delta T$ and $T_1 - \Delta T$ respectively when the current flows in the direction shown. (C) When the current flow is reversed, the temperature reverses also. The case above corresponds to the behavior of copper.

rent at that point flows in the same direction as the heat. Thus, in a copper wire, the current tends to reduce the difference in temperature, whereas in the iron wire the current tends to increase the difference.

In a circuit made up of iron and copper wires with the cold junction at 32°F, the *emf* increases as the temperature of the hot junction increases. But as the temperature approaches a maximum, the rate of increase is reduced until finally it reaches zero. Once past the maximum temperature, the *emf* decreases, meaning that the polarity of the wires is reversed.

The voltage which produces the Seebeck current is the sum of the Peltier *emf* at the junctions and the two Thompson *emfs* along the dissim-

ilar wires. This is the true basis of thermoelectric thermometry.

The Law of Intermediate Temperatures. This law states that the sum of the voltages generated by two thermocouples (Fig. 25), one with its reference junction at 32°F and its measuring junction at a higher temperature (A°F), and the other thermocouple with its reference junction at A°F and its measuring junction at a still higher temperature (B°F) is equal to the voltage generated by one thermocouple with its reference junction at 32°F and its measuring junction at B°F. Because of this law, it is possible to establish a reference temperature of a fixed value. By using a temperature sensitive resistor in the measuring circuit that automatically eliminates the voltage change due to temperature changes at the reference junction, the voltage in the circuit remains constant at the fixed value. Therefore, the only voltage change in the circuit is the result of a change in the temperature of the measuring junction.

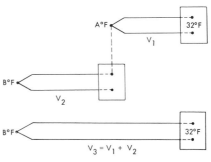

Fig. 25. The Law of Intermediate Temperature permits the establishment of a reference temperature of fixed value.

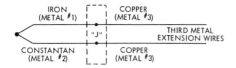

Fig. 26. The Law of Intermediate Metals states that the temperatures of the three metals at junction "J" must be the same.

The Law of Intermediate Metals. This law states that the use of a third metal in a thermocouple circuit does not affect the voltage as long as the junctions of the third metal with the thermocouple metals are at the same temperature (Fig. 26). This law makes it possible to use extension wires of a metal different

from the thermocouple materials. This is actually common practice in industry.

For instance, because of the high cost of platinum, the extension lead wires used with Platinum/Platinum-10% Rhodium thermocouples may both be copper, or one copper and the other an alloy. With Chromel-Alumel thermocouples, the extension lead wires may be copper and constantan, or iron and an alloy.

Of all the materials used for thermocouples, platinum is no doubt the most important. The Platinum/Platinum-10% Rhodium thermocouple is the primary standard for temperatures between 630.5°C and 1063°C.

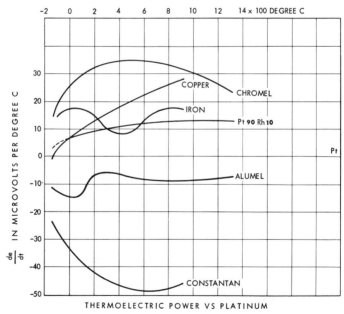

THERMOELECTRIC POWER VS PLATINUM

Fig. 27. The electrical characteristics of various metals when used with platinum as a dissimilar metal in a thermocouple are compared. Notice that copper, iron, chromel, and platinum-10% rhodium are positive with respect to platinum, while alumel and constantan are negative. From this, the reason for the selection of Iron-Constantan, Copper-Constantan, Chromel-Alumel, and Platinum/Platinum-10% Rhodium becomes apparent.

The useful range of this thermocouple actually is from 0°C to 1500°C.

The behavior of other thermocouple materials is determined by using them with platinum as the second material. When selecting a pair of materials for use as a thermocouple, the greater the thermoelectric difference between them, the better the result. Fig. 27 illustrates the characteristics of the common thermocouple materials when compared with platinum.

In addition to the common combinations seen in Fig. 27, others have found application in temperature measurement. Chromel-Constantan, for example, is an excellent combination for temperatures up to 2000°F. Nickel/Nickel-Molybdenum is sometimes used in place of Chromel-Alumel. Tungsten-Rhenium is used for temperatures up to 4200°F. Other combinations for special applications are Chromel-White Gold, Molybdenum-Tungsten, Tungsten-Iridium, and Iridium/Iridium-Rhodium.

The size of the wire and the protection of the thermocouple are also important. The wire size affects both the sensitivity and the maximum operating temperature of the thermocouple. Thermocouple wire sizes range from fine (40 AWG) to heavy (8 AWG). While a 20 gage wire requires only two minutes to reach 80% of its final temperature reading, an 8 gage wire requires nearly nine minutes. The table at the top is a summary of the maximum temperatures for various thermocouples.

Table of Maximum Temperatures for Thermocouples

THERMOCOUPLE	GAGE	MAXIMUM OPERATING TEMP. °F
COPPER-CONSTANTAN T	14	700
	20	600
	24	500
	28	400
IRON-CONSTANTAN J	8	1400
	14	1000
	20	900
	24	700
	28	700
CHROMEL ALUMEL K	8	2500
	14	2000
	20	1800
	24	1600
	28	1600
PLATINUM-10% RHODIUM -PLATINUM S	24	3000
CHROMEL-CONSTANTAN	8	1800
	14	1200
	20	1000
TUNGSTEN 5% RHENIUM TUNGSTEN 26% RHENIUM	18	4200
	20	1800
	24	1600
	28	1600

In most cases, thermocouples cannot be used without protection from the environment in which they are used. The environment may be a reducing atmosphere (where oxygen content is low and hydrogen and carbon monoxide are present) or an oxidizing atmosphere (where oxygen and water vapor are present). For example, iron corrodes in an oxidizing atmosphere and chromel becomes contaminated in a reducing atmosphere. Platinum / Platinum-Rhodium thermocouples always require protection.

The devices used for protecting thermocouples are called thermocouple wells and protecting tubes. They may be made of metals such as iron, steel, nickel, or inconel; silica compounds such as corundum or carbofrax; or metal ceramic compounds such as chromium oxide and aluminum oxide. Sometimes a thermocouple must be enclosed in a primary metal protector as well as a secondary silica protector. The table at the bottom of the page lists some of the more common protecting tube materials.

The selection of the complete thermocouple assembly should be carefully made, and manufacturers have made available a considerable amount of data to aid in this.

Fig. 28. A typical permanent-magnet moving-coil mechanism with U-shaped magnet. This mechanism requires a minimum of electrical energy to move the pointer. (Weston Instruments, Inc.)

The Millivoltmeter. The millivoltmeter used to measure temperature is a permanent-magnet moving-coil type (Fig. 28). When a voltage is applied across the coil, it becomes a magnet and rotates until its magnetic force balances the magnetic force of the permanent magnet. The coil is held in check by spiral springs, and these springs also act as conductors, bringing the voltage into the meter coil. Because the millivoltmeter requires power to move the coil, the voltage due to temperature must be sufficient to produce this power. For this reason, the tempera-

ture range of a millivoltmeter type thermometer must be wide enough to produce at least a six millivolt range electrically. Using an iron-constantan thermocouple, this would mean that the temperature range should be 0° to + 200°F or greater.

Temperature changes at the meter must be compensated for because they affect the temperature of the reference junction located at the meter. Variations in the meter temperature can also cause the electrical resistance of the meter to change.

Table of Protecting Tube Materials

TYPE	RECOMMENDED MAX. TEMP.	COMMENTS
WROUGHT IRON	1200°F	FOR GENERAL USE EXCEPT CORROSIVE ATMOSPHERES
CAST IRON	1500°F	FOR ACID AND ALKALINE SOLUTIONS
304 STAINLESS STEEL	1800°F	FOR CORROSIVE ATMOSPHERES AND SOLUTIONS
NICKEL	2000°F	FOR SPECIAL CHEMICAL APPLICATIONS
INCONEL	2200°F	SUBSTITUTE FOR NICKEL WHEN SULFUR IS PRESENT
CORUNDUM	3000°F	FOR STEEL INDUSTRY, WHERE THERMAL SHOCK MAY BE HIGH
CARBOFRAX	3000°F	FOR APPLICATIONS WITH HIGH THERMAL AND MECHANICAL SHOC
CHRONIUM & ALUMINUM OXIDE	3000°F	FOR BRASS AND BRONZE FOUNDRIES HIGH THERMAL CONDUCTIVI

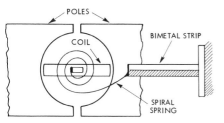

Fig. 29. A bimetallic strip is used to compensate for changes of temperature in the reference junction millivoltmeter.

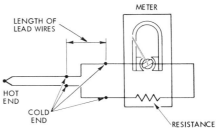

Fig. 30. In the thermocouple pyrometer circuit, proper selection of the length and diameter of the lead wire is very important, since this determines the wire's resistance, which must stay constant with the resistance value printed on the meter scale.

Compensation for changes in the reference junction temperature is generally accomplished by using a bimetallic strip in the coil spring mechanism (Fig. 29). When the temperature changes and the electrical effect tends to move the moving coil in one direction, the bimetallic strip corrects this tendency. A meter is said to be temperature-compensated when a change of 10°F causes less than 0.25% error in its reading.

The changes in the internal electrical resistance of the millivoltmeter may be held to a minimum by using wire which does not change its resistance when its temperature changes. For this reason, manganin wire is frequently used for the internal meter resistors.

The external resistance of the millivoltmeter circuit also affects the accuracy of the system. This includes the resistance of the lead wire and the thermocouple itself. This is generally overcome by making the resistance of the meter itself as high as possible so that changes in external resistance will have little effect. When the instrument is calibrated, a fixed external resistance is used.

This value is usually printed on the meter scale. When installed, best accuracy is obtained when the external resistance is as near to this value as possible. This is done by proper selection of the length and diameter of the lead wire (Fig. 30). The longer the lead wire the greater the resistance. The thicker the wire the less the resistance.

The usual static accuracy of the millivoltmeter thermocouple is ± 1%. The speed of response of a millivoltmeter is generally better than that of the thermocouple itself but, of course, this is true only when the meter is a well-designed mechanism.

The Potentiometer. Unlike the millivoltmeter type, which uses the voltage of the thermocouple to move the meter mechanism, the potentiometer compares the thermocouple voltage with a battery-supplied voltage. The battery supplied voltage is adjusted so that it is equal and opposite the thermocouple voltage. The battery-supplied voltage adjustor is

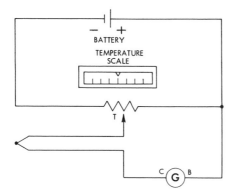

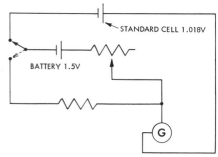

Fig. 32. The galvanometer compares the voltages of the standard cell and the battery.

Fig. 31. In the potentiometer, the thermocouple voltage is measured between points T and C, while the battery-supplied voltage is measured between points T and B, and adjusted so that it is equal and opposite the thermocouple voltage. When the potential on the slidewire at point T is different from that of the thermocouple current flows through the thermocouple and the galvanometer deflects. The direction of deflection depends upon whether the thermocouple potential is greater or less than that at point T. If the slider is moved so that the two potentials are equal no current will flow through the galvanometer. Since the thermocouple potential differs for each measured temperature and a new slider position can restore the zero position of the galvanometer, a scale can be used with the slider to indicate temperature.

calibrated in degrees of temperature (Fig. 31). Thus, for each position of the voltage, there is a temperature reading. Because a battery does not maintain its voltage, it is necessary to adjust quite frequently to a particular value so that the relationship between temperature and battery-supplied voltage remains constant. A standard cell is used for this purpose (Fig. 32). The battery voltage is temporarily disconnected from the thermocouple and connected to the standard cell. By means of an adjustable resistor, the battery voltage is made to equal that of the standard

cell. The standard cell maintains a constant voltage (1.018v) for long periods of time. The comparison of battery and standard cell voltage is called standardization and can be performed manually or automatically. During standardization, the measuring circuit of the instrument is "borrowed" for a short time, with the standard cell replacing the thermocouple.

To explain the operation of such an instrument, it is simpler to use one containing a galvanometer, although this type is no longer common in industry. A galvanometer is a permanent-magnet moving-coil meter like the millivoltmeter. In fact, the millivoltmeter is really a galvanometer for measuring voltage in units of 1/1000 of a volt. The galvanometer in the potentiometer-type instrument usually has no scale; only a mark indicates when no electrical current is passing through. There may be a small scale with marks indicating whether the current is above or below the zero point.

Fig. 33 shows a simple potentiome-

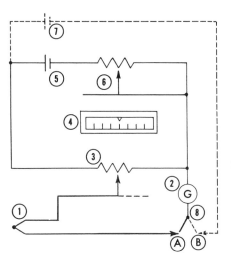

Fig. 33. Schematic of a simple null-balance potentiometer circuit. (1) Thermocouple, (2) Galvanometer, (3) Slidewire and Slider, (4) Scale, (5) Battery, (6) Standardizing Rheostat and Slider, (7) Standard Cell, (8) Standardizing Switch—(A) Thermocouple position and (B) Standard Cell position.

ter circuit. It is called a null-balance circuit since the value to be measured is correct only when the galvanometer is at its zero (null) point. At this point, the circuit is in balance, the thermocouple and battery voltages being equal and opposite.

With the standardizing switch at the thermocouple position, the standard cell is cut out of the circuit. The slider divides the slidewire length so that some of the battery voltage is added to the thermocouple voltage and the total enters the galvanometer. The remaining battery voltage is applied to the galvanometer, entering it on the opposite side. The circuit is at the null point when these two voltages are equal and opposite; the pointer indicates the temperature of the thermocouple.

With the standardizing switch at the standard cell position, the slider and thermocouple are no longer in the circuit, being replaced by the standard cell. The entire slidewire is in the circuit, being connected to the positive terminals of the battery and the standard cell at one end and to the galvanometer at the other. The negative terminal of the standard cell is connected directly to the opposite side of the galvanometer. By positioning the standardizing rheostat slider, the battery voltage is adjusted to a value equal and opposite to that of the standard cell. As long as the battery maintains this voltage, the thermocouple voltage can be read as a temperature because the voltage across the whole measuring slidewire remains constant.

The simple circuit shown in Fig. 33 does not include the resistors necessary to establish the operating range of the potentiometer or to make the instrument suitable for use with a particular type of thermocouple. In modern industrial instruments, the measuring resistors are supplied as a prewired unit for plug-in, or other simple method of installation.

Temperature Variations. Temperature variations at the instrument must be compensated for to eliminate:

1. changes in resistance due to temperature
2. changes in reference temperature

The resistors used in the measuring circuit should be carefully se-

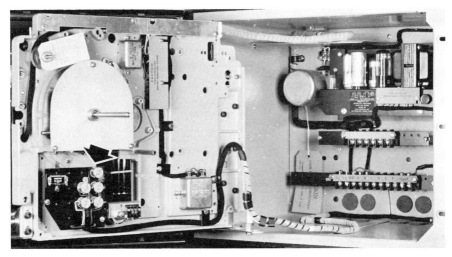

Fig. 34. Measuring circuit showing special resistor and reference junction compensator. (Bristol Co.)

lected so that their resistance remains constant over the range of temperatures expected in use. If this range is unusually wide and best accuracy is necessary, the resistors may be made of manganin which has exceptional stability.

Reference junction compensation is usually accomplished automatically by using a special nickel resistor in the measuring circuit. By enclosing this resistor and the reference junction terminals separately inside the instrument, variations in the temperature of the reference junction are compensated for (Fig. 34). The nickel resistor must be selected so that its variation in resistance causes a voltage equal and opposite to that caused by the change in reference junction temperature.

Balancing Mechanisms. In the simple circuit of the potentiometer, the

Fig. 35. Manual Balance Indicator. The slidewire is adjusted by the knob in the middle of the instrument. By manipulating the knob, the deflection of the galvanometer (located above the temperature scale) can be made to disappear, and the temperature can then be read on the scale. (Foxboro Co.)

balancing is a manual operation of the kind shown in Fig. 35. This is not satisfactory for most industrial

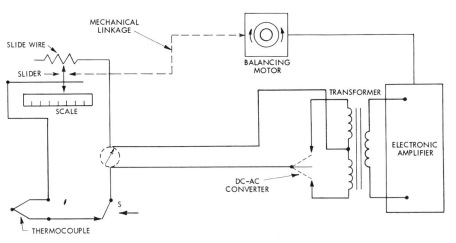

Fig. 36. Electronic potentiometer circuit, showing dc-ac converter, electronic amplifier, and balancing motor.

applications where the instrument must be in continuous balance to provide an accurate record or precise control.

In the older galvanometer-type instruments, many different automatic balance mechanisms were employed, but today most manufacturers have standardized a system that eliminates the galvanometer and substitutes a converter, electronic amplifier, and balancing motor. A typical circuit is shown in Fig. 36.

In this circuit, the dc voltage of the measuring circuit is converted to ac. Then this ac voltage is amplified. The amplified voltage is used to control the balancing motor, which moves the slidewire slider to maintain balance in the measuring circuit. Although the galvanometer is not used, its function of detecting measuring circuit unbalance is performed by the converter, which

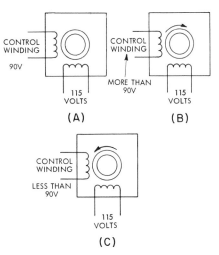

Fig. 37. Balancing motor characteristics: (A) motor stationary at a predetermined voltage on control wiring; (B) motor runs clockwise when motor is lower than in (A); (C) motor runs counterclockwise (reverses) when voltage is higher than in (A).

changes the current that flows in the measuring circuit due to the voltage unbalance from dc to ac. The ac current passes through a transformer and an amplifier and then to the balancing motor, causing the motor to drive the slidewire slider to a position that will balance the measuring circuit. When the measuring circuit is again in balance, no dc current is fed into the converter; hence, there is no ac current, and the motor stops. The slider then indicates the correct temperature.

The balancing motor contains two windings, one of which is supplied with line voltage. The other winding is called the control winding. At a particular voltage on this winding, the motor remains stationary. When this voltage decreases, the motor drives in one direction; when the control voltage increases, the motor drives in the opposite direction (Fig. 37).

The static accuracy of automatically balanced potentiometers is usually better than ± ¼ of 1% which is, of course, considerably better than the accuracy of most industrial thermocouples. Some instruments of this type will respond to a full scale temperature change in a fraction of a second, which is faster than the temperature response of the thermocouple itself (Fig. 38).

Resistance Thermometers. When precise temperature measurement by electrical means is desired, the resistance thermometer is used in a bridge circuit.

The thermometer itself is furnished in the form of a bulb, which consists of a fine wire wrapped around an insulator and enclosed in metal (Fig.

Fig. 38. High speed single point strip chart recorder which responds to a full-scale temperature change in a fraction of a second. (Minneapolis-Honeywell Reg. Co.)

39). The most common shape for a resistance thermometer resembles a bimetal thermometer bulb (Fig. 40).

Platinum wire is the best material for a resistance thermometer since it is useful over a wide range of temperatures (−400°F to +1200°F). Nickel is frequently used because of its lower cost and also because, over its useful range (−250°F to +600°F), its resistance per degree of temperature change is greater than that of platinum. Copper is generally restricted to temperatures below that of nickel. Its full useful range is −328°F to +250°F.

The important considerations in the selection of resistance thermometer wire are:

1. Purity
2. Uniformity
3. Stability
4. High resistance change per degree temperature change
5. Good contamination resistance

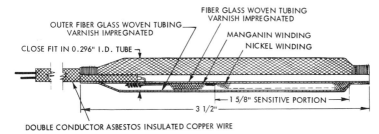

CLOSE FIT IN 0.296" I.D. TUBE

OUTER FIBER GLASS WOVEN TUBING
VARNISH IMPREGNATED

FIBER GLASS WOVEN TUBING
VARNISH IMPREGNATED

MANGANIN WINDING
NICKEL WINDING

1 5/8" SENSITIVE PORTION

3 1/2"

DOUBLE CONDUCTOR ASBESTOS INSULATED COPPER WIRE

Fig. 39. Resistance Thermometer Bulb Element. (Minneapolis-Honeywell Reg. Co.)

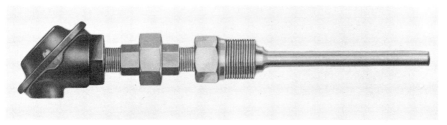

Fig. 40. High Speed Resistance Thermometer Bulb. (Minneapolis-Honeywell Reg. Co.)

Resistance thermometers of the same material should be interchangeable without requiring recalibration of the instrument being used. For this reason, they are manufactured to have a fixed resistance at a certain temperature. Platinum resistance thermometers generally have a resistance of 25 ohms at 32°F. Nickel thermometers generally have a resistance of 100 ohms at 77°F. Copper thermometers generally have a resistance of 10 ohms at 77°F.

Since temperature measurement by resistance thermometers is actually a resistance measurement, the Wheatstone bridge is used, with variations. The bridge may be dc or ac, although for this discussion we shall deal with the dc type in its simplest form.

The simplest form of resistance thermometer uses the indicating millivoltmeter. The Wheatstone bridge circuit is used with this type of meter (Fig. 41).

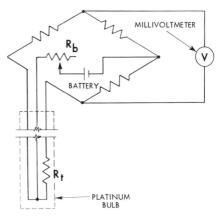

Fig. 41. Platinum resistance bulb used in a Wheatstone bridge circuit with a single indicating millivoltmeter.

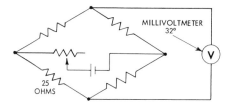

Fig. 42. Wheatstone bridge circuit with 25 ohm resistor in place of the platinum bulb.

As the temperature of the resistance bulb R_t rises, its resistance rises. Because of this, the bridge is unbalanced. This unbalance is detected by the millivoltmeter, causing it to deflect to a point that will restore balance to the circuit. When calibrating the circuit, a precision resistor is substituted for the temperature bulb, and the battery voltage is adjusted by varying R_b until the meter reads the correct temperature for this resistance. For instance (Fig. 42), if a platinum bulb is to be used, a precision resistor of 25 ohms would require that the meter reading be 32°F.

The resistance bulb has three leads (Fig. 43). This is necessary so that the same amount of lead wire is used in both branches of the bridge. This arrangement is generally preferred because the lead length may be lengthened or shortened without affecting the meter reading (Fig. 44).

Resistance thermometers are also used with slidewire instruments of the automatic null-balance type. Except for the circuitry and the lack of standardizing equipment, they are the same as the self-balancing po-

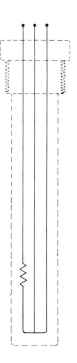

Fig. 43. The resistance bulb has three leads, so that the same amount of lead wire is used in both branches of the bridge.

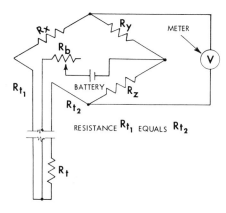

Fig. 44. Lead length does not affect meter readings. R_{t1} is added to R_x bridge arm, while R_{t2} is added to R_z bridge arm, so that lead length has no imbalance effect.

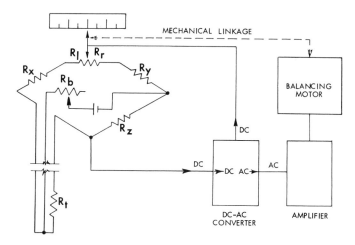

Fig. 45. A typical dc bridge circuit used with resistance thermometer. When $R_x + R_t + R_l = R_y + R_z + R_r$ there is no imbalance, and therefore no dc current, no ac current, no motor movement, and no slider movement. The temperature reading is now correct.

tentiometers. Just as with the potentiometer, the galvanometer has been eliminated, either by using a dc–ac converter or by simply using an ac power supply instead of a battery. Fig. 45 shows a typical dc bridge circuit used with a resistance thermometer. Notice that the slidewire is in a different position from where it was in the simple Wheatstone bridge.

The reason for placing the slidewire in the position shown is to eliminate the effect of a change in resistance between the slidewire and its slider. Any change in the resistance at this point, because of poor contact, has the same effect on both arms of the bridge, thus having negligible effect on the measurement.

The null balance principle in this instrument depends upon the balance between the thermometer bulb resistance and the division of the slidewire resistance. For each position of the slider the amount of slidewire resistance in the two arms of the bridge changes. When the thermometer bulb resistance rises, the resistance in its arm must be reduced, and the resistance in the opposing arm must be increased to obtain balance. When $R_x + R_t + R_l = R_y + R_z + R_r$, the circuit is in balance, and there is no voltage to the converter, amplifier, and motor. The pointer then remains stationary and the temperature reading is correct.

While the accuracy of the millivoltmeter-type thermometer is generally about $\pm 1\%$, the accuracy of the null-balance type is generally better than $\pm 0.25\%$.

The response of the resistance thermometer is about the same as the response of the thermocouple

ROD

ROD THERMISTORS—are made by an extrusion process and sintered at a high temperature. Lead wires are soldered to the ends of the element.

DISC

DISC THERMISTORS—are produced by pressing thermistor powders in a mold and sintering at a high temperature.

BEAD

BEAD THERMISTORS—are made by utilizing the surface tension of a slurry of mixed oxides applied to closely spaced platinum wires. Shrinkage of the oxides occurs at the high sintering temperature used and results in a permanent electrical contact.

Fig. 46. Thermistors display the characteristic of decreasing electrical resistance when their temperatures are increased.

when used under the same conditions and in similar enclosures. Both the resistance thermometer and the thermocouple are usually enclosed in a well of some type which, of course, slows down their response somewhat.

In recent years, thermistors (Fig. 46) have found increasing use in temperature measurement. These are very small, solid, semi-conductors made of various metal oxides. They are available in several shapes such as rods, discs, beads, washers, and flakes. The electrical resistance of a thermistor decreases with an in-

crease in temperature. For temperature measurement, they are used in bridge circuits, like the resistance thermometer. Of course, because of their very small size the bridge current must be kept low.

Radiation Measuring Thermometers. Radiation pyrometers are used for measuring temperatures up to 10,000°F. See Fig. 47. They are also used for measuring higher temperatures of moving objects, or when the use of other sensitive devices is impractical.

The operation of the radiation thermometer involves measuring thermal

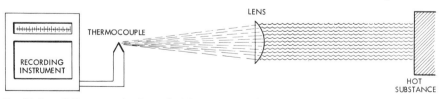

Fig. 47. In radiation pyrometry the radiant heat or energy from the hot substance is translated into **emf** by the thermocouple and indicated in degrees of temperature.

Table of Emmission Factors of Oxidized Metals

MATERIAL	100C	200C	500C
BRASS		0.61	0.59
COPPER (CALORIZED)	0.6		0.6
CAST IRON		0.95	0.84
IRON		0.74	
MONEL		0.43	0.43
NICKEL		0.37	
STEEL		0.79	0.79
WROUGHT IRON		0.94	0.94
STAINLESS STEEL		0.62	0.73

energy which is radiated by a body when that body is heated. The Stefan-Boltzmann Law governing this principle is stated by the formula:

$$W = K\ T^4_a$$

This principle states that the total radiation (W) per unit area per second from a "black" body or surface is proportional to its absolute (Kelvin) temperature raised to the fourth power. The Stefan-Boltzmann constant factor (K) varies with the substance being measured.

The tendency to radiate thermal energy is called emissivity. All substances have different emission factors and the factor may range from 0 to 1. The emissivity of copper, for example, is 0.6. A body or surface which emits all thermal energy that it absorbs (but which reflects none) is called a black body. The emissivity of a black body is 1, the maximum possible emissivity. The emissivity factor is included in the Stefan-Boltzmann constant factor K. The table shown lists the emissivity of various materials.

If used to measure the temperature of a hot ingot of iron in the open, radiation pyrometer readings will be low since iron is a poorer emitter than a black body. When readings are taken while the iron is still in the furnace, the walls and the iron are at the same temperature. Since there is no net energy exchange between walls and iron, the iron can be said to be emitting as much thermal energy as it is absorbing. Thus it approximates the characteristics of a black body, and the reading of its temperature will be accurate.

In an industrial radiation pyrometer, the temperature-sensitive element is either a single thermocouple or several connected thermocouples (a thermopile). Whichever is used, they serve as the input to the same meters or circuits as if they were receiving their thermal energy directly rather than from a radiation unit.

Finally, it should be remembered that in temperature measurement, the primary or sensing element must be carefully selected and properly installed to provide the best sensitivity and response. More than any other measurement, temperature is subject to the details of installation.

Chapter 11 _____ Pressure

THERE are three scales for pressure measurement:
    Gage Pressure Scale
    Absolute Pressure Scale
    Vacuum Scale
The difference between the gage pressure scale and the absolute pressure scale is the location of the zero point. On the gage pressure scale, the zero point is at atmospheric pressure. On the absolute pressure scale, the zero point is at the absolute zero pressure point.

The vacuum scale has its zero at atmospheric pressure and its maximum point at the absolute zero pressure point. Thus, the vacuum scale is used to indicate negative gage pressure. See Fig. 1.

The measurement of atmospheric pressure is essential to the establishment of the gage pressure scale and the vacuum scale. Atmospheric pressure is the pressure exerted by the air surrounding the earth. This pressure varies with altitude since the air nearer the earth is compressed by the air above. At sea level, the atmospheric pressure is 14.7 pounds per square inch (psi). At 5,000 feet elevation, the atmospheric pressure is 12.2 psi. At 10,000 feet elevation, the atmospheric pressure is 9.7 psi. See Fig. 2. The instrument used for meas-

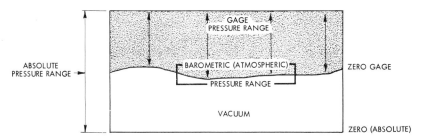

Fig. 1. Gage pressure is pressure above atmospheric pressure, hence the location of zero on the gage pressure scale depends on the barometric reading. Absolute pressure is the pressure above absolute zero pressure. A vacuum is any pressure less than atmospheric pressure.

136

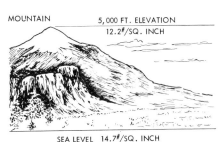

Fig. 2. Atmospheric pressure at sea level, at 5,000 feet, and at 10,000 feet.

uring atmospheric pressure is the barometer. The simplest barometer consists of a long glass tube which is filled with mercury and sealed at one end and then placed in a pan of mercury (Fig. 3). The mercury in the tube settles down, leaving a vacuum above it. The height of the mer-

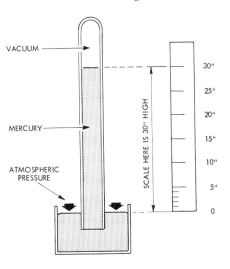

Fig. 3. Simple barometer for measuring atmospheric pressure.

cury in the tube above the level of the mercury in the pan indicates the atmospheric pressure in inches of mercury. Another device for measuring atmospheric pressure is the aneroid barometer (Fig. 4). In this type, a pressure capsule from which all air has been removed is linked to a pointer. The pointer then indicates atmospheric pressure on the scale in pounds per square inch.

For measuring absolute pressures, the principle of the aneroid barometer is used except that, instead of

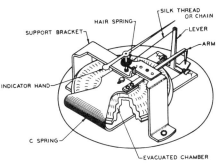

Fig. 4. Aneroid barometer. Aneroid means using no fluid. (Taylor Instrument Co.)

having atmospheric pressure act upon an evacuated pressure element, the pressure to be measured is used. In Fig. 5 the pressure inside the evacuated bellows is at the absolute zero point. Therefore, the pressure indicated by the instrument is in absolute units.

Vacuum measurement is the measurement of pressures below atmospheric. The vacuum scale is graduated in inches of mercury or inches of water. Elastic deformation elements, such as the Bourdon tube, bellows, and diaphragm, are used to measure vacuum just as they are used to measure pressure.

In review, the three pressure scales are shown in Fig. 6. Notice that the absolute pressure scale includes the gage pressure scale and the vacuum scale. Thus, a pressure of 10 inches of mercury absolute may also be expressed as vacuum of 20 inches of mercury or a gage pressure of −20 inches of mercury.

Pressures which do not exceed 1 psi above atmospheric pressure are generally regarded as low pressures.

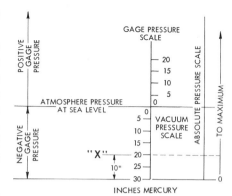

Fig. 6. At "X" the pressure can be expressed as 10 inches of mercury absolute, or as 20 inches of mercury vacuum, or as −20 inches of mercury gage.

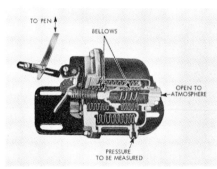

Fig. 5. Cutaway of bellows-type absolute pressure gage. The bellows to the left is evacuated and sealed; the pressure being measured acts on the bellows to the right. The movement of the bellows actuates the pen. (Taylor Instrument Co.)

Instruments for measuring such low pressures are usually calibrated in inches of water (1 pound per square inch above atmospheric pressure equals 27.7 inches of water).

Manometers

The manometer can be used for measuring low pressures. In addition to the simple U-tube manometer, several special types of manometers have been devised to measure low pressures. The Direct Reading Well Type Manometer is one of these. The pressure to be measured is admitted to the well.

Assume that a pressure of 2 psi is applied to the well side of the manometer in Fig. 7. This causes the water in the tube side to rise 55.06 inches above the zero line. At the

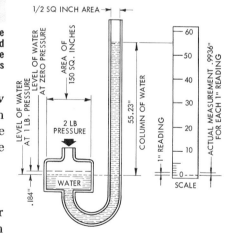

Fig. 7. Direct Reading Well-Type Manometer uses water as the liquid for low pressure measurement. In this case the manometer well has 300 times the area of the tube. The scale is graduated so that each inch reading actually measures .9966 inches.

same time, the water in the well side is lowered. As the area of the well is 300 times greater than the area of the tube, this movement will be considerably less (.184 inches). Because it is desired to read the pressure directly on a scale attached to the tube side, each scale inch must be corrected for the movement of water in the well. Thus, each inch of water read on the manometer scale would actually be less than an inch in length.

In the example shown, each scale inch, after adjustment would be $1 - \dfrac{.184}{55.23}$ inches in length, or .9966 inches. Note that the sum of the change in heights of the water in the two sides of the manometer (55.23 + .184) equals 55.414 inches. This checks, since 2 psi is equivalent to the pressure exerted by a column of water 55.414 inches in height.

Another form of manometer is called a draft gage (it gets its name from its frequent use for measuring furnace drafts). In this well-type manometer, the tube is not vertical but almost horizontal. This has the effect of lengthening the graduations of the scale. A vertical rise of two inches in the tube will actually show up as a six-inch movement of the water in the tube of the instrument in Fig. 8. Note that this type of manometer must be installed in a level position. Levelling devices are usually built into the instrument. Here, again, the scale must be corrected for the lowering of the water in the well.

Water and mercury are the most common liquids used in manometers, but since the measurements produced are in common units of pressure other fluids may be used as long as their specific gravities remain constant under the operating conditions. It must be remembered that the specific gravity of the liquid actually determines the pressure range of the manometer, and the substitution of one liquid for another calls for a correction of the reading. For instance, if a liquid with a specific gravity of 3.0 is substituted for water (specific gravity = 1.0) each "inch of water" shown on the manometer scale is actually equal to 3 inches of water in terms of pressure measurement. There are manometer fluids available whose specific gravities are less than 1.0 as well as others with specific gravities from 1.0 to 3.0. In addition to their usefulness in extending or limiting the manometer scale, they may have physical or chemical properties which make them superior to water or mercury.

Elastic Deformation Elements

Of the elastic deformation elements available for pressure measurement, the diaphragm is best suited for low pressure measurement.

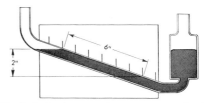

Fig. 8. Inclined manometers are very precise in the measurement of extremely low pressures.

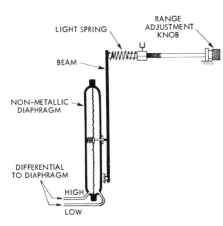

Fig. 9. Non-metallic diaphragms are often used when pressure ranges are small. (Bailey Meter Co.)

One type of diaphragm is non-metallic, employing such materials as leather, teflon, and neoprene. See Fig. 9. Generally, diaphragms of this type are large and non-circular. They are satisfactory for pressure ranges from 0 to .5 inches of water to 0 to 10 inches of water. The diaphragm is

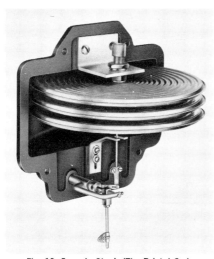

Fig. 10. Capsule Stack (The Bristol Co.)

opposed by a light spring. Indicating, recording, or controlling draft gages are the principal applications of such diaphragms.

Another type of diaphragm is a single, circular, metallic disc, either flat or corrugated, which depends upon its own resilience for its operation.

Pressure Capsules. Frequently, two circular diaphragms are welded or soldered together to form a pressure capsule. These capsules may be used singly or stacked (as in Fig. 10) depending on the pressure range to be measured. The deflection of a pressure capsule depends upon:

1. Diameter of the capsule
2. Thickness of the material
3. Elasticity of the material
4. Design of the capsule (shape and number of corrugations).

It is important that the deflection vs. pressure relationship be linear and that the capsule be made of material which will maintain its accuracy after many deflections. Phosphor bronze, stainless steel, and NI-SPAN C (a nickel alloy) are the most common materials used for pressure capsules. Fig. 11 shows the deflection vs. pressure curves of these three materials.

Phosphor bronze capsules are suitable for most applications for ranges from 0 to .5 inches of water to 0 to 30 psi. They should not be used if chemical corrosion is possible or if wide temperature variations are expected.

Stainless steel capsules are used for corrosive applications. They are

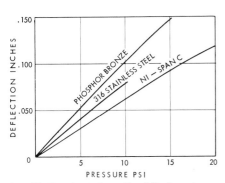

Fig. 11. The chart shows the deflection characterists of the three most widely used materials for low pressure capsules. (The Bristol Co.)

available for ranges from 0 to 8 inches of water to 0 to 50 psi.

NI-SPAN C capsules are virtually unaffected by temperature changes from —50° to 150°F. They are available for ranges from 0 to 4 inches of water to 0 to 30 psi.

Responses of all pressure elements to a full scale pressure change are extremely rapid. This response is, of course, affected by the length and

diameter of pipe or tubing used. The longer the sensing line, the slower the response because of line resistance. The greater the diameter of the line, the slower the response. These dimensions must be carefully selected to avoid excessively slow response. For low pressure measurement, the length of sensing line must be short and the diameter small. For high pressure measurement, the sensing line may be long and the diameter larger. If the pressure to be measured pulsates, a small needle valve should be inserted in the line as a pulsation dampener.

For measuring the pressure of corrosive fluids which would damage the measuring element, seals are available which are used for protection. Fig. 12 shows a typical capsule-type seal. The process fluid acts on a pressure capsule which, along with the measuring element and connecting capillary tubing, is filled with a sec-

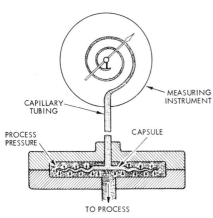

Fig. 12. Process fluid pressure, acting on the secondary fluid within the capsule, forces the secondary fluid up the tubing. This forces the coil to expand or unwind. (The Bristol Co.)

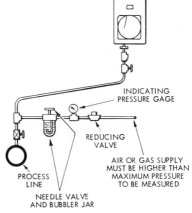

Fig. 13. With a constant air or gas purge pressure, any change in the reading of the combined pressures indicates a changed process pressure. (The Bristol Co.)

ondary fluid. Sometimes it is possible to eliminate the capsule and provide a seal merely by the insertion of an inert liquid between the process liquid and the measuring instrument.

Still another sealing method employs an air or gas purge, as shown in Fig. 13. In this system, the measuring instrument senses the difference between the purge pressure and the process pressure. Since the purge pressure is constant, the variations in process pressure actuate the measuring instrument.

Bellows. For slightly higher pressures, the bellows is a serviceable elastic deformation element. A bellows is a one-piece, collapsible, seamless metallic unit with deep folds formed from very thin-walled tubing. Metals such as brass, phosphor bronze, and stainless steel are among the type used for such bellows. The diameter may be as small as 0.5 inches or as large as 12 inches, and it may have as many as 24 folds.

Generally, only a portion of the total available motion of bellows is used, to prevent their taking a "set" from being expanded to their limit too frequently. A spring is often used to limit their motion. The larger the diameter of the bellows, the lower the pressure that they can measure. Instruments with bellows elements are used for pressure ranges from 0 to 5 inches of water to 0 to 800 psi.

Pressure Springs. Pressure springs of helical or spiral shape, or of the simple C-shaped Bourdon type, are used for measuring higher pressures.

These are all formed from seamless metal tubing with wall thickness varying from .01 inches to .05 inches. Beryllium copper, steel, and stainless steel are among the metals used for such elements. The wall thickness and the material determine the maximum pressure to which such an element may be subjected. A thick-walled steel Bourdon tube is available for measuring pressures as high as 100,000 psi.

Pressure Transducers

Any of the elastic deformation elements may be joined to an electrical device to form a pressure transducer. These transducers may produce a change of resistance, inductance, or capacitance. It is, of course, essential that for each unit change of pressure there is a unit change of electrical characteristic.

Resistance Type. Resistance-type devices used in pressure transducers include:

1. Strain gages
2. Moving contacts

A strain gage is simply a fine wire in the form of a grid (Fig. 14). When

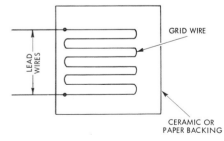

GRID WIRE

LEAD WIRES

CERAMIC OR PAPER BACKING

Fig. 14. A strain gage consists of a wire grid bonded to an impregnated paper or ceramic backing.

the grid is distorted, the resistance of the wire changes according to the formula:

$$R = K \frac{L}{A}$$

where

K = a constant for the particular kind of wire

L = length of wire

A = cross-sectional area.

As the strain gage is distorted by the elastic deformation element, its length is increased and its cross-sectional area is reduced. Both of these changes increase the resistance. Because little distortion is required to change the resistance of a strain gage through its total range, this type of transducer can be used to detect very small movements and, therefore, very small pressure changes.

Because current flows in the strain gage, some heat will be generated which must be compensated for. One method of compensation employs a second strain gage placed close to the measuring unit. These two are used in a bridge circuit so that the heating effect of the two resistive elements is cancelled out, and the only resistance change in the bridge is due to the deformation. Most often, strain gage bridges are ac bridges.

The moving contact type of resistance transducer is most often used with a bellows because of the force required. A typical circuit for such a transducer is shown in Fig. 15.

Inductance Type. Inductance-type pressure transducers consist of three parts: a coil, a movable magnetic core, and the elastic deformation element. The element is attached to the core. As the pressure varies, the element causes the core to move within the coil (See Fig. 5, Transmission). An alternating current is passed through the coil, and as the core moves the inductance of the coil changes. The current passing through the coil in-

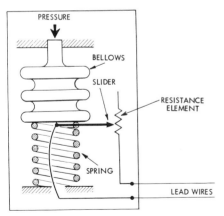

Fig. 15. The moving-contact type of resistance transducer is not as sensitive to every small pressure change as the strain gage.

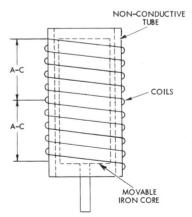

Fig. 16. Greater sensitivity is achieved by using a center tap, which has the effect of using two separate coils. The inductance change in one coil is opposed by an opposite inductance change in the other coil.

creases as the inductance decreases. This type of transducer is used in a current-sensitive circuit.

For increased sensitivity, the coil may be divided in two, using a center tap (Fig. 16). This actually provides two coils. As the core moves inside the coils, the inductance of one coil decreases as the inductance of the other increases.

Still another type of inductance unit used for pressure measurement employs a mutual inductance unit, or differential transformer. In this type, three coils are wound on a single tube (Fig. 17). The center coil is connected to an ac source. Voltage is induced in the two outside coils. When the movable core is centered, the induced voltages in each of the outside coils are equal. Moving the core unbalances these voltages, and the difference between them can be measured.

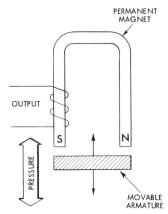

Fig. 18. In the reluctance-type pressure transducer, electrical energy is provided by the field of a permanent magnet rather than an AC source.

Similar to the inductance-type pressure transducer is the *reluctance-type* (Fig. 18). The principal difference is the source of energy which in the case of the reluctance unit is a permanent magnet. AC input is used in the inductance-type. For pressure measurement, the elastic deformation element moves an armature closer to or farther from the permanent magnet. The reluctance of a coil wrapped

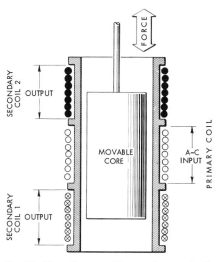

Fig. 17. When the movable core is moved off-center, different voltages result in the two outside coils, which can be measured as an indication of pressure change.

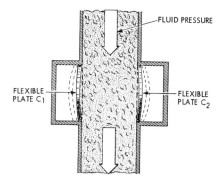

Fig. 19. In the capacitive pressure transducer, changing pressure directly changes the distance between the capacitive plates, thus changing the voltage.

around the permanent magnet varies with this movement.

Capacitive Type. Capacitive pressure transducers (Fig. 19) consist of two conductive plates and a dielectric. As the pressure increases, the plates move farther apart, changing the capacitance. The fluid whose pressure is being measured serves as the dielectric.

Several other types of transducers

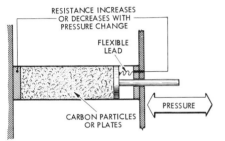

Fig. 20. The carbon pile pressure transducer translates pressure change to resistance change. As pressure change reduces the volume of the carbon pile the resistance decreases.

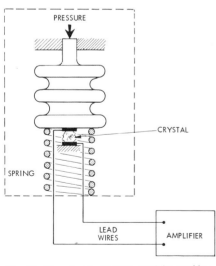

Fig. 21. Piezoelectric Crystals used in combination with bellows as a pressure transducer.

are used with elastic deformation elements for pressure measurement.

1. Carbon pile transducers (Fig. 20). As pressure is applied to a confined mass of carbon particles, the electrical resistance of the carbon pile changes.

2. Piezoelectric transducers. As pressure is applied to crystals of certain materials, a difference in voltage across particular points of their structure occurs. See Fig. 21.

Differential Pressure Measurement

Because of its importance in flow rate and level measurement, precise differential pressure measurement is of prime importance in industrial processes.

All the pressure sensitive elements already described are adaptable to differential pressure measurement. Manometers of all kinds can be used with the differential pressure (ΔP) being equal to the difference in vertical height ($h_1 - h_2$) of the two columns multiplied by the density of the manometer liquid (d_m). Expressed as a formula, this is:

$$\Delta P = (h_1 - h_2) d_m$$

Density is defined as the amount of matter per unit volume and is generally stated in pounds per cubic foot. Water has a density of 62.4 pounds per cubic foot, mercury a density of 848.4 pounds per cubic foot, and glycerine 78.6 pounds per cubic foot.

Consider a U-tube manometer

with water as the fluid. A difference in height of the columns of 1 inch produces this relationship:

$$\Delta P = (1'') \frac{(62.4)}{(1728)} = .03611 \text{ psi}$$

(Note: 62.4 lb./cu. ft. must be converted to lb./cu. in. 1 cu. ft. = 1728 cu. in.

$$62.4 \text{ lb./cu. ft.} = \frac{62.4}{1728} \text{ lb./cu. in.})$$

Using mercury in the same manometer, a 1 inch difference in column height gives:

$$\Delta P = (1'') \frac{(848.4)}{(1728)} = .49097 \text{ psi}$$

In many differential pressure applications, the density of the measured fluid must be taken into account, particularly when the density is quite high and there is a difference in height between the two pressure points. Such an installation is illustrated in Fig. 22.

The difference in height of the liquid columns is not only due to the fact that P_1 is greater than P_2, but also because there is an unbalance caused by the difference in height (the column H) of measured fluid on the two manometer columns. The manometer reading must, therefore, be corrected for the pressure caused by this difference. This pressure equals H × D. Therefore, the difference between P_1 and P_2 is actually $P_1 - P_2 = \Delta P = hd\text{-}HD$.

Sometimes this correction is complicated by the presence of a sealing fluid between the manometer fluid and the measured fluid. A sealing fluid is used when the measured fluid might damage the manometer. In this case in addition to the correction required to overcome the unbalance caused by the difference in height of the columns of measured fluid, any difference in height of the sealing fluid columns must also be corrected.

Such corrections are made by adjusting the zero of the manometer with measuring fluid and the sealing fluid—if used—at their respective zero levels.

The well-type manometer, when used for differential pressure measurement, makes possible readings on one scale. The higher pressure is admitted to the well and the lower pressure to the tube (Fig. 23). The

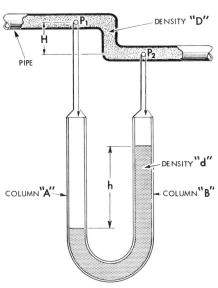

Fig. 22. Differential pressure installation for a dense liquid with pressure connections at different heights.

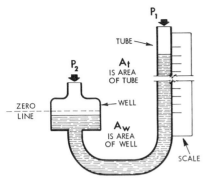

Fig. 23. The reading can be made directly on the scale (if adjusted) when the well-type manometer is used for differential pressure measurement.

reading is made directly on the scale which is corrected for the movement of the fluid in the well as mentioned previously. The relationship between differential pressure and the height of the fluid in the tube is as follows:

$$P_2 - P_1 = (1 + \frac{A_t}{A_w}) \ d \times h$$

where

d = density of the liquid

h = height of the fluid in the tube as read on the scale (unadjusted).

$\dfrac{A_t}{A_w}$ = ratio of the areas of the tube and well

$\dfrac{A_t}{A_w}$, is usually between $\dfrac{1}{300}$ and $\dfrac{1}{600}$

With this ratio fixed at $\dfrac{1}{500}$, each scale inch is actually

$1 - \dfrac{1}{500}''$ in length or .998″

When water or mercury is used as the manometer fluid, the readings are in standard units; when some other fluid is used, the readings must be corrected for the density of the substitute fluid.

The Inclined-Tube manometer, a variation, permits the scale to be expanded so that lower differential pressures may be measured precisely. The relationship between differential pressure and the position of the fluid in this type manometer (See Fig. 8) is expressed:

$$P_2 - P_1 = D \ (1 + \frac{A_t}{A_w}) \ d \sin \alpha$$

where

D = density of the fluid

d sin α = height of the fluid

α = angle of the inclined tube

d = length of fluid along the inclined tube.

The mercury float manometer is a modification of the well type manometer. Because the buoyant force on the float is sufficient to move a recording mechanism, the mercury float manometer can be used as a differential pressure recording instrument (Fig. 24). The manometer fluid does not have to be visible; therefore, the manometer may be made of metal, permitting its use at high pressures—up to 5,000 psi. Another feature of this kind of manometer is the interchangeability of the tube columns (range tubes) to permit a change in the differential range of the instrument. The relationship between the differential pressure

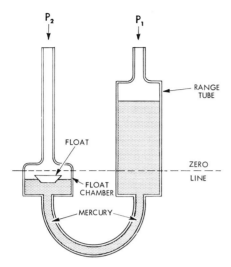

Fig. 24. The mercury float manometer can be used as a differential pressure recording instrument.

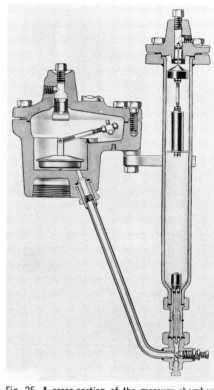

Fig. 25. A cross-section of the mercury chamber of a mercury float manometer. The check valves are located in the upper and lower sections of the high pressure chamber, on the right of the instrument. (American Meter Co.)

and height of the fluid in the well (or height of the float) is as follows:

$$P_2 - P_1 = (1 + \frac{A_w}{A_t}) \, d \times h$$

It can be seen that, by changing the range tubes, the ratio $\frac{A_w}{A_t}$ is changed, thus changing the range of the meter. The differential pressure ranges available with such instruments vary from 0 to 10 inches-of-water to 0 to 200 inches-of-water. Very low differential pressure ranges from 0 to .2 inches-of-water to 0 to 1.5 inches-of-water can be accommodated by substituting oil for mercury. When such a substitution is made special oil seals are required inside the meter body, and the instrument can be used only at low pressures.

This kind of instrument (Fig. 25) usually includes check valves to prevent excessive movement of the mercury when the instrument is subjected to differential pressure above its normal range or when occasional reversal of pressures occurs. Accuracy of such a meter is excellent.

The bellows or dry-type differential meter uses two matched bellows enclosed in separate chambers of the

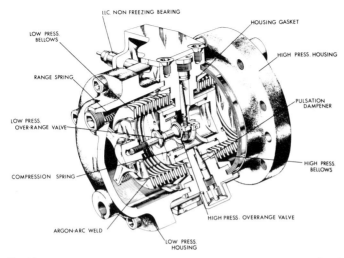

Fig. 26. Bellows-Type Differential Pressure Meter. (Industrial Instruments Corp.)

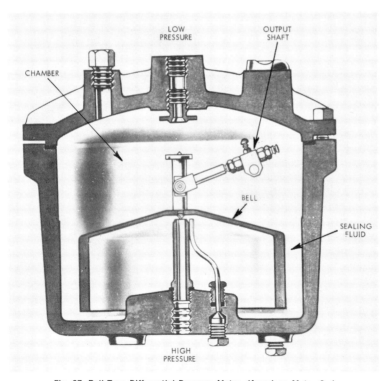

Fig. 27. Bell-Type Differential Pressure Meter. (American Meter Co.)

meter body (Fig. 26). The two pressures are admitted separately to each chamber, thus causing each bellows to be compressed. Because of the difference in the pressures, their compression will not be equal. The two bellows are attached to a common shaft which moves an amount equal to the difference in the movement of the two bellows. The shaft movement is opposed by a spring which determines the amount of bellows unbalance necessary to produce the shaft motion. This spring thus determines the range of the meter. In a typical meter of this type, the bellows are filled with a hydraulic fluid which is permitted to flow from one bellows into the other. This provides a smooth "damped" motion of the bellows. By including a valve in the hydraulic system which shuts off the passage of the fluid between the bellows, the meter is protected against differential pressures above its normal range. In addition, an adjustable restriction in the hydraulic line permits slowing or speeding up the action of the bellows. Such a meter is available for pressures up to 10,-000 psi and differential ranges from 0 to 20 inches-of-water to 0 to 400 psi. Accuracy of such a meter is ± .5% of range.

The bell-type differential pressure meter is a simple instrument that can be used for measuring low range differential pressures from about 1 to 20 inches of water. Meter bodies suitable for pressures up to 250 psi are available. In this kind of meter

(Fig. 27), a bell is floated in a shallow pool of liquid in the meter body. The higher pressure is admitted to the underside of the bell and the lower pressure to the outside. The movement of the bell is opposed by a spring which determines the range

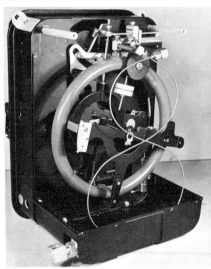

Fig. 28. Ring Balance Meter. Top: the front of the instrument with recording chart. Bottom: the ring with the flexible connections. (Hagan Controls Corp.)

of the meter for any particular bell. The weight and the thickness of the bell also determine the range since the weight affects its buoyancy, and its thickness establishes the ratio of the area of the under surface to the area of the outer surface. The heavier the bell, the more differential pressure required to cause it to move upward.

There are several kinds of weight-balance type differential pressure meters. One of these is the ring balance meter (Fig. 28). This is not really a manometer but rather a weight balance. In this type of meter, the mercury contained in the ring is displaced by the differential pressure. The ring is balanced on a knife edge and counterbalanced by a weight. The pressure connections to the ring are flexible, allowing the ring to rotate. The equation for balance is:

$$P_2 - P_1 = \frac{d}{r} \left(\frac{W}{A} \sin \theta \right)$$

where

d = radius of the arc described by the weight

r = the radius of the ring

W = the weight

A = area of the tube

θ = angle through which the ring moves due to differential pressure.

Notice that the density of the fluid does not appear in this equation. The liquid is used only to provide a seal; mercury is most commonly used.

The bellows, ring balance, and tilting U-tube instruments discussed above are motion-balance devices. In addition to motion-balance instruments, force-balance differential pressure-sensing instruments are also common, used mostly as transmitters. They may be pneumatically or electrically actuated. A diaphragm or capsule serves as the sensing element.

In the pneumatic instrument, the differential pressure displaces the sensing element, which in turn deflects a torque tube which positions a flapper-nozzle mechanism (See Fig. 3, Transmission).

The electrical counterpart of a force-balance differential sensor employs the same type sensing element as the pneumatic. But instead of the flapper-nozzle mechanism, an electrical amplifying system is used. An inductance bridge circuit is frequently used with the sensing element, displacing a core in an inductance coil (See Fig. 7, Transmission).

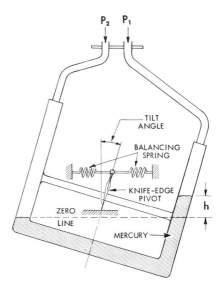

Fig. 29. Tilting U-tube Manometer.

Another weight-balance-type pressure meter is the tilting U-tube manometer. The methods of operation of the ring balance and the U-tube types are similar. The angular deflection of both is proportional to the differential pressure. See Fig. 29.

The two pressures are admitted to the ends of a tube containing liquid. The tube, which is either circular or U-shaped, permits free movement of the liquid, and is balanced on a pivot.

When one of the pressures is greater than the other the fluid is forced to move, upsetting the balance of the tube. For each change in differential pressure there is a new position of the tube, and this may be indicated on a scale graduated in units of differential pressure. There is usually a counterweight or spring attached to the tube which will return it to balance when the differential pressure is removed.

Chapter 12 _____ Flow

THE physical properties of fluids which are important in flowmetering are:

1. Pressure
2. Density
3. Viscosity
4. Velocity

Pressure has already been defined as force divided by area. Density is weight divided by volume, and is usually expressed in pounds per cubic foot.

Viscosity. The *viscosity* of a fluid refers to its physical resistance to flow. Molasses is more viscous than water, and water much more viscous than gas. There are several viscosity units, the most widely used being the centipoise. The viscosity of water at 68°F is 1.0 centipoise; the viscosity

of kerosene at 68°F is 2.0 centipoises. The viscosity of liquids decreases as the temperature rises; the opposite is true of gases.

Velocity. The *velocity* of a flowing fluid is its speed in the direction of flow. It is an important factor in flowmetering because it determines the behavior of the fluid. When the average velocity is slow, the flow is said to be *laminar* (Fig. 1). This means that the fluid flows in layers with the fastest moving layers toward the center and the slowest moving layers on the outer edges of the stream. As the velocity increases, the flow becomes *turbulent*, with the layers disappearing and the velocity across the stream being more uniform (Fig. 2). In this discussion, the flow is assumed to be turbulent and the term "velocity" refers to the average velocity of a particular cross-section of the stream.

$$\text{Velocity} = \frac{\text{rate of flow (ft. per sec.)}}{\text{area of pipe (sq. feet)}}$$

Reynolds Number. In flowmetering, the nature of flow can be de-

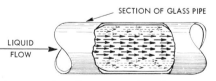

Fig. 1. Laminar flow occurs when the average velocity is slow. The layers are fast moving in the center and become slower on the outer edges of the stream.

153

SECTION OF GLASS PIPE

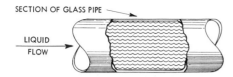

LIQUID
FLOW

Fig. 2. Turbulent flow occurs when the average velocity is fast. The layers disappear and the velocity is more uniform across the stream.

scribed by a number—the Reynolds Number, which is the average velocity × density × internal diameter of pipe ÷ viscosity. In equation form, this is expressed:

$$R = \frac{v D \rho}{\mu}$$

where

v = velocity

D = inside diameter of pipe

ρ = fluid density

μ = viscosity.

Although the Reynolds Number has no dimensions of its own, it is important that the dimensions used for determining it be in agreement.

From the Reynolds Number, it can be determined whether the flow is laminar or turbulent. If the Reynolds Number is less than 2000, the flow is laminar; if greater than 4000, the flow is turbulent. Between these two values, the nature of the flow is unpredictable. In most industrial applications, the flow is turbulent.

Although measurement can be made without consideration of the Reynolds Number, greater accuracy is possible when a correction based upon it is made.

Flow Calculations

The greatest number of rate-of-flow meters for fluids are those which measure the differential pressure across a restriction in the pipe line. The most common restriction is the concentric orifice plate.

Fig. 3 is a cross-section of a typical orifice plate installation showing the variation in pressure that occurs across the plate. Notice that the main flow stream takes the shape of the Venturi tube with the narrowest path slightly downstream from the plate. This point is called the *vena contracta*. At this point, the pressure is at its minimum. From this point on, the fluid again begins to fill the

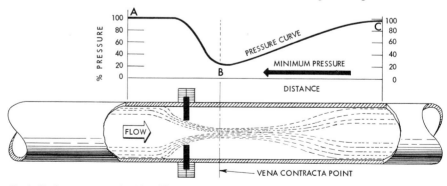

Fig. 3. Maximum pressure in this orifice plate installation is at A; minimum pressure is at B. Because of loss of pressure across the plate, downstream pressure rises only as high as point C.

pipe and the pressure rises. The pressure, however, does not recover completely. There is a loss of pressure across the plate. The principal consideration in selecting an orifice plate is the ratio of its opening (d) to the internal diameter of the pipe (D). This is often called the beta ratio. If the d/D ratio is too small, the loss of pressure becomes too great. If the ratio is too great, the loss of pressure becomes too small to detect and too unstable. Ratios from .2 to .6 generally provide best accuracy.

Several procedures have been developed for calculating the correct size of an orifice to make it suitable for measuring a particular range of rate of flow. The fundamental equation on which all these procedures is based is:

$$Q = E \, A_o \sqrt{2gh}$$

where

Q = flow rate (volume per unit of time)

E = efficiency factor

A_o = area of orifice in square feet

g = acceleration due to gravity 32 feet/sec/sec

h = differential pressure across orifice in feet.

The efficiency factor E is required since the actual flow through an orifice is not the same as the calculated flow. Values of E have been determined by tests and are found in tables. It is different for each combination of d/D ratio and Reynolds Number. In some equations the letter K is used to express this factor, in others the letter C. It may be called flow coefficient. This factor or coefficient has no units since it is a ratio of the actual to the theoretical.

Concentric orifice plates are $\frac{1}{16}$ inches or $\frac{1}{8}$ inches thick in the smaller sizes (up to 10 inches), and $\frac{1}{4}$ inches thick for larger sizes. The upstream edge should be square and as sharp as possible and the upstream face as smooth as possible. The plate should be flat and the orifice exactly centered in the pipe.

The fundamental equation cannot be used in calculating either flow rates or orifice sizes. It must be changed to a working equation.

A typical working equation for liquids is:

$$Q = 19.65 \times d^2 \times E \times \sqrt{h}$$

where

Q = gallons per minute

19.65 = units constant

d^2 = orifice diameter in inches

E = efficiency factor

h = differential pressure in inches.

As stated above, values of E are found in tables or on graphs such as Fig. 4.

Example: for Reynolds No. of 10,-000

B ratio of .6

the value of E is .673

The orifice plate, flow nozzle, and venturi tube operate on the same principle, and the same equation is used for all three. In addition to the difference in flow coefficient (E), there are other factors for each that determine which element should be used.

Venturi Tube. The *venturi tube* is the most expensive and the most ac-

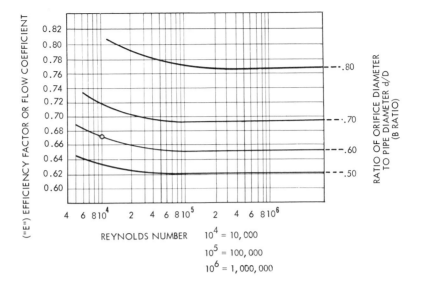

Fig. 4. Given a Reynolds Number of 10,000, and a beta ratio of .6, the graph indicates an "E" value of .673.

curate. High beta ratios (above .75) can be used with good results. The pressure recovery of the venturi tube is excellent, which means that there is little pressure drop through it. Functionally, the venturi tube is good since it does not obstruct abrasive sediment; in fact, because of its shape it resists wear effectively.

Flow Nozzle. The *flow nozzle* is simpler and cheaper than the venturi tube. It is slightly less accurate and does not provide as good pressure recovery. The flow nozzle can be used with higher beta ratios (above .75), but it is not quite so wear resistant as the venturi.

Orifice Plate. The *orifice plate* is quite simple and inexpensive. It is the easiest to install and to replace. There is much data available for

calculation of correct sizes. The orifice plate is not so accurate as either the venturi or flow nozzle and does not have as good recovery. It cannot

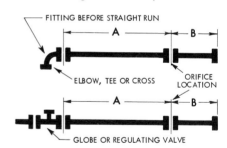

Fig. 5. When beta ratio = .6, upstream distance A must be at least 13 pipe diameters after the elbow, tee, or cross; after globe or regulating valve, upstream distance A must be at least 31 pipe diameters. In both cases, downstream distance B is 5 pipe diameters. Straight run requirements become less as ratio of orifice diameter d to inside pipe diameter D decreases. For example, when d/D is .4, the distances A become 9D after elbows and 19D after valves. (Not drawn to scale.)

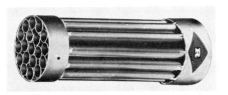

Fig. 6. Straightening vanes are installed above the orifice to reduce turbulence and make accurate measurement possible. (Robertson Mfg. Co.)

be used with high beta ratios. Functionally, the orifice plate is subject to erosion and damage, but its easy replacement offsets this. Hence, it is the most widely used of the primary flow elements.

There must be a long continuous run of straight pipe leading up to any of these primary elements (Fig. 5). Considerable information is available concerning the length of straight pipe required between such devices as elbows and valves and the primary elements. When insufficient straight pipe is not possible, the disturbances can be reduced or eliminated by the installation of *straightening vanes*. One kind of straightening vane consists of a bundle of tubes joined together (Fig. 6).

Pitot Tube. Another primary flow element used to produce a differential pressure is the *pitot tube*. In its simplest form, the pitot tube consists of a tube with a small opening at the measuring end. This small hole faces the flowing fluid (Fig. 7). When the fluid contacts the pitot tube, the fluid velocity is zero and the pressure is at a maximum. This small hole, or "impact opening" as it is called, provides the higher pressure for differential pressure meas-

urement. While the pitot tube provides the higher pressure for differential pressure measurement, an ordinary pressure tap provides the lower pressure reading.

The pitot tube actually measures the velocity of fluid flow and not rate of flow. However, the flow rate can be determined from the velocity using this formula:

$$Q = K A V_1$$

where

Q = flow rate (cubic ft. per sec.)
A = area of flow cross section in feet
V_1 = velocity of flowing fluid (ft. per sec.)
K = flow coefficient of pitot tube (normally about .8).

There is no standardization of pitot tubes as there is for orifice plates, venturi tubes, and flow nozzles. Each pitot tube must be calibrated for each installation.

Pitot tubes may be used where the flowing fluid is not enclosed in a pipe or duct. For instance, a pitot tube may be used to measure the flow of river water, or it may be suspended from an airplane to measure air flow.

Any of the differential pressure type instruments previously described may be used with the pitot tube.

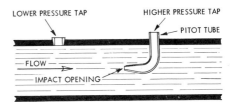

Fig. 7. The pitot tube is an economical device for providing a differential pressure reading.

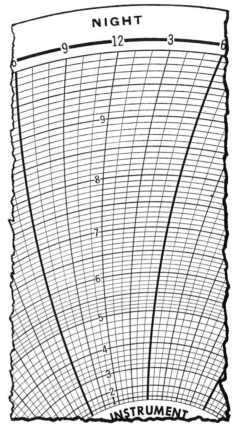

Fig. 8. This square root chart is calibrated so that the square root of the differential pressure being recorded can be read directly, reading flow from the pressure chart itself.

Measurement Conversion Methods

Several methods for converting differential pressure measurement directly to flow measurement are available. The simplest method is to use a square root chart. The observer can directly read the square root of the differential pressure (flow) being recorded at any given instant. See Fig. 8. In most cases, however, a square

root extracting mechanism is built into the meter.

In the Ledoux Bell Fluid Meter (Fig. 9) conversion is achieved by shaping the inside of the bell so that it moves the same distance vertically when almost completely submerged in mercury (at low differential) as it does when hardly submerged (at high differential). In a mercury float-type

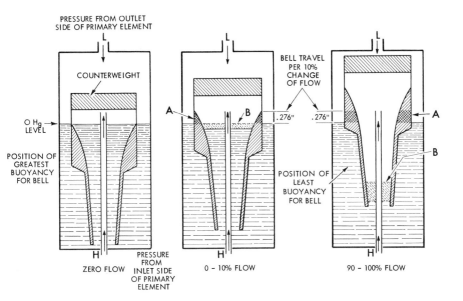

PRESSURE FROM OUTLET
SIDE OF PRIMARY ELEMENT

COUNTERWEIGHT

O Hg
LEVEL

POSITION OF
GREATEST
BUOYANCY
FOR BELL

H   PRESSURE
ZERO FLOW   FROM
          INLET SIDE
          OF PRIMARY
          ELEMENT

BELL TRAVEL
PER 10%
CHANGE
OF FLOW

A   B
          .276"

H
0 - 10% FLOW

.276"   A

B

POSITION OF
LEAST
BUOYANCY
FOR BELL

H
90 - 100% FLOW

IN THE ILLUSTRATION ON THE LEFT, NO FLOW IS PASS-
ING THROUGH THE PRIMARY ELEMENT. THE BUOYANCY
GIVEN TO THE BELL BY THE MERCURY IS OVERCOME BY
THE COUNTERWEIGHT, AND THE BELL SETTLES DOWN ON
TOP OF THE STANDPIPE.

IN THE CENTER ILLUSTRATION, FLOW HAS STARTED
THROUGH THE PRIMARY ELEMENT AT A RATE EQUAL TO
10% OF THE MAXIMUM, CONSEQUENTLY THE BELL HAS
BEEN RAISED 10% OF ITS TRAVEL, OR .276". THIS IS AC-
COMPLISHED BY SO SHAPING THE INSIDE BELL SURFACE
THAT THE VOLUME OF THE BELL WALL A EMERGED FROM
THE MERCURY EXACTLY EQUALS THE VOLUME OF THE
MERCURY B DECREASED BELOW THE ZERO LEVEL INSIDE
THE BELL.

WHEN THE FLOW RATE CHANGES FROM 90 TO 100%
MAXIMUM, AS IN THE ILLUSTRATION ON THE RIGHT, THE
BELL MUST MOVE THE SAME AMOUNT, OR .276", IN OR-
DER THAT THE PEN CAN TRAVEL THE SAME 10% ON THE
CHART. HOWEVER, THE CHANGE IN THE DIFFERENTIAL
PRESSURE WHEN THE FLOW INCREASES FROM 90 TO 100%
IS ABOUT 19 TIMES THE INCREASE FROM 0 TO 10%, RE-
SULTING IN A MUCH LARGER VOLUME OF MERCURY DE-
PRESSED INSIDE THE BELL, AND THUS AN EQUIVALENTLY
LARGER VOLUME OF BELL WALL EMERGED FROM THE MER-
CURY. THIS LARGER WALL VOLUME A CAN ONLY BE OB-
TAINED BY MAKING THE WALL THICKER, SINCE THE VER-
TICAL EMERGENCE (.276") REMAINS AS BEFORE.

Fig. 9. The Ledoux Bell Fluid Meter. (Illustration and accompanying explanation adapted from lecture
notes of the Bailey Instrumentation Course, Bailey Meter Co.)

manometer, the range tube may be
similarly shaped.

In pneumatic flow transmitters
(Fig. 10) the square root extraction
is performed by the pneumatic system. Likewise in electric flow transmitters, it is done in the circuitry. See
Fig. 11.

The measurement of gas flow, to
be accurate, demands knowledge of

the temperature and pressure, since
the volume of gas varies directly
with temperature and inversely with
pressure (See Chapter 11.). The measurement provided is in standard cubic feet per minute. Automatic methods for accomplishing this may be
mechanical or electrical.

A typical mechanical method employs the Sorteberg Force Bridge

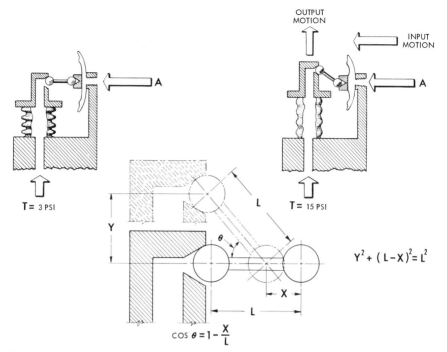

$$Y^2 + (L-X)^2 = L^2$$

$$\cos \theta = 1 - \frac{X}{L}$$

Fig. 10. In this pneumatic square root extractor, as the input pressure A increases, the capsule expands. This causes the floating link L to move against the exhaust outlet of the bellows. The bellows expands due to increased pressure in the now sealed bellows, producing the output motion. The output motion Y is the square root of the input motion X. (Moore Products Co.)

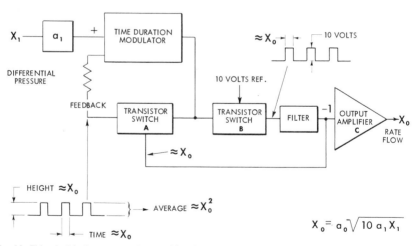

$$X_0 = a_0 \sqrt{10\, a_1 X_1}$$

Fig. 11. This electrical square rooter provides the square root of one or two inputs. When two inputs are introduced, the square rooter adds them and produces the square root of the sum. This system employs a high gain time duration modulator. Time duration is adjusted automatically to balance X_1 against a feedback voltage having an average value proportional to X_0. To give the feedback voltage an average value proportional to X_0, both height and width of the waveform are made proportional to X_0. (DeVar-Kinetics Division, Consolidated Electrodynamics Corp.)

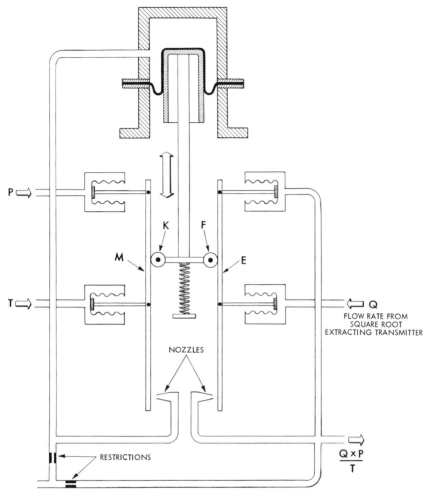

Fig. 12. Pneumatic signals proportional to Pressure and Temperature (forces P and T) act on the bar M. Any unbalance causes movement of wheel K to restore balance. Any unbalance on bar E caused by repositioning the wheel F requires a change in output pressure to restore balance. Total balance is achieved only when the product of signal P and signal Q, divided by the magnitude of signal T, equals Output Pressure.

shown in Fig. 12. This device provides simultaneous multiplication and division and can continuously solve the equation

$$Q_1 = \frac{Q \times P}{T}$$

where Q_1 is flow (Q) compensated for pressure (P) and temperature (T).

In one electrical method, a linear-differential transformer is used. The core of this transformer (Fig. 13) is positioned by

$$\sqrt{\frac{P \times H}{T}}$$

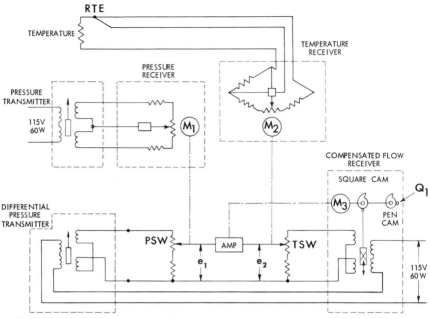

Fig. 13. Electrical method of obtaining a flow reading compensated for pressure and temperature. The differential pressure transmitter determines the voltage across the Pressure Slidewire PSW. The pressure receiver motor M_1 positions the slider on PSW, determining the voltage e_1. The temperature receiver motor M_2 positions the slider on the Temperature Slidewire TSW, determining e_2. When voltages e_1 and e_2 are unequal, the amplifier causes motor M_3 to rotate the square cam. This moves core X in the Compensated Flow Receiver Unit to restore balance. Simultaneously, the pen cam rotates and its follower positions the pen to indicate Q_1 which is flow rate corrected for temperature and pressure. (Bailey Meter Co.)

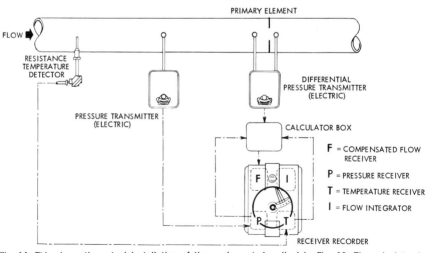

Fig. 14. This shows the actual installation of the equipment described in Fig. 13. The calculator box houses the Pressure Slidewire, the Temperature Slidewire, and the Amplifier. (Bailey Meter Co.)

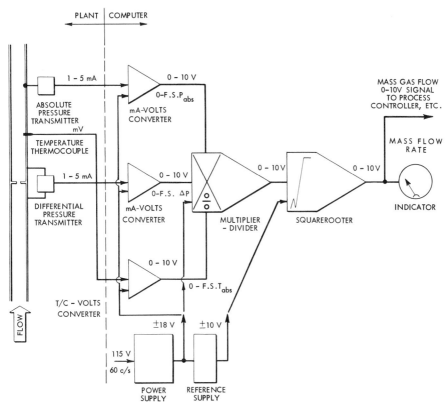

Fig. 15. The internal circuitry of the separate modules shown here is beyond the scope of this text. The modulation of pulse height and width is the basis of their operation. (DeVar-Kinetics Division, Consolidated Electrodynamics Corp.)

The square root extraction is accomplished by using a cam to position the core. The multiplication of differential pressure (H), pressure (P), and the inverse of the temperature (T) is done electrically. In a typical recorder, a resistance thermometer measures temperature, an elastic deformation inductance transducer measures pressure, and a bellows or diaphragm-actuated inductance transducer measures differential pressure. See Fig. 14.

Another electrical method (Fig. 15) has similar measuring transducers. The outputs of these transducers are converted into 0 to 10 volt signals by transistorized signal-converter modules. These converted signals are then fed into transistorized multiplier, divider, and square root extracting modules. The output of the whole circuit is a 0 to 10 volt DC signal, which can be the input of voltmeter-calibrated inflow units or of a compatible controller.

RATE OF FLOW

Fig. 16. Flow rate in a rotameter varies directly as the annular area varies. The differential pressure remains constant.

Variable-Area Meter. In the variable-area flowmeter, the differential pressure across the meter is held constant. Hence, the rate of flow varies as the metering area varies. The differential is maintained by a free floating element which rises and falls as the flow rate increases or decreases. As the float rises, the metering area is increased. The weight of the float and the weight of the flowing fluid determines the amount of rise of the float.

Rotameter. In the rotameter, which is the most common form of variable area meter, the float travels in a tapered tube. The metering area is the annular area (in the form of a ring) between the float and the tube.

The same fundamental equation used for the orifice meter also applies to the variable area meter:

$$Q = A \sqrt{2gh}$$

In the working equation for the rotameter, the differential pressure is replaced by a factor which causes it to remain constant. This factor in-

volves the volume of the float and the area of the float as well as the density of the float and the density of the fluid. The area of the float must be applicable to the taper of the tube; the actual metering area occurs at the bottom of the float (Fig. 16). Thus, the working equation becomes:

$$Q = K A_m 2_g \sqrt{\frac{V_f}{A_f} \left(\frac{\rho_f}{\rho} - 1 \right)}$$

where

Q = rate of flow
K = taper
A_m = area between float and tube measured at bottom of float
g = 32.2 ft/sec
V_f = volume of float
A_f = area of float
ρ_f = density of float
ρ = density of flowing fluid

Using this equation, the rate of flow through the rotameter can be calculated for any position of the float.

The rotameter is subject to error due to changes in the density of the

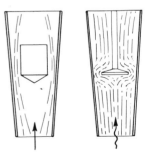

Fig. 17. Left: Special float shape is not required where viscosity does not vary. Right: Where viscosity varies, floats must be shaped so as not to react to viscosity changes.

viscosity of the flowing fluid.

To overcome small changes in fluid density, the float should be of material twice as dense as the flowing fluid.

To overcome the effect of small changes in the viscosity of the flowing fluid, the float shape should be made so that it is as insensitive to these changes as possible (Fig. 17).

Turbine Meter. The pulse generating turbine flowmeter (Fig. 18) consists of a precision turbine wheel mounted on bearings inside a length of pipe and an electromagnetic coil mounted on the pipe at a right angle to the turbine wheel. Fluid passing through the pipe causes the turbine wheel to turn at a speed which varies with the velocity of the flowing fluid. As each blade of the turbine wheel passes the coil, it interrupts the magnetic field of the coil, producing an electrical pulse. The frequency of the pulses, therefore, varies with the velocity of the fluid flow. The electrical pulses become the input to an electrical circuit which provides continu-

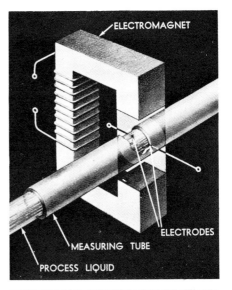

Fig. 19. Electromagnetic Flowmeter. (Foxboro Co.)

ous indication of the fluid velocity.

Electromagnetic Meter. The electromagnetic flowmeter (Fig. 19) consists of a tube of non-conducting material with two electrodes mounted opposite one another on the tube wall. The ends of the electrodes are

Fig. 18. Pulse Generating Turbine Flowmeter. (Cox Instruments Co.)

in contact with the fluid flowing in the tube. Surrounding the tube is a magnet with its field at right angles to the electrodes. The flowing fluid must be an electrical conductor.

As the moving electrical conductor (the fluid) flows through the non-conductive tube through the magnetic field, a voltage is produced which can be picked up by the electrodes. The voltage produced depends upon:

1. the strength of the magnetic field
2. the distance between the electrodes
3. the velocity of the conductive fluid flowing through the tube

Therefore, if the strength of the magnetic field and the distance between the electrodes is held constant, the voltage produced will be entirely due to the rate of flow of the flowing fluid. This voltage is then amplified and connected to suitable indicating or recording instruments. This is the principle of operation of the electromagnetic flowmeter.

Mass Flow Measurement

Recent demands for the measurement of flow *in weight rather than volumetric units* have resulted in the development of mass flow measurement. This requires continuous measurement of density as well as flow rate. One mass flowmeter consists of an electromagnetic flowmeter with a radioactive density-measuring unit. See Fig. 20. The outputs of these two units are fed into an electrical computing circuit to produce a single

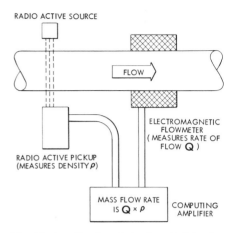

Fig. 20. A radioactive device is added to the electromagnetic flowmeter which gives density together with rate of flow. The result is mass flow measurement.

output proportional to flow in weight units (lbs./min.).

Several other specially designed instruments are available for measuring mass flow. One of these, a constant-speed impeller, imparts an angular momentum to the flowing fluid. See Fig. 21. A turbine wheel downstream from the impeller is displaced by this angular momentum. The turbine wheel's movement is opposed by a spiral spring. The torque exerted by the spring to restrain the revolution of the turbine is proportional to mass flow. A pointer attached to the turbine shaft can be made to indicate the mass flow on a suitable scale or the shaft movement itself may be used to actuate totalizers or controllers.

Still another mass flowmeter (Fig. 22) senses the change in temperature of a heated thermopile due to the change in flow rate. Two Platinum-Rhodium thermocouples (A & B) are

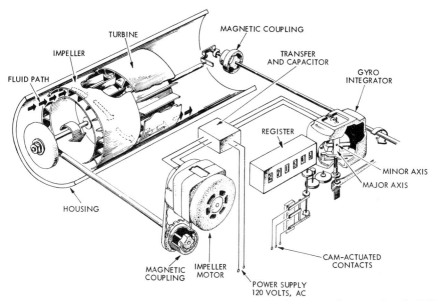

Fig. 21. The GE mass flowmeter uses a motor-driven impeller to impart angular momentum to fluid. A spring-restrained turbine recovers the angular momentum. (Black, Sivalls, and Bryson.)

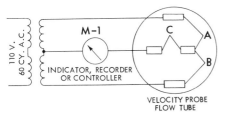

Fig. 22. Mass flow can be measured by using the amount of heat that the flowing fluid picks up from a heated thermopile. (Hastings-Raydist.)

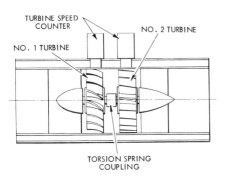

Fig. 23. The Twin Turbine Flowmeter. Because of the difference in the blade angles of the two turbines, they tend to rotate at different speeds but cannot because of the spring coupling. They rotate as one with one displaced from the other by an angle proportional to mass flow rate times velocity, and at a speed proportional to average velocity. (Potter Aeronautical Co.)

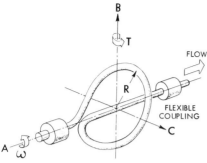

Fig. 24. The Gyroscopic Flowmeter. This element is driven by a constant speed motor about axis A. When fluid flows through it, there is a tendency for it to rotate about axis B. This results in a deflection which can be measured; it is directly proportional to mass flow. (Decker Corporation.)

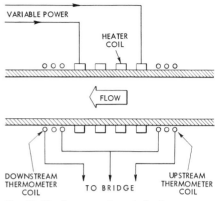

Fig. 25. The flowmeter depends for its operation on the difference in temperature along a pipe due to fluid flow through the pipe. The amount of current required to maintain a constant temperature differential is a function of the mass flow rate. (Flow Measurements Corp.)

immersed in the fluid stream. They are heated by alternating current. A change in flow results in a change of temperature in each of the thermocouples, producing a change in total DC output of the thermocouples. A third thermocouple (C) is used, but is not heated. It merely compensates for changes in ambient temperature. All three thermocouples are combined in a DC-measuring circuit. Since the change in flow rate is proportional to the change in the output of the two sensing thermocouples and

because the change in temperature is proportional to the change in density, the measurement is one of mass flow.

Several other variations in mass flowmeters also deserve mention:

1. The twin-turbine mass flowmeter (Fig. 23)
2. The gyroscopic mass flowmeter (Fig. 24)
3. The thermal flowmeter (Fig. 25).

Chapter 13 _____ Analysis

CONTINUOUS production processes involve the conversion of raw materials, or the combining of several ingredients, into a single final product. To be able to measure and control the physical and chemical properties of the constituent materials as they are being processed is essential to obtaining uniformly satisfactory quality in the finished product. The means of accomplishing this are provided by instruments called analyzers.

In recent years there has been a considerable increase in the number of analyzers, and an expansion in their field of application. It is possible here to describe only a representative few.

Analyzers sometimes require complicated sampling systems and special sensing devices. It should be noted, however, that generally the actual measurement is of temperature, electrical characteristics, or other simple variable, which can be measured using conventional instruments. In this chapter the measure-

ment of the following physical and chemical properties will be briefly discussed:

Density and specific gravity
Viscosity and consistency
Acidity and alkalinity
Conductivity—electrical and thermal
Combustibility
Chromatography

DENSITY AND SPECIFIC GRAVITY

The density of a material is its weight per unit of volume. The specific gravity of a liquid is the ratio of its density compared with the density of water at 4°C. The specific gravity of a gas is the ratio of its density compared with that of air at 32°F at 14.7 pounds per square inch absolute pressure. Liquid density or specific gravity can be measured by several methods:

Hydrometers
Weight of Fixed Volume
Displacement
Differential Pressure

169

Fig. 1. Thermo-hydrometer which contains a thermometer so that corrections in the density reading due to temperature can be made. (Taylor Instrument Co.)

Hydrometers

A hydrometer (Fig. 1) is a floating instrument which displaces a volume of liquid equal to its own weight. It is usually made of hollow glass or metal, and is weighted at one end to make it float upright. The less dense the liquid, the greater the volume displaced, and the lower the position of the hydrometer in the liquid. The density or specific gravity scale ap-

pears on the upper portion of the instrument. The reading is taken by noting the point on the scale to which the liquid rises. The hydrometer contains a thermometer which must be checked when a reading is taken so that any density changes due to temperature can be corrected for.

To permit remote reading of a hydrometer, a metal rod can be used as a weight. Suspended in an electrical coil, the rod acts as the variable arm of an inductance bridge. The movement of the hydrometer and rod due to changes in liquid density is duplicated by the movement of a matching motor-positioned metal rod in the indicating or recording instrument (Fig. 2). Such a hydrometer can be used for continuous measurement, but it must be placed in an enclosure which permits the liquid to flow through it. The level of the liquid in the enclosure is maintained by the use of an overflow tube. Usually the temperature of the liquid is measured continuously with a thermocouple or similar device so that density corrections due to temperature can be made.

Weight of Fixed Volume

Another method of measuring liquid density is to weigh continuously a fixed volume of the liquid. This can be done using a mechanical balance (Fig. 3) or an electrical load cell (Fig. 4). A load cell is an electromechanical device containing a strain gage. When the mechanical portion is deflected due to a weight, the

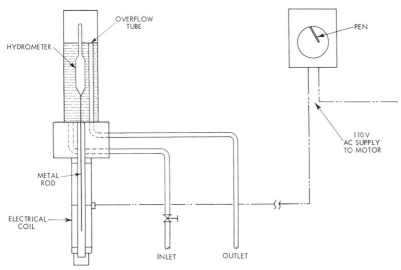

Fig. 2. Specific gravity meter designed to transmit the measured variable signal to a remote instrument in which a matching motor-positioned metal rod operates the recording pen. (Fischer & Porter Co.)

strain gage is distorted, causing a change in electrical resistance. The strain gage is used as the variable resistance in a bridge network, making possible remote indication or recording of the density. For continuous measurement, the fixed volume can be enclosed in a chamber through which the liquid flows in and out at a constant rate.

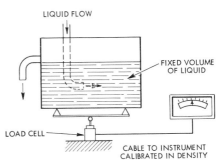

Fig. 4. An electric load cell can also be used for measuring liquid density by weight.

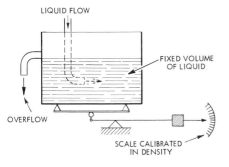

Fig. 3. Liquid density can be measured by weight using a mechanical balance.

Displacement

In a typical displacement type liquid density meter (Fig. 5) the displacer element is enclosed in a chamber of fixed volume. As the density of the liquid changes, the buoyant force acting on the displacer changes. The displacer is attached to a balance beam which moves slightly as the

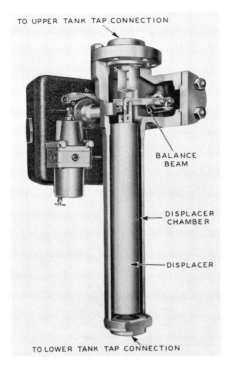

TO UPPER TANK TAP CONNECTION

BALANCE BEAM

DISPLACER CHAMBER

DISPLACER

TO LOWER TANK TAP CONNECTION

Fig. 5. Liquid density meter with displacer, which operates on the principle that when a body (in this case, the displacer) is immersed or partly immersed in any liquid it loses weight equal to the weight of liquid displaced. (Mason-Neilan Div. of Worthington Corp.)

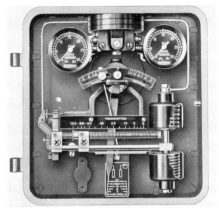

Fig. 6. Pneumatic transmitter used with displacer type density element shown in Fig. 5. (Mason-Neilan Div. of Worthington Corp.)

brated in units of density or specific gravity.

In the electrical system (Fig. 7) the balance beam moves a small iron rod in an inductance coil, similar to that described for use with the hy-

buoyant force changes. The other end of the balance beam acts either as the actuating mechanism of a pneumatic or an electrical measuring system.

In the pneumatic system (Fig. 6) the beam moves the flapper in a flapper-nozzle device. When the force acting on the displacer increases due to an increase in the density of the liquid, the flapper is pressed against the nozzle, thus increasing the air pressure to the receiver, which may be an indicator or a recorder. The receiver is cali-

Fig. 7. Electronic transmitter used with displacement type density element shown in Fig. 5. (Mason-Neilan Div. of Worthington Corp.)

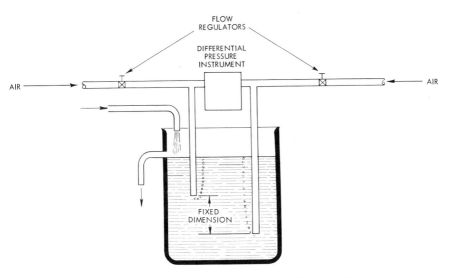

Fig. 8. Measuring specific gravity or density by the bubbler method using single container.

drometer. In this case, however, the inductance coil must provide a greater change in electrical output for a small change in position of the iron rod. This can be obtained using a differential transformer. The output of this unit is used as the variable arm of the inductance bridge.

Differential Pressure

Liquid density may also be measured using differential pressure instruments. One common method is a variation of the bubbler system used for level measurement (Fig. 8). Air is piped to two bubbler tubes immersed in the liquid, with their lower ends at different levels. The air pressure to each bubbler tube is regulated so that it is slightly higher than the pressure of the column of liquid in which the tubes are immersed, thus permitting air bubbles to be released slowly. As the density of the liquid

changes, the pressures at the ends of the tubes change, since they are equal to height × density. Because the ends of the tubes are at different levels, the difference in pressures at these points can be due only to the change in density of the column of liquid, which is equal in height to the difference in levels of the tube ends. The air pressures, in addition to passing to the bubbler tubes, enter a differential pressure measuring unit calibrated in units of density or specific gravity. In summary, as the density of the liquid decreases, the air pressures in the bubbler tubes and the differential unit decrease. Thus a change in liquid density is measurable as a change in differential pressure.

A variation of the bubbler system differential pressure method of density measurement requires the use of two similar vessels—one containing

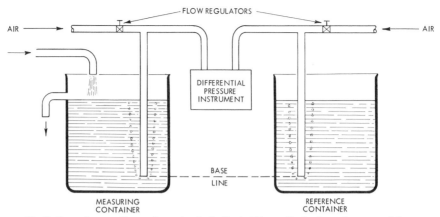

Fig. 9. Measuring specific gravity or density by the bubbler method using reference container.

a reference liquid (such as water) and the other the process liquid which flows through it (Fig. 9). The levels of the two liquids are held constant at the same height. Bubbler tubes are immersed in each vessel with their ends at precisely the same

level. Since the liquid levels above the tube ends are equal, any difference in the pressures to the bubbler tubes and the differential unit are due to the change in density of the process liquid. The differential unit may therefore be calibrated in units

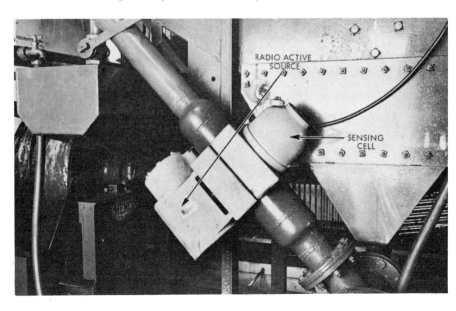

Fig. 10. Radioactive density measuring device. (Ohmart Corp.)

of density or specific gravity.

Radioactive Sensing Cell

The density of a liquid can also be measured using radioactivity. A source of radioactive energy, such as radium or cobalt 60, is placed at one side of a vessel, with its rays directed across the vessel. A radioactive sensing cell, such as a Geiger tube, is placed on the opposite side of the vessel or tube so that it receives the amount of radioactive energy remaining after passing through the vessel walls and the liquid (Fig. 10). The amount of radiation absorbed by all materials varies directly with their density. Such a method is best for liquids that do not permit a sensing element to be immersed because of corrosion, abrasion, or other limitation.

VISCOSITY

The viscosity of a fluid expresses its resistance to flow. When measuring viscosity the nature of the fluid must be known, because the viscosity of some liquids varies with temperature, or changes considerably after the fluid has been shaken or when it is flowing. Such fluids are generally classified as non-Newtonian. Fluids whose viscosity is constant at any given temperature are classified as Newtonian. Before attempting to measure fluid viscosity, it is necessary first to determine the classification of the fluid. Newtonian fluids permit viscosity measurement by any

of the instruments that are described in this section. Non-Newtonian fluids must be tested for their particular characteristics to determine their suitability for viscosity measurement.

There are several systems of units for expressing viscosity. Absolute viscosity is a measure of the resistance of a fluid to internal deformation. The most common unit for expressing absolute viscosity is the centipoise. Kinematic viscosity is the ratio of the absolute viscosity to the mass density. The common unit of kinematic viscosity is the centistoke.

$$\text{centistokes} = \frac{\text{centipoises}}{\text{grams per cubic cm}}$$

The equipment that has been developed for continuous measurement of viscosity is based upon several laboratory types:—

1. Falling ball or piston
2. Rotating spindle
3. Measured flow through orifice

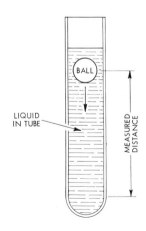

Fig. 11. Falling ball viscosity device.

Fig. 12. Variable area Viscorator with rotameter. Note: a rotameter cannot be used in horizontal position as shown. (Fischer & Porter Co.)

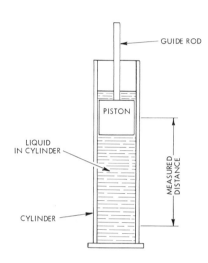

Fig. 13. Cylinder (piston) viscosity device.

Falling Ball or Piston

In the falling ball laboratory device (Fig. 11), the time required for a ball to fall a certain distance through the liquid is measured. The time is proportional to the viscosity. The continuous viscosity measuring apparatus based upon this principle employs a rotameter (Fig. 12). A metering pump draws some of the liquid from the main stream and pumps it through the rotameter at a fixed rate. The differential pressure across the rotameter is constant, therefore any movement of the float is due to a change in viscosity. The

rotameter can be calibrated in viscosity units.

In the falling piston laboratory device (Fig. 13), the time required for a piston to fall a certain distance in a cylinder containing the sample liquid is measured. The time required varies with changes in viscosity. The continuous type employing this principle adds mechanical equipment, which automatically raises the piston after each fall, and at the

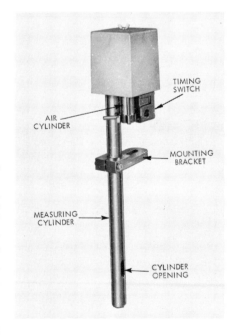

Fig. 14. Norcross Viscometer. (Norcross Corp.)

same time draws a new sample into the cylinder (Fig. 14). Although this type is not really continuous, the operation can be speeded up sufficiently to make it satisfactory for continuous measurement.

Rotating Spindle

The rotating spindle apparatus for measuring viscosity in the laboratory (Fig. 15) consists of a spindle rotated in a container of the sample liquid. The principle involved is that the viscosity is directly proportional to the torque required to drive the spindle. Some units of this type rotate the container rather than the spindle; the principle, however, remains the same. The continuous viscosity measuring unit based on this principle resembles the laboratory

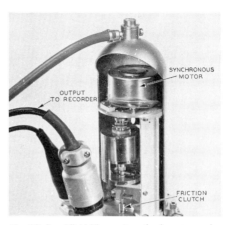

Fig. 16. Brookfield Viscometran for in-process viscosity measurement. (Brookfield Engineering Laboratories, Inc.)

apparatus, with the addition of a means of allowing the liquid to flow into and out of the container (Fig. 16).

Measured Flow Through Orifice

A simple apparatus for measuring the kinematic viscosity of oils and other viscous liquids in the laboratory is the Saybolt Universal Viscosimeter (Fig. 17). This apparatus consists of a temperature controlled vessel with an orifice in the bottom. In use, the orifice is first plugged, and the liquid to be tested is poured into the vessel. The temperature of the liquid is regulated to a desired value. The plug is then quickly removed and, at the same time, a stop-watch is started. When the liquid reaches the desired volume, the stop-watch is stopped. The units of viscosity measurement with this apparatus are Saybolt Universal Seconds.

Saybolt Universal Seconds = Centistokes × 4.635.

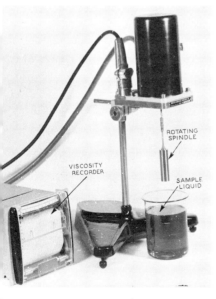

Fig. 15. Rotating spindle apparatus for measuring viscosity. (Brookfield Engineering Laboratories, Inc.)

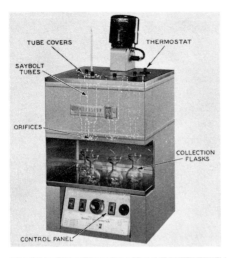

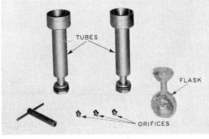

Fig. 17. Saybolt Universal Viscosimeter. (Precision Scientific Co.)

For more viscous liquids the orifice is changed and the resultant measurement is expressed as Saybolt Furol Seconds.

Saybolt Furol Seconds = Centistokes × .470

An adaptation of the Saybolt Viscosimeter for continuous measurement substitutes a capillary tube for the orifice. The actual measurement is of the differential pressure across the capillary tube. The flow through the capillary tube and the temperature of the liquid are accurately controlled. The absolute viscosity varies

directly with the differential pressure.

Although the measurement made may result in only an indication of the apparent viscosity values, this information is sufficient to make the installation worth while. The important aspect is the reproducibility of the results.

ACIDITY AND ALKALINITY

The measurement of the acidity or alkalinity of a liquid is frequently of prime importance in industrial processes. The scale on which this variable is measured is the pH scale (Fig. 18). On this scale, pure water, which is neutral (neither acid or alkaline), has a value of 7. The strongest acid has a value of −1 and the

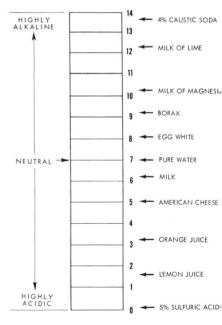

Fig. 18. pH Scale.

strongest alkaline has a value of 14. The theory of pH measurement involves the breakdown of certain chemical compounds when combined with water. As these compounds (electrolytes) break down, tiny electrically charged particles are released. Some are positively charged; these are hydrogen ions (H +). Some are negatively charged; these are hydroxyl ions (OH −). In pure water there are more hydrogen ions and in alkaline solutions more hydroxyl ions. The pH scale is based on the concentration of hydrogen ions in a certain volume of water. A more complete explanation of pH theory is beyond the scope of this book.

The measurement of pH requires the use of specially designed electrodes. Two electrodes are used for

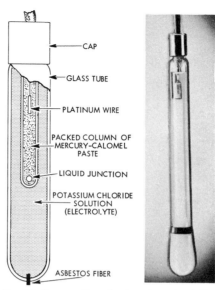

Fig. 20. Cross section showing elements of the reference electrode in the illustration on right. (Minneapolis-Honeywell Reg. Co.)

each installation. One produces a change in voltage as the pH of the solution in which it is immersed changes. The other electrode maintains a constant voltage. The most common pH-sensitive electrode is the glass electrode (Fig. 19), and the most common reference electrode is the calomel electrode (Fig. 20).

Together these electrodes form an electrolytic cell whose output equals the sum of the voltage produced by the two electrodes (Fig. 21). This voltage is applied as the input to a null-balance millivolt potentiometer similar to that used with a thermocouple. Included in the circuit is a temperature compensating resistor which is immersed in the solution. Its resistance changes with the temperature of the solution, so that the

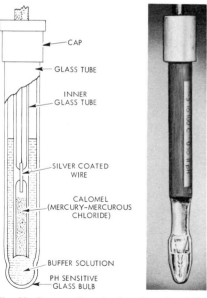

Fig. 19. Cross section showing elements of the glass electrode in the illustration on right. (Minneapolis-Honeywell Reg. Co.)

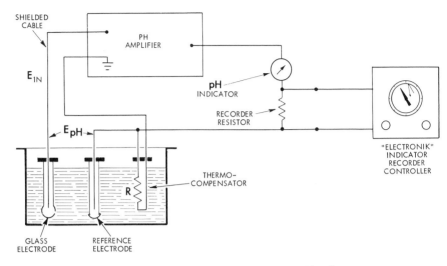

Fig. 21. Simplified diagram of circuit used for electrometric pH measurement.

pH measurement is correct at the operating temperature.

CONDUCTIVITY
(Electrical)

pH measurement, as previously described, is concerned with the hydrogen ion concentration in a solution. All ions in a solution, however, affect its ability to pass an electric current. Measurement of this ability (conductivity) is useful in many industrial processes. Such a measurement can be made by immersing a pair of electrodes of known area a certain distance apart, and then measuring the resistance between them. Conductivity is expressed in mhos measured between two electrodes, each having an area of 1 square centimeter and placed 1 centimeter apart (Fig. 22).

A mho equals $\dfrac{1}{1 \text{ ohm}}$ and it repre-

sents the ability of a substance to sustain one ampere of current at one volt of potential. The conductivity electrodes used in industry often have areas greater or smaller than 1 square centimeter, and are placed closer or farther apart than 1 centimeter. The dimensional relationship

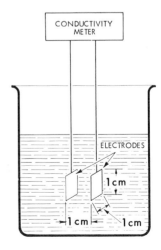

Fig. 22. Conductivity expressed in mhos.

between the actual electrodes and those of the standard conductivity cell is termed the cell constant. These constants range from .1 to 100.

The conductivity cell can be used with an ac Wheatstone bridge (Fig. 23). As with the pH measuring system, a temperature compensating resistor is used in the circuit to correct for variations in the temperature of the solution.

Since the measurement is an indication of the total ions present in a solution, the scale of the instrument can be calibrated in per cent concentration of electrolyte. This is frequently an important consideration in determining the purity of water, or the completeness of a chemical reaction.

THERMAL CONDUCTIVITY

Gases differ in their ability to conduct heat. The thermal conductivity of air at 32°F is established as 1.0.

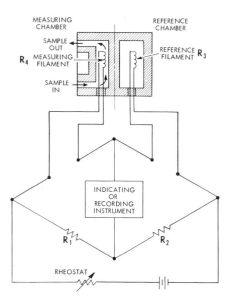

Fig. 24. Detail of thermal conductivity bridge and cell.

Here is a list of thermal conductivities of other gases:

CO_2	.585
CO	.958
Helium	6.08
Hydrogen	7.35
Nitrogen	1.015
Oxygen	1.007

The measurement of the thermal conductivity of a gas mixture provides knowledge about the proportions of its constituents. The most common method of making this measurement involves the use of a hot wire thermal conductivity gas-analysis cell. Such a cell (Fig. 24) consists of two chambers, each containing a wire filament. One chamber permits the sample gas to flow through it, while the other is sealed and contains a reference gas (such as air).

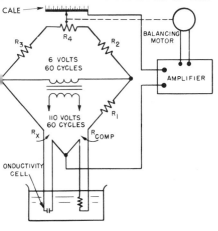

Fig. 23. Conductivity cell used with Wheatstone bridge. (Minneapolis-Honeywell Reg. Co.)

The temperature of the filament in the sampling chamber rises as the thermal conductivity decreases, because the heat of the filament is unable to pass out of the chamber through its walls. The preferred circuit used with thermal conductivity cells is the Wheatstone bridge, using two cells (four chambers) as shown in Fig. 25.

Although it is a simple matter to determine the proportion of two gases in a mixture, it is considerably more difficult to analyze a complex gas. Special techniques have been developed to accomplish this, such as passing the sample through one chamber, then through an apparatus which removes one constituent of the sample, and finally through another chamber (Fig. 26). The difference in the thermal conductivity in each of the chambers is, therefore, due to the constituent removed. Hence, the percentage of this constituent can be determined.

Typical applications of Thermal Conductivity Gas Analyzers are as follows:

MIXTURE	SUITABLE REFERENCE GAS
Hydrogen in Air	Air
Helium in Air	Air
Hydrochloric Acid Vapor in Air	Air
Ammonia in Air	Air

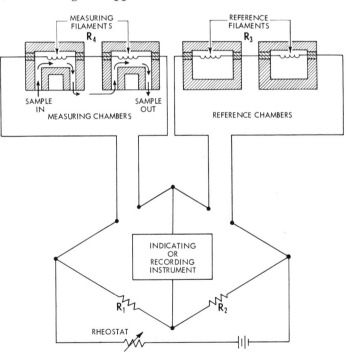

Fig. 25. Two cell (four chamber) thermal conductivity bridge.

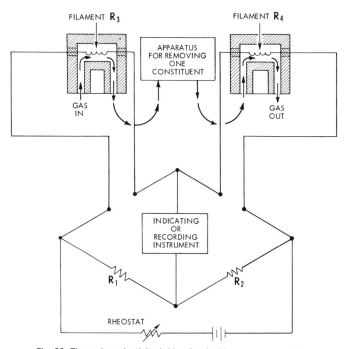

FILAMENT R_3

FILAMENT R_4

APPARATUS FOR REMOVING ONE CONSTITUENT

GAS IN

GAS OUT

INDICATING OR RECORDING INSTRUMENT

R_1

R_2

RHEOSTAT

Fig. 26. Thermal conductivity bridge for double pass gas analysis.

COMBUSTIBILITY

Combustion is a process to which analysis instrumentation has been applied for many years. The amount of heat developed when a fuel is burned depends upon the completeness of combustion. The products of complete combustion, in addition to heat, are carbon dioxide and water vapor. When sulfur is present, sulfur dioxide is a combustion product. When carbon monoxide is given off, it is an indication that combustion is not complete. An instrument that measures the amount of carbon monoxide in fuel gas can, therefore, be used to determine combustion efficiency. A thermal conductivity gas analyzer is suitable for this application (Fig. 27).

The flue gas is passed through one thermal conductivity chamber and then into an apparatus that converts the carbon monoxide into carbon dioxide. The resultant gas is then passed through a second thermal conductivity chamber. The difference in the output of the two chambers is due to the carbon monoxide present in the flue gas. Air or carbon dioxide can be used in the reference chambers of the two cells.

The combustion process presents another opportunity for the application of analyzers—the continuous analysis of fuel gas to determine its combustibility. A thermal conductiv-

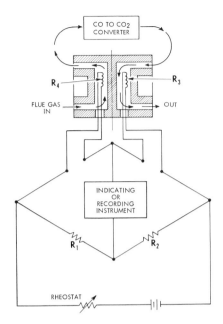

Fig. 27. Thermal conductivity bridge for flue gas analysis.

ity analyzer is used for this measurement to provide information about the percentage of combustible constituent in the fuel gas.

CHROMATOGRAPHY

Chromatography is the name given to a method of analysis that permits the continuous measurement of the amounts of each constituent in a complex vapor or gas mixture. There may be many constituents in the mixture. The method involves combining the sample gas with a carrier gas and passing the combination of gases through a column, which is made of metal tubing and filled with an adsorbent such as activated alumina, silica gel, or activated carbon (Fig. 28).

The effect of passing the gases through the column is the separation of the constituents of the sample gas. Each constituent travels through the column at a different rate, because each is retained for a different period of time by the column adsorbent. The carrier gas, which forces the sample gas through the column, emerges from the column continuously, so that the constituents of the sample gas actually leave the column in combination with the carrier gas. The most common carrier gases are helium, nitrogen, air, or hydrogen. A typical sample gas might contain such constituents as ethane, propane, acetylene, butane, pentane, among others.

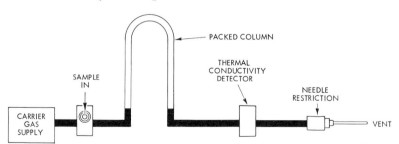

Fig. 28. Gas analysis by packed column method.

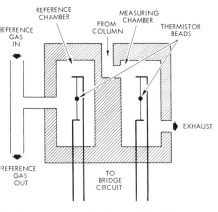

Fig. 29. Thermal conductivity cell for chromatography using thermistor as sensing device.

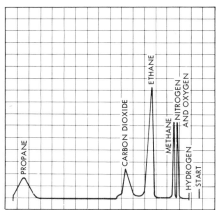

Fig. 30. Typical chromatographic chart.

Thermal Conductivity Cell

Thermal conductivity cells are generally used as the detecting elements (Fig. 29). During operation a metered amount of sample gas is injected into the carrier gas stream, the combination passing to the measuring chamber of the cell. At the same time, the carrier gas is passed separately through the reference chamber. The cell, therefore, measures the difference in the thermal conductivity of the carrier gas and of the carrier gas plus each constituent as it leaves the column. When the last constituent has emerged from the column, a new sample is injected into the carrier gas stream, and the analysis is repeated. The output of the thermal conductivity cell is applied to a bridge circuit. The output of the bridge circuit is amplified and becomes the input to a strip chart recording instrument. The record made by the instrument is a series of peaks and valleys (Fig. 30). By comparing the height of each peak with that produced as the result of the passage of a calibrated sample, the percentage by volume of each constituent can be determined.

This has been a very brief description of a complicated process of analysis. For best results, the following variables must be controlled and recorded:

Flow rate
Pressure
Temperature

In addition, the column material must be carefully selected, and the sample injection apparatus must be capable of excellent reproducibility.

Chapter 14

Control

THE automatic control of a process requires knowledge of the behavior of the process as well as of the devices used for its control. Frequently, there are a number of process variables such as temperature, pressure, density, level, and several means by which these variables may be controlled. Regulating the amount of heat to a process will affect not only the temperature but perhaps also the pressure and density. Regulating the flow of material to a process will also affect the level of material in storage vessels within the process. It is important, therefore, to select the means that most affect the variable to be controlled. Following this selection, a study of the effect of a change in the control means on the variable should be undertaken. The simplest study method and the one that requires only the equipment to be applied to the operating process

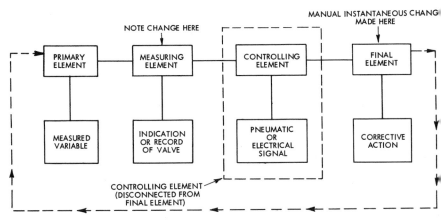

Fig. 1. The step function response method is the simplest way to study the effect of a change in the control means on the measured variable.

is the step function response method. See Fig. 1. This consists of applying an instantaneous change in the control means and then recording graphically the result of the change on the measured variable. The controller action is eliminated during this operation.

To accomplish the step function response study, the final element position is manually changed a small amount instantaneously and the resultant effect on the measured variable, sensed by the primary element, is recorded by the measuring element. The record produced is called the process reaction curve. Two typical process reaction curves resulting from a step change are shown in Fig. 2.

Curve A describes a simple process in which the measured variable begins to change as soon as the step change in the final element position is made. This means that there is little or no *resistance* to an energy change in the process. At the start, the rate of change is very rapid, but as the process continues the rate of change slows down. This means that the process is storing up some of the energy change. This characteristic of a process is called *capacity*. The rate of change is termed the *process reaction rate*.

Curve B describes a more complicated process in which there is resistance, more than one capacity, and another process characteristic called *dead time*. Notice that nothing at all happens to the value of the measured variable at the start and for a short time thereafter. This is due to the effect of dead time. When the variable does begin to change it does so slowly at first. Then it speeds up un-

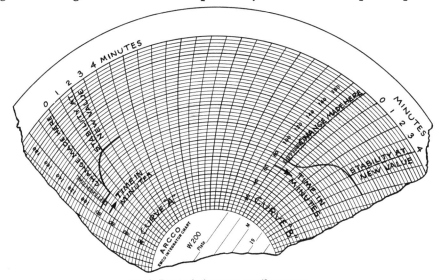

Fig. 2. Two typical process reaction curves.

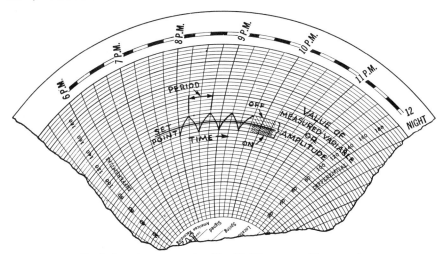

Fig. 3. Control pattern produced by ON-OFF or two position control.

til it approaches the final value when it slows down again. This change in *reaction rate* is caused by a combination of *capacity* and *resistance* and particularly by the passage of energy from one capacity through a resistance into another capacity. This characteristic is called *transfer lag*.

A process which produces a *reaction curve* similar to curve A may be controlled by the simplest form of controller.

A process which produces a *reaction curve* similar to curve B pre-

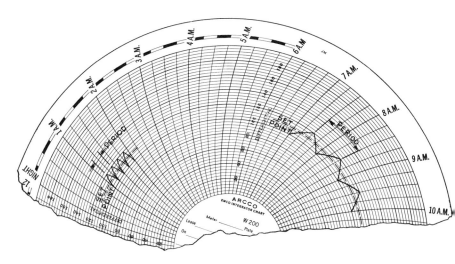

Fig. 4. Control pattern on the left is produced by fast reaction rate; the pattern on the right by slow reaction rate.

sents quite a different problem. Selecting a controller for this process demands an understanding of the control actions available and of their ability to handle the process characteristics.

On-Off Control

ON-OFF or two position control, when applied to a process, produces a control pattern as shown in Fig. 3.

Note the following characteristics: the faster the process reaction rate, the shorter the period (Fig. 4); the greater the differential between the ON and OFF positions, the longer the period and the greater the amplitude (Fig. 5). Dead time causes the value of the measured variable to go beyond the limits set by the differential since the presence of dead time means a delay in the corrective action of the controller. The greater the dead time, the greater the amplitude

and the period (Fig. 6). Transfer lag effect differs from dead time effect in that it is not a delay in response but, rather, a slowing down of the response. The presence of transfer lag in a two position control system will produce a pattern as shown in Fig. 7.

Notice that the measured variable exceeds the controller differential values as it does when dead time is present. Instead of the sharp peaks which appear when there is no transfer lag, these are rounded off since, with transfer lag, all the changes are more gradual.

A two position control system performs best when:

1. The reaction rate is slow
2. There is little or no dead time
3. There is little or no transfer lag

Proportional Control

Proportional control, when applied to a process that is stable, produces

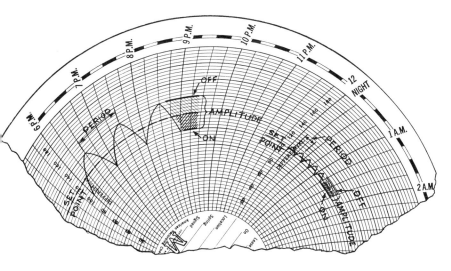

Fig. 5. Pattern on the left is the result of a large differential; pattern on the right, of a small differential.

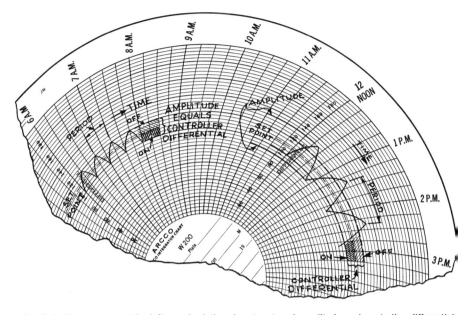

Fig. 6. In the pattern on the left, no dead time is present and amplitude and controller differential are equal; in the pattern on the right, dead time is present and amplitude and period are increased.

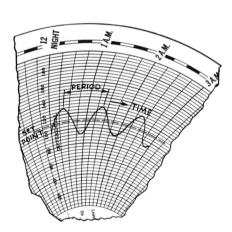

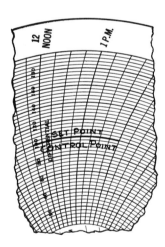

Fig. 7. Pattern showing presence of transfer lag.

Fig. 8. Pattern produced by proportional control when process is stable.

a control pattern like the one shown in Fig. 8.

Unfortunately, however, an industrial process is rarely stable. Fig. 9 shows a typical process in which

steam is used to heat water to a particular temperature. The control system should maintain the temperature of the water at set point.

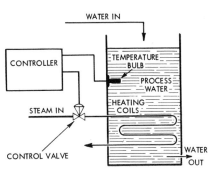

Fig. 9. A simple temperature control system.

Ideally, the water enters the process at a fairly constant temperature and enters and leaves at a constant rate. The steam pressure and, therefore, its temperature also remain constant. If any of these conditions change, the control system must make the necessary corrections to maintain the exit water at constant temperature. The changes are called *load changes*. Fig. 10 is a graph of the desired result of the control system's

response to a change in input conditions (load change).

If the reaction curve produced by a step function response study of the process shows that dead time and transfer lag are present, proportional control alone will not be satisfactory.

It must be remembered that with proportional action there is a fixed relationship between the position of the final element and the amount of deviation of the measured variable from the set point. In the temperature control process shown above, this means that the steam valve has a particular position for each temperature value above or below the set point of the temperature controller. The system is thus dependent upon the valve passing the necessary amount of steam at each position to bring the temperature back to the control point after a departure. If the valve position called for by the controller does not allow sufficient steam

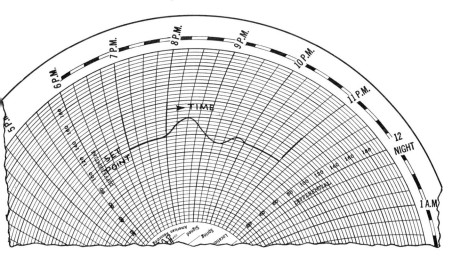

Fig. 10. Ideal response curve produced by load change.

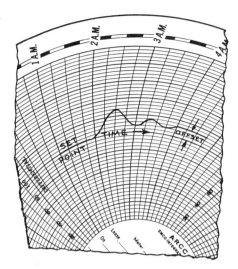

Fig. 11. Pattern illustrating effect of offset.

down after such a load change but not at the set point. Fig. 11 is a graph of such a situation—the departure from set point that results is called *offset*.

The faster the reaction rate of the process, the worse the result; the process settles down faster but the offset becomes larger. See Fig. 12.

If the reaction curve (Fig. 13) indicates that there is dead time or transfer lag present, the result is still worse. In addition to a large offset, the time required for stability is considerably longer.

We can conclude, therefore, that proportional control will *not* be satisfactory when:

to pass, the system will not be able to restore control at set point. This is precisely what happens when a load change is large enough or lasts long enough. The system will settle

1. The process reaction rate is fast.

2. There is considerable dead time or transfer lag (examination of the process reaction

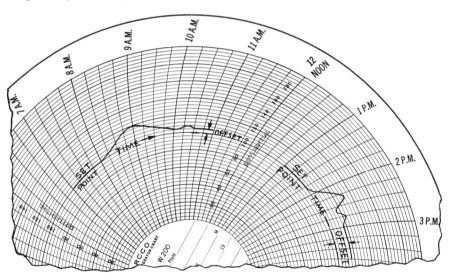

Fig. 12. Pattern on left shows result of slow reaction rate; pattern on right shows result of fast reaction rate, which increases the offset.

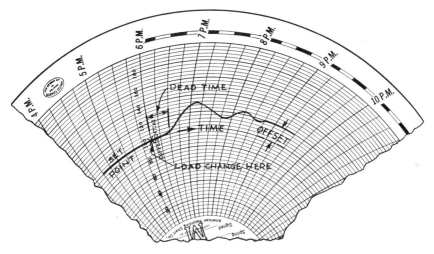

Fig. 13. Reaction curve that indicates the presence of dead time.

curve provides this information—Fig. 2).

3. If the load changes which occur are rapid, large, or for
long periods (examination of
the record of the control system provides this information
—Figs. 10, 11 and 12).

With proportional control systems,
there are three modifications available to improve the system performance:

1. Proportional Band Adjustment
2. Adjustable reset response
3. Adjustable rate response

Proportional Band Adjustment

Proportional Band Adjustment actually is a sensitivity adjustment. As
stated above, in proportional control
there is a particular position of the
final element for each unit of departure of the measured variable from
set point. A narrow proportional

band means that the measured variable must depart from set point only
a small amount for the final element
to move to its limit. The narrower
the proportional band, the closer the
result is to two position control (Fig.
14). The proportional band adjustment affects the response of the sys-

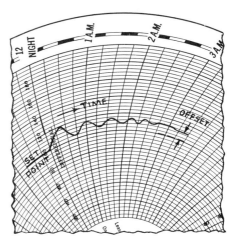

Fig. 14. With a narrow proportional band, stability
time is long and offset is small.

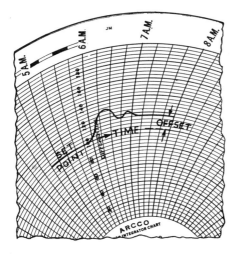

Fig. 15. With a wide proportional band, stability time is short and offset is large.

tem to a load change as shown in Fig. 15.

The faster the reaction rate, and the greater the dead time or lag, the wider the proportional band must be.

Adjustable Reset Response

Reset response, when added to proportional control, acts to eliminate the offset produced by a load change. This happens because reset response continues to change the signal to the final element as long as the measured variable is not at set point. The rate of motion of the final element in a proportional + reset control changes with the amount of deviation from set point.

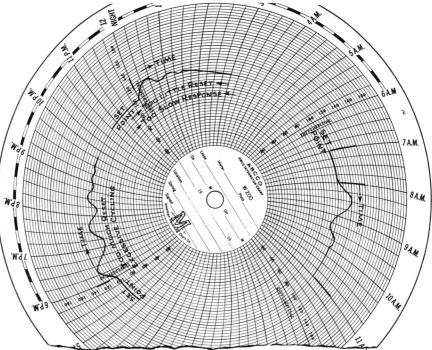

Fig. 16. Pattern on left shows that too much reset results in excessive cycling; pattern in center shows that too little reset results in too slow a response; pattern on right shows correct reset results in good response.

In the temperature control process described above, a change in the steam pressure results in less heat being supplied to the process for a particular valve opening. This is a load change. The result of this change with proportional control would be the exit water temperature would be changed, because the valve position called for by the controller would not be able to supply the correct amount of heat to maintain set point. The addition of reset response permits the valve position to be changed. The amount of reset response is adjustable, the adjustment affecting the length of time necessary to return to set point. See Fig. 16.

Notice that the offset is eliminated in all cases but that the amount of reset determines the length of time required to do this. It is possible to have so much reset that it overcorrects and, instead of becoming stable,

the system becomes completely unstable as shown in Fig. 17.

Since proportional band and reset response are both adjustable, it should be noted that the adjustment of either one affects the other. The effect of reset adjustment has already been illustrated. Adding reset response to a proportional controller calls for a widening of the proportional band setting. See Fig. 18.

We can conclude from this discussion of proportional plus reset response that when properly adjusted it will overcome most of the limitations of proportional control alone. There are, however, two conditions which cannot be completely satisfied by proportional + reset control:

1. Excessive dead time, or lag
2. Large, rapid load changes

Adjustable Rate Response

Rate response, when added to a

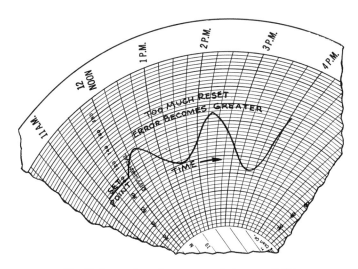

Fig. 17. Too much reset causes error to become greater.

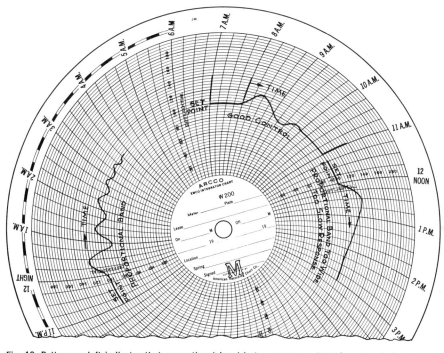

Fig. 18. Pattern on left indicates that proportional band is too narrow; pattern in center indicates that proportional band is providing good control; pattern on right indicates that proportional band is too wide, with the result that reset response is too slow.

proportional + reset controller, acts to overcome the disturbance caused by dead time or lag and large, rapid load changes. This is possible because rate response makes its contribution to control in accordance with the rate—not the amount—of departure of the measured variable from set point.

Without rate response, a proportional + reset controller, used to control a process having considerable dead time and lag, would produce the result shown in Fig. 19 when subjected to a load change.

Just as the addition of reset to a proportional controller requires a change in proportional band setting,

the addition of rate response to a proportional + reset controller requires a change in proportional band

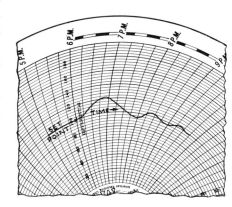

Fig. 19. Pattern produced when process has considerable dead time and lag.

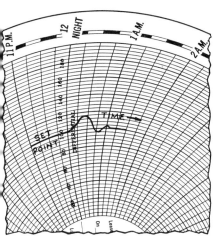

Fig. 20. Pattern indicates that proper corrections to proportional band and reset response have been made.

and reset settings. The proportional band should be made narrower and the reset action should be increased.

The result of the addition of rate response to a proportional + reset

controller when the proper corrections to proportional band and reset response have been made is shown in Fig. 20.

Both the amount of deviation and the stability time have been considerably reduced; and since rate response itself is adjustable the effect of such adjustment should be noted. See Fig. 21.

When adjustments of proportional band, reset response, and rate response are properly made in the controller, the system should be able to maintain control at set point under any of the following conditions:

1. Process reaction rate may be fast or slow.

2. Dead time or transfer lag may be present.

3. Load changes may be large or small, fast or slow.

When applying a controller to a

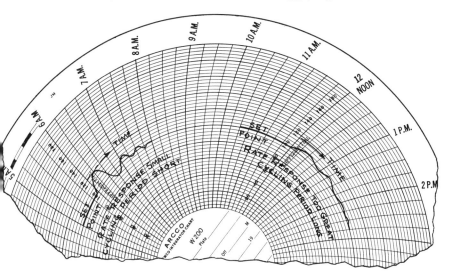

Fig. 21. Pattern on left shows how small adjustment to rate response results in short cycling period; pattern on right shows how too great an adjustment results in long cycling period.

process, the order in which the available adjustments are made is important.

1. The proportional band adjustment should be made first. If reset or rate response adjustments are available, they should be set at 0 during the adjustment of proportional band.
2. The rate response adjustment should be made before the reset adjustment. When adjusting rate response, reset should be at 0.
3. Reset response adjustment should be made last since its only function is to eliminate the offset resulting from the adjustment of the other two responses.

The control responses described above are all available in pneumatic, electric, and hydraulic controllers.

Pneumatic Controllers

There are two kinds of pneumatic controller available. One kind—the flapper-nozzle type—has been described previously in Chapter 8.

The other kind—the force balance type—operates entirely on a balance of air pressures. The value of the measured variable is converted to an air pressure by a pneumatic transmitter. The set point is converted to an air pressure by a manually adjustable valve.

The schematic (Fig. 22) of the force balance pneumatic control unit is shown in two sections:

1. The unbalance detector section
2. The amplifier section

The unbalance detector section consists of a stack of pressure chambers:

1. Set point chamber
2. Measured variable chamber
3. Positive feedback chamber
4. Negative feedback chamber

separated by flexible diaphragms. This section compares two pairs of pressures: set point pressure and measured variable pressure; positive feedback pressure and negative feedback pressure; and produces a single output signal in the form of motion of the baffle shaft. Since the baffle shaft is attached to all the diaphragms its movement is the result of the total unbalance of both pairs of pressures acting upon the diaphragms.

The amplifier section consists of a pair of pressure chambers:

1. Jet back pressure chamber
2. Output pressure chamber

separated by flexible diaphragms. This section produces the pneumatic output to the final element.

When the measured variable pressure increases slightly due to a change in the value of the measured variable, the increase pushes upward on diaphragm A and downward on diaphragm B. Since diaphragm B has twice the area of diaphragm A, the effect of the increase is to create a greater downward force. The baffle shaft, therefore, is forced downward. This causes a restriction in the passage of air from the jet, causing the

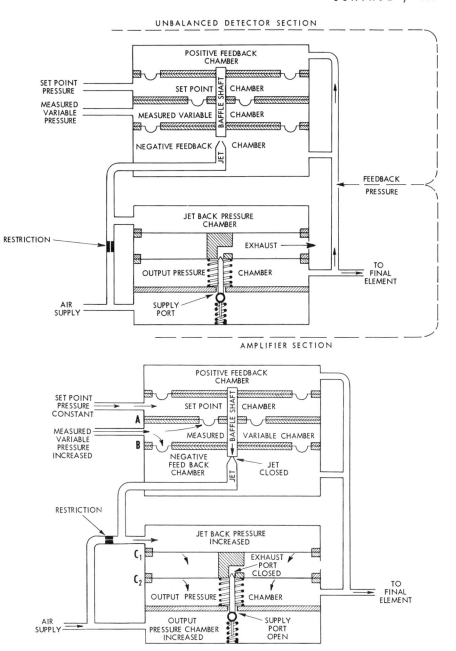

Fig. 22. Top: Schematic of force balance pneumatic control unit. Bottom: Change in the value of the measured variable increases measured variable pressure in the unit. The spring in the output pressure chamber is a biasing spring. Its function is to provide a fixed load on the double diaphragm so that the output pressure signal is always positive (3# to 15# or 6# to 30#).

pressure in the jet chamber of the amplifier section to increase. Double diaphragm C_1, C_2, therefore, moves downward against the spring, carrying with it the valve stem. This closes the exhaust port and opens the supply air port, allowing air to pass through the supply port to the output pressure chamber and to the final element. The output pressure continues to increase until the upward force acting upon diaphragm C_2 equals the downward force acting upon C_1. The force on C_2 is due both to the air pressure and the spring. When the upward pressure on diaphragm C_2 equals the downward pressure on C_1, the valve stem is returned to its original position, shutting off the supply of air to the output pressure chamber. Now the

pressure to the final element has reached a new value.

For ON-OFF action, a change of only 2% in the measured variable pressure moves the baffle shaft enough to produce a full range change in the output pressure to the final element.

In the proportional action unit (Fig. 23), the set point pressure, in addition to entering the set point chamber, passes through a fixed restriction to the positive feedback chamber. An adjustable restriction is placed in the positive feedback line to this same chamber. The result of this arrangement is that the pressure in the positive feedback chamber affects the amount of motion of the baffle shaft for each change in the measured variable pressure. For each unit of

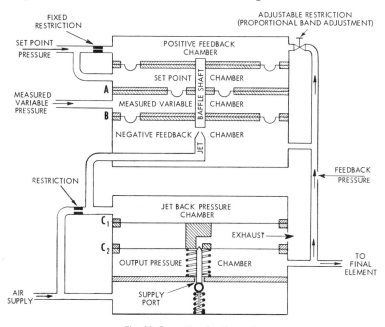

Fig. 23. Proportional action unit.

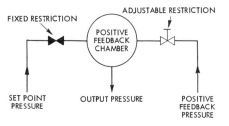

Fig. 24. Schematic of adjustable pressure divider circuit.

vider circuit, it is possible to establish different ratios between the positive feedback chamber output pressure and the positive feedback pressure. This is done by adjusting the amount of the restriction in the positive feedback line. The set point pressure may be considered as a constant, and since its restriction is fixed it contributes a constant reduced pressure to the positive feedback chamber. The adjustment of the restriction in the positive feedback line is, therefore, a proportional band adjustment.

change of the measured variable pressure, there is, therefore, a new position of the baffle shaft and a new controller output pressure.

The two restrictions in this pneumatic circuit form an adjustable pressure divider circuit and are shown schematically in Fig. 24.

With this adjustable pressure di-

With the adjustable restriction fully closed (Fig. 25), there is no positive feedback but only a negative feedback pressure which opposes any

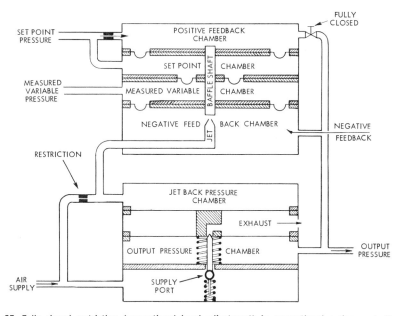

Fig. 25. Fully closed restriction (proportional band adjustment) in proportional action controller has the following effects: no positive feedback; negative feedback pressure opposes changes in measured variable pressure, which must change a great amount to close jet; output pressure changes slowly.

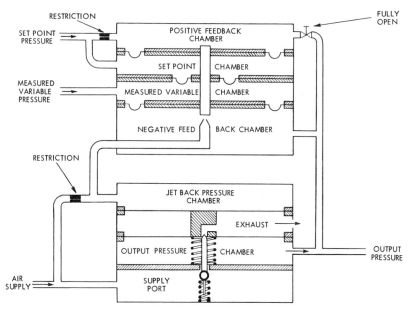

Fig. 26. Fully opened restriction (proportional band adjustment) has the following effects: it provides maximum available positive feedback; the measured variable pressure must change only slightly to close jet; output pressure changes rapidly.

change in the measured variable pressure. This means that the measured variable must change a considerable amount to produce a full range change in the output pressure to the final element. Therefore, completely closing the needle valve provides the widest proportional band possible.

With the adjustable restriction fully open, there is very little difference between the positive and negative feedback pressures, which cancels out most of the feedback effect. See Fig. 26. The motion of the baffle shaft depends almost entirely upon the difference between the set point and measured variable pressures, as in the ON-OFF type. There-

fore, completely opening the needle valve provides the narrowest proportional band possible.

Fig. 27 shows a proportional + reset controller. The proportional controller remains unchanged except that the set point pressure does not pass through a restriction into the positive feedback chamber. A reset section is added. It consists of a reset chamber and a reset reference chamber which are separated by a diaphragm. The diaphragm acts to close or open an exhaust port connected to the reset chamber.

When the measured variable is at set point, the pressures in the feedback chambers and the pressures in

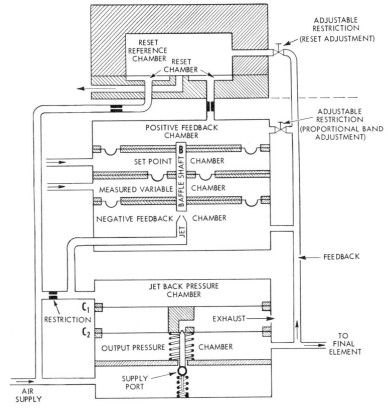

RESET REFERENCE CHAMBER

RESET CHAMBER

ADJUSTABLE RESTRICTION (RESET ADJUSTMENT)

POSITIVE FEEDBACK CHAMBER

ADJUSTABLE RESTRICTION (PROPORTIONAL BAND ADJUSTMENT)

SET POINT CHAMBER

BAFFLE SHAFT

B

MEASURED VARIABLE CHAMBER

NEGATIVE FEEDBACK CHAMBER

JET

FEEDBACK

JET BACK PRESSURE CHAMBER

C_1

RESTRICTION

EXHAUST

C_2

OUTPUT PRESSURE CHAMBER

TO FINAL ELEMENT

SUPPLY PORT

AIR SUPPLY

Fig. 27. Force balance pneumatic controller with proportional + reset action.

the set point and measured variable chambers are equal, and the output pressure of the controller remains constant. See Fig. 28.

When the measured variable departs from the set point, the pressures in the set point and measured variable chambers become unbalanced and the baffle shaft changes position. See Fig. 29. Assuming that the measured variable pressure exceeds the set point pressure, the baffle shaft would move up, allowing air to enter the negative feedback chamber from the jet. At the same time, the double diaphragm in the amplifier

section would move up, reducing the pressure in the output chamber.

The output pressure change passes to four separate locations simultaneously:

1. To the final element, which moves to a new position as the output pressure changes;

2. To the negative feedback chamber, where the lowering of the pressure tends to allow the baffle shaft to move downward (a direction opposite to the original movement);

3. Through an adjustable restriction to the positive feedback chamber, where the lowering of the

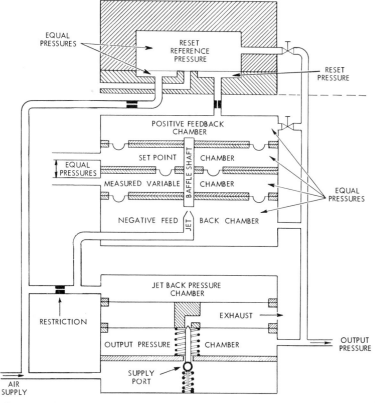

Fig. 28. Pressures when measured variable is at set point. There is no change in output pressure of the controller.

pressure tends to allow the baffle shaft to move upward (in the same direction as the original movement);

4. Through an adjustable restriction to the reset reference chamber, where the lowering of the pressure causes the diaphragm in the reset unit to move upward, allowing air to escape from the reset chamber.

The reset chamber receives its pressure from the air supply line after it has passed through a fixed restriction. Note the pressure divider circuit.

Reset action is obtained, therefore, by slowly changing the reset pressure to the divider circuit. The rate at which the reset pressure is varied is determined by the setting of the reset adjustment. When the reset reference chamber pressure is greater than the reset chamber pressure, the diaphragm halts the escape of reset pressure; this pressure then builds up until it is greater than the reference pressure. At the same time, the positive feedback pressure is increased causing the output pressure to increase which, in turn, increases

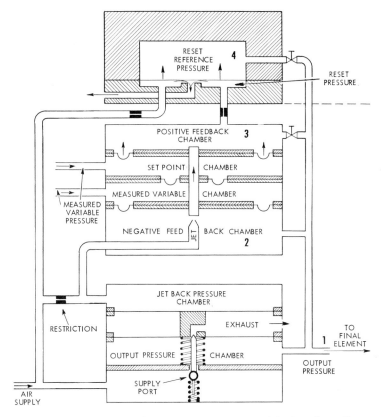

Fig. 29. Increase in the measured variable signal pressure has the following effects: 1) output pressure changed; 2) pressure in negative feedback chamber lowered; 3) pressure in positive feedback lowered; 4) pressure in reset reference chamber lowered.

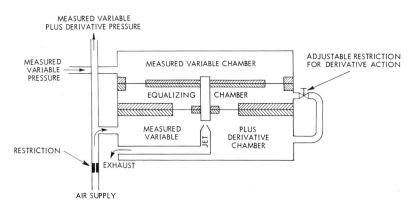

Fig. 30. Derivative action amplifier.

the reset reference pressure and begins the cycle all over again. As long as the positive and negative feedback chamber pressures are unbalanced due to a difference between set point and measured variable pressure, reset action continues and the output pressure continues to change.

Thus the requirement of automatic reset response has been satisfied—namely, the continuous repositioning of the final element as long as there is an offset between set point and control point.

To achieve derivative action in this type of controller, a derivative amplifier is interposed between the proportional and power amplifiers. The derivative amplifier is a complete force balance unit in itself. See Fig. 30.

When there is a change in the measured variable pressure, there is a greater change in the measured variable plus derivative pressure, and the baffle shaft in the proportional amplifier moves more than if there were a change in measured variable pressure alone. See Fig. 31. The gain in the movement of the baffle shaft depends upon:

1. the setting of the adjustable restriction in the derivative amplifier. This is a rate setting.

2. the rate of change of the measured variable.

The effect of derivative action, therefore, is to cause the proportional amplifier to produce an output greater in magnitude than would be produced by proportional action alone and at a rate related to the rate of change of the measured variable.

The pneumatic force-balance controllers just described are commonly called the "stacked diaphragm" type. A similar instrument employing bellows instead of diaphragms has also been developed. Except for this substitution the principle of operation is the same.

Fig. 32 is a schematic of a pneumatic force-balance controller using bellows units to effect the balance. The set point pressure is introduced by a remote pressure regulator. The measurement input is supplied by a pneumatic transmitter. The set point and measured variable pressures each enter one of the four bellows which act upon opposite sides of a force balance "floating disc". Any unbalance between the set point and measurement pressures causes this disc to move. The plate acts as a flapper. The nozzle against which the flapper presses is mounted on another plate immediately above the "floating disc" and separated from it by a lever, which provides proportional band adjustment. Proportional band adjustment is accomplished by rotating the nozzle to different positions from the fulcrum of the lever, thus changing the magnitude of floating disc motion necessary to produce the full change in controller output. Two other bellows also act upon the floating disc; the reset bellows and the proportional bellows. These receive as their input the feedback pressure from the air relay. The reset bellows acts upon the side of the floating disc opposite to

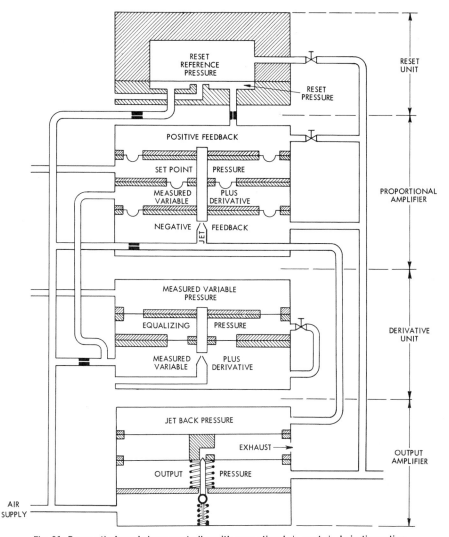

Fig. 31. Pneumatic force balance controller with proportional + reset + derivative action.

the proportional bellows so that its effect on the nozzle-flapper position is counter to that of the proportional bellows. The adjustable restriction and capacity tank in the line to the reset bellows permit adjustment of the reset time. The adjustable restriction and capacity tank in the line to proportional bellows permit adjustment of the rate time.

Electric Controllers

Electric controllers for proportional, proportional + reset, and proportional + reset + derivative

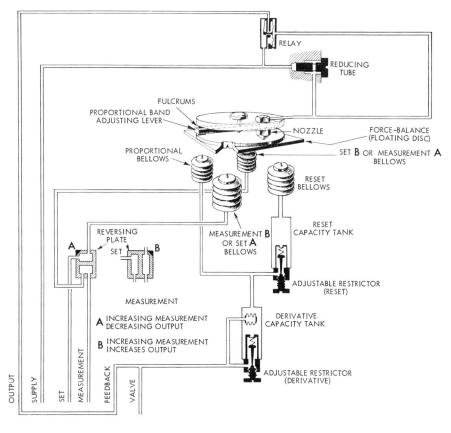

Fig. 32. The movement arms of the four bellows are fixed by the position of the proportional band adjusting lever. (Foxboro Co.)

actions may be divided into two types:

1. The null-balance type in which there is an electrical feedback signal to the controller from the final element
2. The direct type in which there is no such feedback signal

Shown in Fig. 33 is a schematic of an electrical null-balance controller.

As with the pneumatic controller, the various control actions are accomplished by modifying the feed-back signal. This is done by adding properly combined electrical resistances and capacitances to the feedback circuit just as restrictions and chambers were added in the pneumatic circuits.

1. For *proportional action*, the only addition required is one which permits adjustment of the proportional band—a sensitivity adjustment. This can be done by inserting a variable resistor in the feedback line,

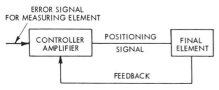

Fig. 33. Schematic of electrical null balance controller.

thus providing regulation of the magnitude of the feedback signal. Since the feedback signal depends upon the position of the final element, the amount of movement of the final element which will produce electrical balance in the controller is established by the setting of the variable resistor. See Fig. 34.

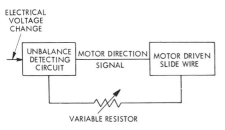

Fig. 34. Proportional action is provided by addition of variable resistor, which permits adjustment of proportional band.

2. For *proportional + reset action,* the feedback signal must be modified by the addition of a resistor-capacitor arrangement, as shown in Fig. 35.

Any change in the feedback voltage from the final element slidewire causes a current to flow into the capacitor C where it is stored as a voltage. The capacitor is then said to be "charged." This results in a voltage drop across resistor R. For a current to continue to flow through R, the capacitor must remain charged. Hence, it must continue to receive current. It receives this current by a continuing change of the feedback voltage. The final element and its slidewire must, therefore, continue to change position to produce the necessary voltage change.

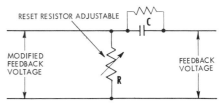

Fig. 35. Feedback signal modified to provide proportional + reset action.

It does so as long as there is an unbalance signal from the controller. When the error signal is eliminated by the measured variable being at set point, the reset action ceases. The setting of the resistor R determines the rate at which reset action proceeds.

3. For *proportional + derivative action,* the feedback signal must be modified by the addition of another resistor capacitor network, as shown in Fig. 36. With this arrangement, any change

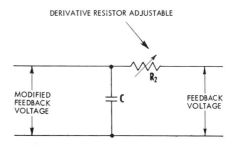

Fig. 36. Feedback signal modified to provide proportional + derivative action.

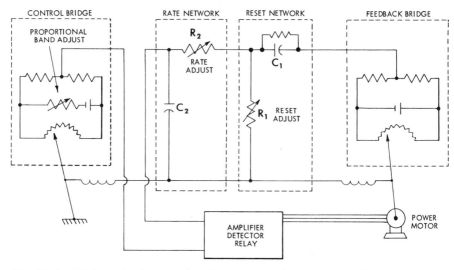

Fig. 37A. A null-Balance electrical controller with proportional + derivative + reset action. (Leeds & Northrup Co.)

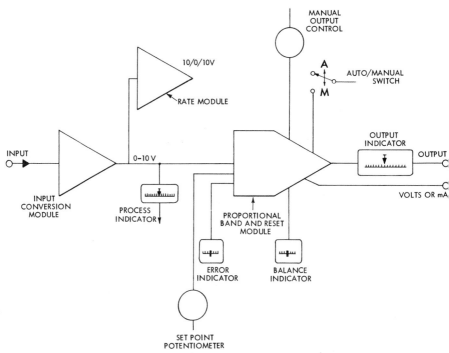

Fig. 37B. A direct-type electric controller with proportionai + derivative + reset action. (DeVar-Kinetics Division, Consolidated Electrodynamcs Corp.)

in the feedback voltage causes the capacitor C_2 to draw more or less current, thus delaying the effect of the change in the feedback voltage. This permits the final element to move more than it would with proportional action alone.

The setting of the resistor R_2 determines the rate at which the capacitor is charged. Therefore, the modified feedback voltage varies with the rate of change of the feedback voltage from the final element slidewire. Since the final element slidewire position changes as the value of the measured variable changes, the modified feedback voltage changes with the rate of change of the measured variable. Derivative action is thus accomplished.

Fig. 37A shows a null balance electric controller with proportional + rate + reset response. It includes a control bridge, a feedback bridge, a detector-amplifier relay, and a power motor. Also shown are the rate and reset networks.

The power motor positions the sliders of two different slidewires, one in the control bridge and another in the feedback bridge. In some electric controllers the power motor may also be used to position the final element.

The detector receives as its input signal any difference in voltage between the control bridge and the feedback bridge. This signal is amplified sufficiently to actuate the relay, which causes the power motor to run in a direction which repositions the sliders to reduce the input signal to zero.

The control bridge contains the proportional band (sensitivity) adjustment. This adjustment determines the relationship between the input signal to the control bridge and its output signal.

The direct-type electric controller operates on a different principle. There is no feedback signal from the final element. Fig. 37B is a schematic of a typical direct-type electronic controller with proportional + reset and rate responses. This controller operates from a 0 to 10 volt d.c. input signal. If the primary element does not provide such an input the conversion module provides the operating voltage.

The percentage of total input voltage is shown on the process indicator. The matching set point voltage of 0 to 10 volts is introduced by a precision potentiometer. Any difference between the input signal voltage and the set point voltage enters the proportional + reset module. It also is shown on an error indicating meter.

Proportional band adjustment is accomplished by a precision potentiometer which regulates the output of the amplifier in the proportional + reset module. For reset response the regulated output of the amplifier is further changed by a precision potentiometer in the reset RC network. For rate response the input signal voltage is modified by an RC network before entering the proportional + reset module. The output of the rate module is then proportional to the rate of change of the input signal voltage. The output meter indicates

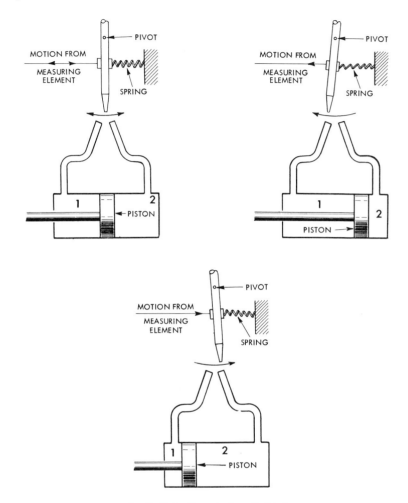

Fig. 38. Hydraulic controller with jet pipe.

the percentage of total output voltage being produced.

To facilitate switching to manual control, a balance-indicating meter is provided. The manual adjuster must be positioned so that the meter is at the null position when switching from automatic to manual control. A capacitor in the instrument circuit eliminates the need for manual ad-justment when switching from manual to automatic. This feature is called *automatic bumpless transfer*.

Hydraulic Controllers

There are hydraulic controllers which will provide the three control responses. Essentially the hydraulic controller resembles the pneumatic

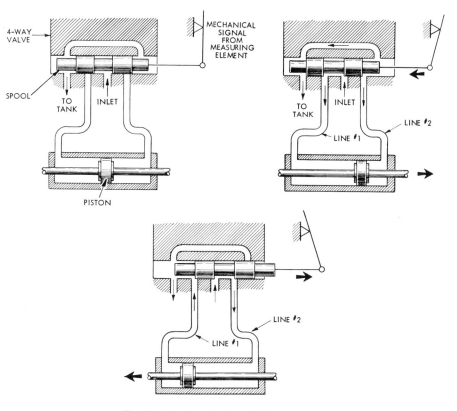

Fig. 39. Hydraulic controller with four-way valve.

except that the system must remain completely closed. In place of the flapper-nozzle and air relay of the pneumatic controller, jet pipes and pistons or four-way valves are used.

The jet pipe resembles the pneumatic nozzle; it directs a fluid stream into either of two receiving chambers of a double-acting cylinder.

When the jet pipe shown in Fig. 38 is moved to the left by the measured variable, more fluid enters Chamber 1 than enters Chamber 2. This causes the pressure in Chamber 1 to increase, moving the piston to the right.

The piston movement can be used to position a final element.

The four-way valve can be used instead of a jet pipe in the same manner. See Fig. 39.

When the valve spool is moved to the left, the fluid path to Line 1 is opened and the path to Line 2 is closed. This causes the piston to move to the right. Similarly, when the valve spool is moved to the left, the fluid path to Line 1 is closed, and the path to Line 2 is opened. The piston then moves to the left. Thus, the action of the four-way

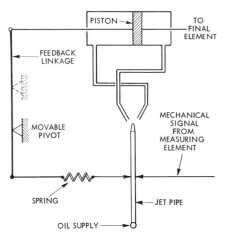

Fig. 40. Proportional action in jet pipe hydraulic controller.

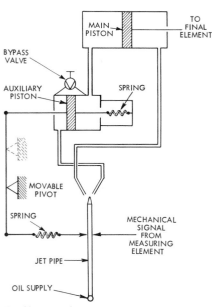

Fig. 41. Proportional + reset action in jet pipe hydraulic controller.

valve resembles the action of the jet pipe system.

On-Off action is accomplished in a hydraulic controller by a very rapid movement of the piston to its extreme positions when the measured variable departs from the set point by a small amount. The set point is established by positioning the jet pipe or valve spool at neutral for a particular value of the measured variable.

Proportional action requires a feedback signal from the piston to the jet pipe or spool. Proportional action is accomplished by the addition of a feedback linkage from the piston. When the jet pipe in Fig. 40 is moved to the right, due to a change in the value of the measured variable, the piston moves to the right. Attached to the piston is the feedback linkage which acts to bring the jet pipe back to its neutral position, stopping the movement of the piston. Thus there is a piston position for each value of the measured variable. Changing the location of the pivot provides proportional band adjustment by regulating the amount of piston motion required to restore the jet pipe to its neutral position.

Automatic reset action may be added to the proportional controller by modifying the feedback signal. Fig. 41 illustrates a jet pipe hydraulic controller with proportional + reset control action. The reset action is accomplished by the addition of an auxiliary piston with a bypass. When the jet pipe is moved to the right, both the main piston and the

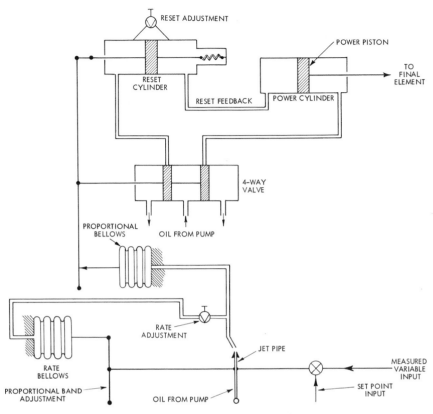

Fig. 42. Proportional + reset + derivative action in hydraulic controller.

auxiliary piston move to the right. The feedback linkage is attached to the auxiliary piston. This linkage returns the jet pipe to its neutral position. Due to the presence of the by-pass, the auxiliary piston returns to its mid position, moving the jet pipe to the right again. This causes more motion of the main piston in the original direction.

Derivative action may be added to a hydraulic proportional + reset controller. In Fig. 42, which does not describe an actual controller, a four-way valve is used to provide the power to the reset and power cylinders. The proportional bellows provides the actuation of the four-way valve. There are two separate feedback systems, one for reset action and another for rate action. The reset feedback signal is provided by the power cylinder. Reset action permits the power piston to continue to move as long as the proportional bellows receives a signal from the jet pipe that indicates there is a difference between the set point and measured variable values. The adjustable restriction in the bypass line of the reset cylinder determines the reset time. The rate feedback signal is provided by the linkage from the rate bellows, which acts to move the jet pipe back to a neutral position. The adjustable restriction between the jet pipe and the rate bellows determines the rate time. As required, rate action delays the feedback to the jet pipe, thus allowing the proportional bellows to act longer than if the rate action were not present. Proportional band adjustment is provided by adjusting the point at which the proportional bellows acts on the lever system that connects the four-way valve spool and the reset piston.

Control Valves

Of the many different final elements, the control valve is by far the most common and the most varied in type.

A valve is essentially a variable orifice and behaves according to the following formula. (Note the similarity between this formula and the one given for the orifice plate in Chapter 5.)

$$Q = K \, d^2 \sqrt{\Delta p}$$

Q = rate of flow

K = flow coefficient constant— corrected for units

d = nominal valve size

Δp = pressure drop across valve

When applied to valves, the formula is usually modified by substituting a valve coefficient C_v for Kd^2.

The equation then becomes:

$$Q = C_v \sqrt{\Delta p} \quad \text{(for liquids with specific gravity} = 1.0)$$

Most control valve manufacturers provide C_v values which are based upon actual performance tests.

When selecting a control valve for a particular application, this formula is used to determine the C_v required for maximum flow, since it is most important that the valve be capable of passing the maximum amount of fluid. Before such a calculation can be made, however, the correct differential pressure must be determined. This determination must, of course, be accurate if the calculation is to be reliable. The time spent in studying the pressure losses in the piping upstream and downstream from the valve will be well invested. If it is suspected that the differential pressure across a valve may vary, the lowest estimate of differential pressure should be used in the calculation of C_v. It should be remembered also that, for compressible fluids, when the pressure drop across the valve is greater than one-half the entering pressure the flow rate does not increase in accordance with these formulas.

Here, then, are the valve formulas for various fluids using common units of measurement:

$$Q_l = C_v \sqrt{\frac{\Delta p}{G}}$$

Q_l = flow rate of liquid in gpm at flowing temperature

G = specific gravity

$$Q_s = 3C_v \sqrt{P_2 \Delta p}$$

Q_s = flow rate of dry saturated steam in pounds/hour

P_2 = downstream pressure in pounds per square inch absolute

$$Q_g = 61 \, C_v \sqrt{\frac{P_2 \, (\Delta p)}{G}}$$

Q_g = flow rate of gas in cu. ft. per hour (at 14.7 pisa and 60°F).

In the cases of gas and steam flowing at elevated temperatures correction factors must be applied.

Since the amount of fluid passing through a valve at any time depends upon the opening between the plug and seat, there is a relationship involving stem position, plug shape, and rate of flow. The stem position is,

of course, determined by the operator, which receives its signal from the controller. There are many different types of valve bodies, each of which has its own flow characteristic. In addition, globe valves are obtainable with specially shaped plugs to provide particular flow characteristics.

Valve characteristics are usually described graphically in terms of % flow vs. % lift (or travel).

Here are illustrations and graphs of several basic valve types:

1. Quick opening globe valve (Fig. 43)
2. Linear globe valve (Fig. 44)
3. Equal percentage globe valve (Fig. 45)
4. Saunders-type valve (Fig. 46)
5. Butterfly valve (Fig. 47)

The selection of a control valve

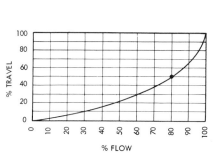

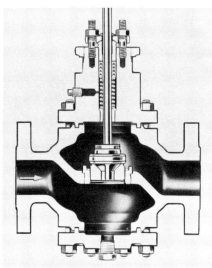

Fig. 43. Quick opening globe valve with graph showing plug characteristics. (This valve and following valves Taylor Instrument Companies)

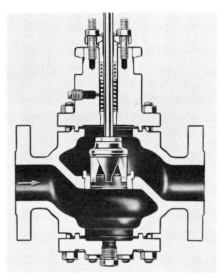

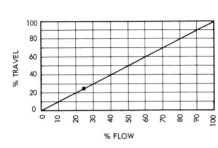

Fig. 44. Linear globe valve with graph showing plug characteristics: At 50% open, there is 50% flow; at 25% open, 25% flow, and so on.

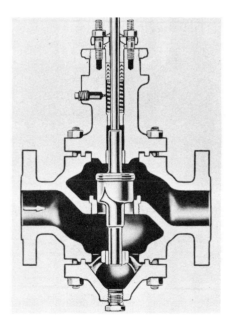

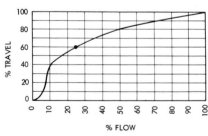

Fig. 45. Equal percentage globe valve with graph showing plug characteristics: Almost constant rate of change of flow for unit changes in lift.

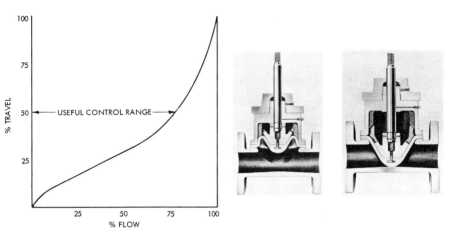

Fig. 46. Saunders patent valve showing plug characteristics: Approximately linear to 50% open.

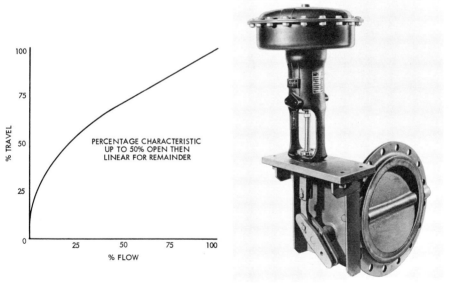

Fig. 47. Diaphragm operated butterfly valve with graph showing characteristics: equal percentage up to 50% open, then linear for remainder of lift.

for a particular application should be carefully made and based upon analysis of the process characteristics. If the process reaction rate is fast and the expected load changes are small, the valve characteristic will not affect the control very much. If, however, the process rate is slow and the load changes large, the valve characteristic becomes important. The nature of the load changes should be examined and compared. Some load changes are linear; others are not. If most of the load changes are linear, the valve should have a linear characteristic; similarly, if the load changes are non-linear, the valve should have a non-linear characteristic (equal percentage). Using a non-linear valve in a process with linear load changes introduces difficulties that make good control harder to attain.

In addition to the flow characteristics of a valve, there are other factors which influence the selection of a valve type. There are valves which will resist corrosion, operate with fluids of particularly high or low temperatures, high or low pressures, or high or low velocities. Fluids containing suspended solids require special consideration; there are special valve types for such service. It may be important that a valve be capable of extremely tight closing; for example, the single-port globe valve permits tighter closing than the double-port type. The quantity of fluid being passed may limit the selection. Globe valves are generally manufactured only in sizes up to 16 inches, so other types must be used for greater flows than can pass through a 16 inch valve.

The foregoing information represents only a limited review of control valves. Most of the fundamental considerations have been presented, but it is suggested that the manufacturers be consulted for information concerning particular problems.

part three

*PART THREE concerns itself with the
application of instruments to actual processes.
The previous sections have dealt with the
operating principles of measuring and controlling instruments. The characteristics of a
process, and the means by which control
devices accommodate these characteristics
have been explained. The variables to be
measured and controlled are presented in the
same order as in previous sections. To point up
the "systems concept" more than one method
of handling each application is described. It
is expected the student will be able to develop
other combinations. Part Three also includes
appendixes which the student will find useful
in his continued study of instrumentation.*

Chapter 15 _____ Application

THERE are two types of industrial manufacturing processes: the batch type process, in which there is no flow of product material from one section of the process to another; and the continuous type process, in which product material is subjected to different treatments as it flows through the process. There are processes that combine the features of the batch and continuous types. In such processes, several product materials are treated and stored in batch operation. Then these stored materials are drawn off as required into a continuous process.

The control of batch type operations is simpler to understand and, except for the problem of controlling the flow of the product material, such systems exhibit all the features of the continuous systems. The discussion that follows of the measurement and control of variables in process systems will be mainly concerned with batch type operations, but the principles apply to continuous systems.

TEMPERATURE

Steam Heat

Fig. 1 shows a simple batch type temperature control system. The product material is to be heated by steam coils to a desired temperature and held at that temperature for an extended period. A pressure spring actuated temperature recorder controller with pneumatic control is used.

Food products like ketchup, or chemicals such as plastic or rubber compounds, are typical of the materials treated in this manner. The product material is admitted into the vessel through the manual inlet valve until it reaches the required level. The manual steam valve is then opened, permitting the steam to enter the heating coils.

If the rate of temperature increase begins as soon as the manual valve is opened, ON-OFF control may be satisfactory. In this case, the control valve will remain fully open until

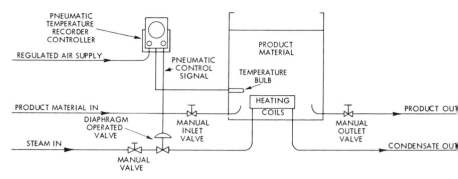

Fig. 1. Steam heat is used in this control system to provide the desired temperature.

the temperature of the product is above set point, when it will completely close. Closing the valve will cause the temperature to fall. As soon as it drops below the set point, the valve opens again. This rise and fall of temperature, and opening and closing of the control valve, is repeated over and over again. It is important that the temperature of the material be held within the allowable limits. The temperature bulb must be very sensitive and the controller and valve must respond quickly, making the entire control system fast acting. If the rate at which the temperature increases is not fast but begins increasing as soon as the manual valve is opened, proportional control should be used. In this case the control valve remains wide open until the temperature enters the proportional band, when it begins to close. When the temperature reaches the set point, the valve will cease to close, and will then remain at a position that will maintain the desired temperature. Usually there will be some overshoot initially and the valve will close too

much and oscillate slightly before settling down to a fixed position.

In a well designed system the valve will be near its midway position when the temperature is at set point. This allows the valve to open or close as much as necessary, enabling it to throttle the flow to maintain the set point.

As long as the heating fluid is at a constant temperature and the product material does not change its heating requirements, the proportional system will be able to control the temperature correctly. If, however, the temperature of the heating fluid changes, or the material because of physical or chemical changes requires more or less heat to maintain its temperature, automatic reset action must be added to the proportional controller. Reset action permits the control valve to take a different position for the same deviation from the set point, allowing more or less of the heating fluid to enter the heat exchanger, thus making up for the change in its heat content or a change in the product's heat requirements.

If changes in the temperature of the product material are very slow in reaching the temperature element, or if the action of the control valve is extremely slow, rate action must be added to the controller. Rate action permits the control valve to change its position with the rate at which the product temperature changes.

The valve should be of the air-to-open type for safety. If the air pressure fails, the valve closes, preventing overheating of the material.

Gas or Oil Heat

Fig. 2 shows another simple batch type temperature control system. Again the material is to be heated to a desired temperature and held at that temperature for an extended period. Instead of a steam coil, a gas or oil burner is used to provide the heat. The temperature sensitive element is a thermocouple or resistance bulb, and the electric controller signal is connected to a motor-operated valve. Such an installation may be used for melting metals or for heating the materials used in the manufacture of such products as varnish or glass.

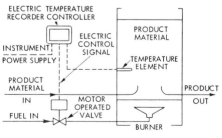

Fig. 2. In this system, the fuel used could be either gas or oil.

Since the gas or oil burner should not be turned on and off repeatedly, ON-OFF control cannot be used.

The proportional controller is the null-balance type, containing a slidewire. The control valve mechanism also contains a slidewire. These two slidewires are connected into the electronic control circuit. The slider on the instrument slidewire is positioned by a reversible motor which receives its impulse from the measuring circuit. The slider on the control valve slidewire is positioned by the valve motor. Therefore, for each measured temperature there is a corresponding valve position. The proportional band adjustment of the controller determines the amount of valve motion for each unit of deviation of the measured temperature from set point.

If the amount of heat required to maintain the set point varies or if the heat supplied by the burner varies, automatic reset action must be added. This permits the valve position to be changed if the position called for by proportional action does not provide the correct amount of heat. This is accomplished by adding a resistance-capacitance network between the instrument slidewire and the control valve slidewire.

If the system responds very slowly to temperature changes, rate action must be added. This provides the means for the valve to change its position with the rate of change of temperature. This too is accomplished by adding a resistance-capacitance network between the instrument slidewire and the valve slidewire.

The resistance-capacitance networks for producing reset action and rate action are described in Part Two. Rate action is rarely added to a proportional controller without the addition of reset action.

The control valve mechanism should include safety equipment to provide valve closure should the fuel supply cease. The valve should also close mechanically if there is a power failure. The control instrument frequently contains a mechanism which acts to close the valve if the power to the instrument fails. The slider on the instrument then travels to the upper end of the scale on battery power, actuating the mechanism which causes the valve to close. This same mechanism may also be used to actuate an audible alarm.

Electric Heat

A batch type control system in which the process heat is provided by electric heaters is shown in Fig. 3. Although in the drawing the heaters are shown at the bottom of the vessel, they may actually be contained in a jacket surrounding the

vessel. Glue, wax or various syrups are frequently heated in this manner.

These heaters are operated by an electrical contactor which, in turn, is actuated by the controller. The primary element is either a thermocouple or a resistance thermometer, and the controller is the electrical null-balance type with slidewire. Proportional action is achieved by regulating the TIME ON-TIME OFF ratio. If the temperature falls below the set point, the heaters remain ON longer; if the temperature rises above the set point, the heaters remain OFF longer. For every unit rise or fall of process temperature there is a new ratio. If reset is needed it may be added; this permits the ratio to change as long as the temperature remains above or below the set point.

If the electrical heaters are large, and turning them ON and OFF repeatedly is impractical, only part of the electric heat is controlled. This arrangement requires that the uncontrolled heaters should *not* be capable of heating the product to set point. The controlled portion provides the additional heat required.

Another method of controlling electric heaters employs a device which varies the voltage to them. One such device is a variable transformer which can be motor driven. The control system resembles that used for the motor operated valve.

A saturable reactor may also be used to vary the voltage to the heaters (Fig. 4). A saturable reactor is a

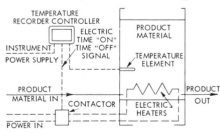

Fig. 3. A control system in which process heat is provided by electricity.

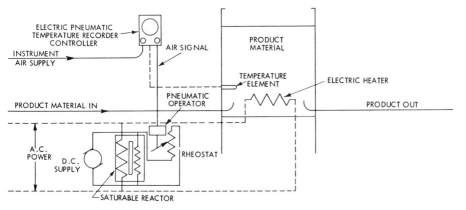

Fig. 4. The voltage to this temperature control system is varied by the saturable reactor.

magnetic amplifier which controls alternating current power in a load circuit by varying direct current in a control circuit. Simply described, it resembles a transformer with a dc primary and an ac secondary circuit. The controller contains an electrical measuring circuit using the electrical primary element as the input device. The control circuit is pneumatic, receiving its error signal from an electronic amplifier which actuates a pneumatic relay. The pneumatic signal is fed into a diaphragm-operated rheostat. This regulates the amount of dc voltage in the saturable reactor which, in turn, regulates the amount of ac going to the heaters. All control actions are available with this type of system.

PRESSURE

The regulation of fluid pressure in a pipe line is a frequent pressure control problem. Water pressure must be regulated for heating systems or distribution systems. Gas or oil pressure must be regulated before entering burners. Pressure regulators are commonly used for such service. They may be divided into three classes:

1. Direct operated
2. Pilot operated
3. Instrument pilot operated

Direct operated regulators may be weight-loaded, pressure-loaded, or spring-loaded (Fig. 5). With all of these the pressure entering the regulator acts against the loading force. When this pressure rises, the loading force acts to change the valve opening to maintain the desired outlet pressure. Regulators may be self-contained as in Fig. 5, which means there is no external connection to the pipe line, or they may be externally connected, as shown in Fig. 6.

Pilot operated regulators may have internal or external pilots (Fig. 7). A pilot is a small regulator which is interposed between the pressure connection to the regulator and the loading chamber. Controlled pressure is piped to the pilot, which varies the

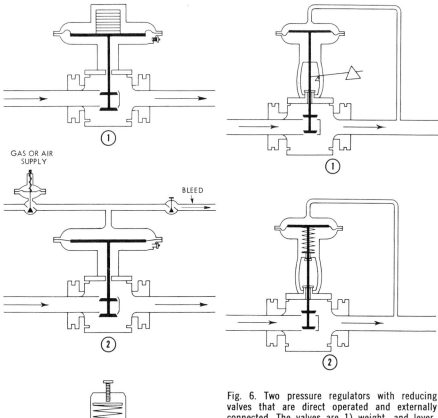

Fig. 6. Two pressure regulators with reducing valves that are direct operated and externally connected. The valves are 1) weight- and lever-loaded, and 2) spring-loaded.

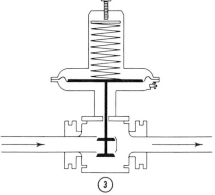

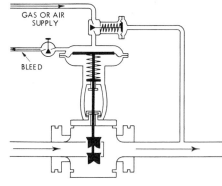

Fig. 5. Three pressure regulators with direct operated, self-contained reducing valves which are 1) weight-loaded, 2) pressure-loaded, and 3) spring-loaded.

loading on the regulator. The addition of the pilot improves the control since only a slight change in the con-

Fig. 7. The reducing valve in this pressure regulator is pilot operated.

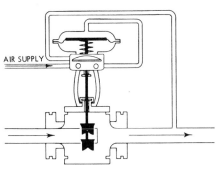

Fig. 8. The reducing valve in this pressure regulator is operated by an instrument pilot.

The regulation of pressure inside a closed vessel is a common control application. Gas holders (tanks for gas supply) require such control. Liquid oxygen, nitrogen, or hydrogen are stored in vessels in which the pressure must be regulated. Frequently a relief valve is all that is required; these open in proportion to the magnitude of the overpressure. They are generally self-contained spring-loaded regulators.

trolled pressure is required to produce a full range change of the regulator.

Instrument pilot operated regulators (Fig. 8) provide more flexible control. In general, the pilot is a pneumatic controller with a bellows or pressure spring as the sensing element. The controller usually includes proportional band adjustment for varying the sensitivity. The regulation is actually performed by a control valve.

When more precise pressure control is required, an instrument pilot and a control valve is used (Fig. 9). The instrument pilot may be a pneumatic pressure controller providing an air signal to a control valve. A variation of this system uses a pressure controller with an electrical output. The electrical signal is sent to an electro-pneumatic relay which provides the air signal required to operate the control valve. The electrical signal is introduced for faster control response, especially when the distance between the sensing point and the control point is great.

A hydraulic control system is often used for furnace pressure or draft control in industrial furnaces or boilers. This choice is made because hydraulic systems possess sufficient power to operate heavy dampers or large butterfly valves. Any of the elastic deformation pressure sensing elements may be used to vary the hydraulic signal. A hydraulic piston is used to position the final element. A typical hydraulic control system for controlling furnace draft is shown in Fig. 10. The draft pressure is

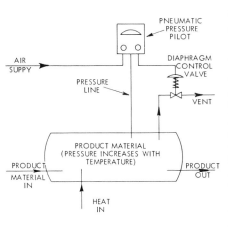

Fig. 9. The pneumatic pressure pilot and the diaphragm control valve insure more precise pressure control.

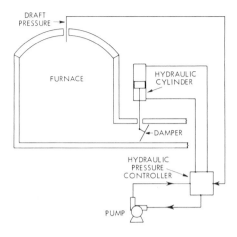

Fig. 10. Hydraulic system used in the control of industrial furnaces and boilers.

sensed by a diaphragm which controls the hydraulic pressure to a double-acting cylinder which positions the outlet damper on the furnace.

Proportional, proportional + reset, and proportional + reset + derivative actions may be included in such a system.

LEVEL CONTROL

The control of liquid level is necessary in many industrial processes. The control of fuel oil or water level in a combustion system is important for continuous operation. Controlling the level of the components of a mixture in a blending operation is a frequent requirement in the petroleum or chemical industries. The control of level in water or sewage treatment plants is essential. In general, all continuous processes require that the level of supply ingredients be controlled.

In the previous discussion of level measuring devices, two classes of devices were established:

1. Direct—in which the varying level of the material is used for actuation.
2. Indirect—in which a variable which changes with level is used for actuation.

The same classification may be applied to level control.

Direct Operated Devices

Among the direct operated level control devices are:

1. Ball Floats
2. Displacers
3. Electrodes
4. Capacitance Probes

The simplest ball float liquid level controller is the float operated lever type (Fig. 11). The float rides on the surface of the liquid, and is attached to one end of a lever system. The other end of the lever system operates a valve which regulates the flow

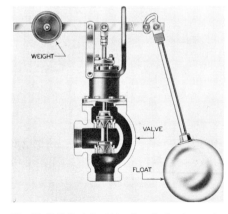

Fig. 11. Ball float liquid level controller for use in open tanks. (Fisher Governor Co.)

of liquid into the vessel. This type is suitable only for open vessels.

Ball float operated liquid level controllers are also available for use in closed tanks. This requires that the float shaft, which transmits the float motion to the lever system outside the tank, pass through a sealed bearing or stuffing box (Fig. 12).

In some applications the float cannot be located in the vessel. For these a float cage is mounted on the side of the vessel with one pipe connection going to the top of the vessel and the other to the bottom (Fig. 13). Any change in liquid level in

Fig. 14. Liquid level controller operated by pilot to provide greater accuracy. (Fisher Governor Co.)

the tank is matched by a change of level in the float cage.

When greater sensitivity and more versatile control is required pilot operated float controllers are used (Fig. 14). In these the float lever system actuates a pneumatic or hydraulic relay. The control valve is then operated by pneumatic or hydraulic pressure. This arrangement makes it possible for the float mechanism to be a considerable distance from the valve.

Ball floats are also used to actuate magnetic switches (Fig. 15). The magnetic switch can be used to operate a solenoid valve or pump motor. In a typical magnetic operated float switch the float is enclosed in a chamber mounted on the side of the vessel and attached to it is a magnetic piston. When the float rises

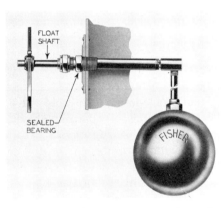

Fig. 12. Ball float liquid level controller for use in closed tanks. (Fisher Governor Co.)

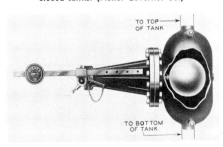

Fig. 13. Float cage used when liquid level controller cannot be located in the tank. (Fisher Governor Co.)

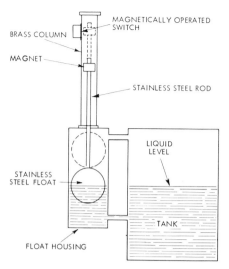

Fig. 15. Level controller which uses the movement of the float to operate the electric switch magnetically.

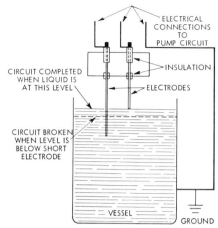

Fig. 16. Conductive electrodes are used in level control of conductive fluids.

and carries the piston to the level of the magnetic switch the electrical circuit is completed or broken.

Displacer elements, when used for level control, provide greater sensitivity and permit the use of a proportional control system which can be either pneumatic or electric. These have been described in the section on density measurement.

Electrode liquid level controllers are used for controlling the level of conductive fluids such as water. The

electrodes are electrically insulated from the vessel. They are of different lengths; when the conductive fluid is in contact with two electrodes an electric circuit is completed (Fig. 16). This action can be used to start a pump or operate a solenoid valve, thus admitting or shutting off the flow of fluid into the vessel.

Capacitance probes may also be used to control the level of some dry materials and many liquids, of which liquid latex is a typical example. These probes consist of an outer shell and a center rod of metal which serve as the plates of a capac-

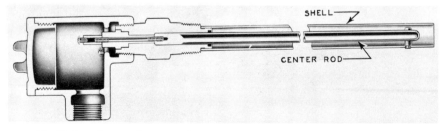

Fig. 17. Capacitance probes are used where there are special problems of level control. (Fisher Governor Co.)

itor (Fig. 17). The liquid in the vessel serves as the insulating (dielectric) material. When the liquid falls below the level of the probe the capacitance changes. This change in capacitance triggers an electronic circuit which operates an electric relay. Thus the capacitance probe position establishes the point of level control. See Fig. 18. Long capacitance probes which are suspended in the vessel providing a gradual

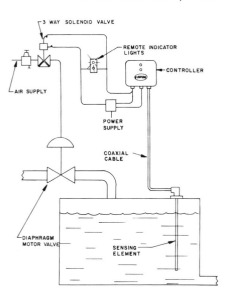

Fig. 19. Drawing showing the application of long capacitance probe as the sensing element in a level control system. (Fisher Governor Co.)

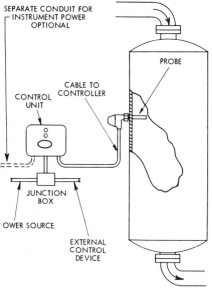

Fig. 18. Installation drawing of capacitance probe used as the sensing element in a level control system. (Fisher Governor Co.)

change in capacitance as the liquid level changes have been applied for proportional control of the level of some liquids (Fig. 19). The control system may be either pneumatic or electric.

Indirect Operated Devices

Of the indirect operated level measuring devices, the differential pressure types are most often selected for control. Their principal use is for controlling the level of volatile liquids in pressure vessels. The petroleum and chemical industries have many applications of this kind. The level of liquid oxygen, nitrogen, and hydrogen in pressure vessels may also be controlled using differential pressure instruments.

Frequently such a liquid level installation employs a transmission system which may be pneumatic, electric, or hydraulic. The level is measured using a differential pressure measuring instrument and a signal is transmitted to a remote controller mounted close to the control valve or pump which admits liquid into the vessel. See Fig. 20. As a rule, proportional action with

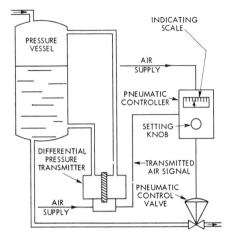

Fig. 20. Pneumatic transmitter used in liquid level control system.

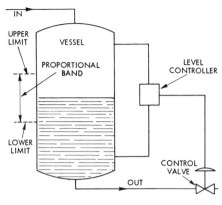

Fig. 21. Controller with proportional action and wide proportional band is used to "average" liquid level in vessel.

a wide proportional band will provide good control. Of course, if the changes in flow out of the vessel are sudden or prolonged, reset and rate action may be added.

In liquid level applications, it is often more important that the flow out of the storage vessel should be held constant than that the level should be held at a particular point. The flow through the outlet valve varies as the level in the vessel varies, which is the result of the change in pressure on the valve because of level changes. The level in the vessel is permitted to rise or fall slowly between limits. Such a system is called "averaging" liquid level control. This is accomplished using a controller with proportional action and a very wide proportional band to allow the valve to move slowly to new positions. The control valve should be equipped with a positioner to insure smooth motion. If the level

reaches the upper or lower limit, the controller quickly closes or opens the valve. Limit stops in the controller provide this safety feature. See Fig. 21.

Pressure vessels in which the pressure may fluctuate, and in which either "average" or pin point control is required, present a need for cascade control. Here the output signal of the level controller is used to

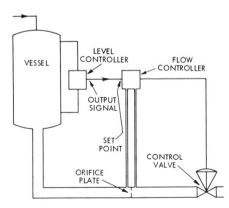

Fig. 22. In the pneumatic cascade control system, output signal of level controller becomes set point of flow controller.

change the set point of a flow controller which regulates the outflow from the vessel (Fig. 22). For "averaging" control the proportional band is set wide, while for pin point control the band is made narrow. "Averaging" liquid level control and cascade control of the type described is a frequent requirement in petroleum refineries to insure constant continuous flow of product material from storage to process.

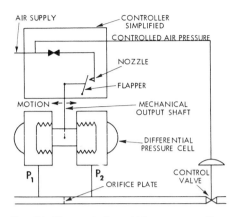

Fig. 23. Flow controller which uses an orifice plate to create differential pressure.

FLOW CONTROL

Almost all industries employ flow controllers. Electric power generating stations require them for controlling fuel flow, steam flow, and water flow. Gas distribution companies need them to regulate the amount of gas being supplied to their customers. The food and beverage industries use them for cooking, heating, and drying. Flow controllers are necessary in the steel industry to conserve water, fuel, and power. In refineries and chemical plants flow controllers are extremely important to insure continuous production of uniform products.

Rate Control

Of the flow rate measuring devices described in previous sections, the differential pressure type employing an orifice plate is most often used for flow control (Fig. 23). The differential pressure produced by the orifice plate serves as the input to the measuring element. The measuring element may be either the mercury-float type or the bellows type. The motion of the float or bellows is used to actuate the control mechanism. In a pneumatic controller the flapper is moved, producing an output air signal which is used to posi-

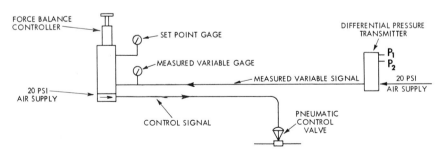

Fig. 24. Pneumatic control system with separated transmitter and controller.

tion a diaphragm-operated control valve. The control mechanism includes a means for establishing the set point. If the measured rate of flow exceeds the set point rate, the control valve closes to reduce it. Likewise, if the measured rate of flow is below the set point rate, the control valve opens to increase it. Since the amount of fluid that will pass through a valve is affected by the pressure of the fluid, it is necessary to correct the valve position for any variation in the fluid pressure. The addition of automatic reset action provides this.

Because differential pressure piping can be run only over limited distances so that measuring lag is not excessive, transmitters are often used. Typical of such an installation is one employing a pneumatic pressure signal in the transmitter. See Fig. 24. This pneumatic pressure becomes the input to the force balance controller. The set point is applied to the controller as a pneumatic pressure and the air output of the controller goes to the control valve. It should be noted that in the system just described the control signal varies with the differential pressure and not the flow rate. This condition may be corrected by including a square root extracting mechanism in the system since flow rate varies approximately as the square root of the pressure. This square root extracting mechanism may be included in the transmitter, the controller, or at the valve.

Electric or hydraulic controllers are also used for flow control. Electric systems are particularly useful when the distance between the point of measurement and the final element is great. Although there are

Fig. 25. Electro-hydraulic operator (Fisher Governor Co.)

electric operators for the final element, usually pneumatic or hydraulic operators are used because they are more powerful. This requires that the electric signal from the controller be converted to a pneumatic signal. Electro-hydraulic operators are available as units attached to the valve itself as illustrated in Fig. 25.

Other flow rate measuring devices such as the rotameter, electromagnetic flowmeters, and turbine type flowmeters also are adaptable to flow control. When using the rotameter, an electrical output signal is obtained by attaching an armature to the float, and positioning this armature in an inductance coil. The recorder controller contains a reversible motor which positions an armature in a matching induction coil. The two coils form an inductance bridge. The same motor action which positions the armature also provides the control signal which may be either pneumatic or electric. The electromagnetic flowmeter and the turbine meter produce electric signals which can be used as controller inputs.

Ratio Control

Frequently the blending of two fluids is required in a process. Flow ratio control accomplishes this. The uncontrolled fluid flow is called the "wild flow." It is measured using any of the conventional methods. In a simple system (Fig. 26) this measurement is converted in a transmitter into a signal which may be used to establish the set point of a controller which regulates the flow

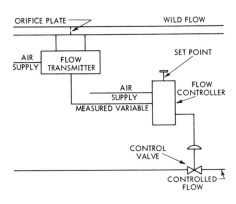

Fig. 26. Simple system showing how "wild flow" is converted to a useful control signal.

of the controlled fluid. Thus the rate of flow of the controlled fluid varies with the measured rate of the wild flow. In another system of flow ratio control (Fig. 27), the flow that is not controlled is called the independent flow. The flow that is controlled is termed the dependent flow. In this system the measured independent flow becomes the input to a pneumatic flow transmitter which converts the measurement to an air pressure. This air pressure passes through a fixed restriction, and enters a pneumatic ratio unit, which is an adjustable pressure divider. The other input to this pressure divider is an adjustable reference pressure. The output of the pressure divider becomes the input to an amplifying relay. When the ratio set needle valve is fully open the input pressure to the amplifying relay equals the pressure from the transmitter. When the needle valve is fully closed the input pressure to the amplifying relay equals 1/25th of the pressure from the transmitter. This means

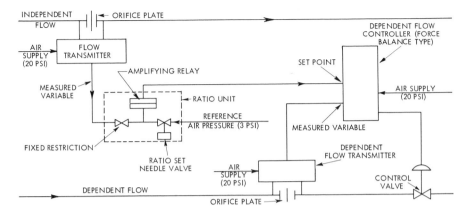

Fig. 27. Pneumatic flow ratio control system.

that by adjusting the needle valve it is possible to establish the relationship between the independent flow measurement and the output of the ratio unit. For instance, the output of the ratio unit may vary its full range of 3 psi to 15 psi for a variation of only 25% of the measured independent flow, or it may require a change of 200% in the measured flow to produce the full range ratio unit output.

The output of the ratio unit is used as the set point input of a force balance controller. The dependent flow is also measured and this measurement is converted by a pneumatic transmitter into an air pressure. The pneumatic output of this flow transmitter becomes the measured variable pressure of the force-balance controller. The controller output then regulates a diaphragm operated valve in the dependent flow line so that the dependent flow is held at the setpoint. Since the setpoint represents a particular percentage of the

independent flow the result is that the dependent flow is held to this percentage of the independent flow.

Ratio control is not limited to flow applications although this is the most frequent use. It is also possible to control the ratio of two temperatures or two pressures in much the same manner.

Cascade Control

One form of cascade control has already been described in which the output signal of a level controller is used to vary the set point of a flow controller. In the type shown in Fig. 28, the output of a temperature controller does this. The temperature is detected by the temperature bulb of a transmitter which converts it into an air pressure signal. This pneumatic signal is used as the measured variable input of a force balance type (temperature) controller. This controller also has an air signal as its set point input. The output of this controller becomes the set point in-

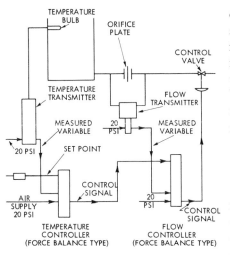

Fig. 28. Temperature-flow cascade control system.

controller to form a cascade control system makes the entire system much faster acting with respect to changes in supply pressure. Using such a system the temperature of a product can be more accurately controlled by regulating the flow of the product into the vessel.

ANALYSIS CONTROL

One of the most rapidly expanding phases of instrumentation is that of controlling processes using analyzers. This has come about as a result of the development of new equipment and techniques.

Chromatography

Outstanding in this field is the application of chromatographic analyzers to the control of petroleum refinery processes. Of critical importance to this technique is the creation of sampling systems. Metering pumps have been perfected which accurately feed the fluids into the measuring apparatus. After the sampling and analyzing systems have been satisfactorily installed the components to be controlled are selected using a "peak-picker" (it will be recalled that the chromatographic record is a continuous curve with a series of peaks). The output signal for each component is a millivolt signal which varies with the height of the peak for that component (Fig. 29). This output signal becomes the input to a controller. The controller accepts this signal and positions a final element in agreement with it.

put of a second force balance (flow) controller whose measured variable input is a pneumatic signal from a flow transmitter. The output of the flow controller is used to position the control valve which regulates the flow of heating fluid in the line containing the primary element (orifice plate) of the flow transmitter.

The result of this arrangement is that as the temperature in the vessel changes the flow of heating fluid into the vessel is controlled. This could be accomplished by a temperature controller and valve alone. However, this simpler system would not be able to change the flow rate rapidly enough to overcome variations in pressure in the heating fluid line. Such changes would be sensed by the temperature controller only after they pass through the process. Sometimes this delay cannot be tolerated and cascade control is required. The addition of the flow

Fig. 29. "Peak-picker" used in sampling and analyzing systems. (Perkin-Elmer Corp.)

This controller signal is maintained until the next time this component is measured when a change may be called for. If more than one component is to be controlled the interval between control impulses is longer than for a single component. The controller is the direct type requiring no feedback signal from the final element.

Such control systems are relatively new and it is to be expected that the users and manufacturers will develop new techniques which will result in wider application of chromatographic control.

Viscosity

The continuous control of viscosity is another example of analysis control. Coating or dipping processes using such materials as plastics or adhesives can be improved by the application of viscosity control.

Consider a process in which the viscosity of a fluid may be controlled by regulating the flow of solids and liquids which make up the fluid. Assume that only one solid and one liquid are involved. Fig. 30 shows a schematic of such a process with the required instrumentation indicated. Continuous viscosity measurement is made using a rotating spindle apparatus. The electrical signal which is proportional to the vis-

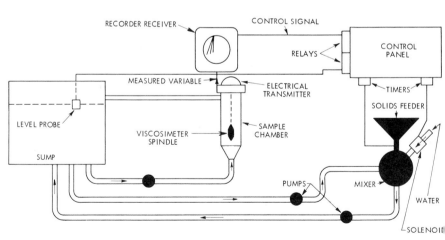

Fig. 30. Automatic viscosity control.

cosity is in the form of a capacitance change. This signal enters a capacitance bridge recorder-controller. This controller provides an output signal used to operate a feeder of the dry material as well as a valve which regulates liquid flow. When the viscosity becomes too low the controller provides increased flow of dry materials. When the viscosity becomes too high the controller provides increased liquid flow. When the viscosity is within the desired range both solids and liquids are admitted according to a predetermined ratio. This ratio may be established using timers to regulate the TIME ON-TIME OFF cycles of the dry materials feeder and the liquid valves. If the materials are admitted to a mixing tank a level control device would be required. This would prevent the admission of either liquid or dry materials if the level in the tank is too high.

Electrolytic Conductivity

Another analysis instrument which lends itself to control applications is the electrolytic conductivity measurement type (Fig. 31). Frequently the purity of boiler feed water is controlled by this method. The electrolytic conductivity element is inserted in the feed water line. There it detects changes in the electrolytic conductivity of the water due to the presence of impurities. When the element detects that the impurity level is too high the feed water is diverted to a treatment section. At the same time a new supply of feed water is admitted to the feed water line to the boiler. The control of such a process may be accomplished using completely electric components, as shown here.

The controller is of the ON-OFF type, actuating the solenoid valves which direct the flow of feed water to the boiler or to the treatment

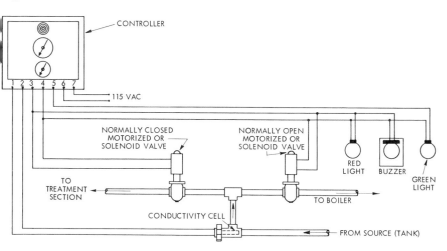

Fig. 31. System for monitoring the purity of boiler feed water.

section, and admit a fresh supply of treated water when needed.

There are many other analysis instruments which can be adapted for control and their number is increasing rapidly. The principal problem is to provide a continuous measurement of the variable using a transducer whose output is suitable for use as the input to a conventional controller. Electronic controllers lend themselves best to such service.

Appendix 1 _____ Glossary

THE following terms and definitions have been chosen for their clarity and because they have become the standard language in the instrumentation field. Some of them have been selected from the list compiled by the Terminology Committee of the Instruments and Regulator Division of the American Society of Mechanical Engineers. The Instrument Society of America has also been used as a source.

The glossary has been intentionally expanded beyond the scope of this book to give students an appreciation of how broad the instrumentation field is. It is hoped that this will encourage the student to advance his study of the subject.

A

ABSOLUTE PRESSURE   The pressure of a liquid or gas measured in relation to a vacuum (zero pressure).

ABSOLUTE ZERO   The temperature at which the molecular motion that constitutes heat ceases, and at which an ideal gas, kept at constant volume, would exert no pressure. This temperature (−273.15°C or −459.67°F) is theoretically the coldest temperature possible, and is the 0° point on the absolute temperature scale.

ACCELERATION   The time rate of change of velocity, expressed in feet (or centimeters) per second per second.

ACCURACY   The difference between the reading of an instrument and the true value of what is being measured, expressed as a percent of full instrument scale.

ACTION   Generally refers to the action of a controller, and defines what is done to regulate the final control element to effect control. Types of action include ON-OFF, proportional, rate, and reset.

AMBIENT CONDITIONS   The conditions of temperature, pressure, humidity, etc., existing in the medium that surrounds an instrument.

AMMETER   An instrument that indicates the quantity of flow of an electric current in a circuit.

AMPLIFICATION   The process of obtaining an output signal that is greater than the input signal through auxiliary power controlled by the input signal.

AMPLIFICATION FACTOR The ratio of a change in plate voltage to a change in grid voltage, with the plate current held constant.

AMPLIFIER A device for increasing the strength of a signal.

AMPLITUDE The greatest distance through which a vibrating body moves from the mid-point.

ANALOG COMPUTER An apparatus that converts mathematically expressed variables into mechanical or electrical equivalents.

ANODE Usually applied to the most highly positive electrode which attracts electrons in an electron tube.

ATMOSPHERIC PRESSURE The pressure exerted on a body by the air, equal at sea level to about 14.7 pounds per square inch.

ATTENUATION The amount of decrease of the amplitude of a signal as it passes through any part of a control system.

AUTOMATIC CONTROL The process of using the differences between the actual value and desired value of a variable to take corrective action without human intervention.

AUTOMATIC CONTROL SYSTEM Any combination of automatic controllers connected in closed loops with one or more processes.

AUTOMATIC CONTROLLER A device that measures the value of a variable and operates to correct or limit deviation from a selected reference. It includes means for both measurement and control.

AUTOMATION In mass production manufacturing, the technique of using self-directing, self-regulating, and self-correcting machines instead of human labor and control.

B

BASE Center section of a junction, or bipolar, transistor. Small current flow through the base is used to control the output of the transistor. See JUNCTION TRANSISTOR.

BATCH PROCESS Applies where a given amount of material is processed in one operation to produce what is required.

BELLOWS A pressure sensing element consisting of a convoluted metal cylinder closed at one end. Pressure difference between the outside and inside of the bellows causes it to expand or contract along its axis.

BIMETALLIC ELEMENT The temperature sensitive bimetal of a bimetallic thermometer. The bimetal is composed of two or more metal alloys mechanically associated so that the bimetal bends in a particular direction when heated.

BLACK BODY The ideal radiator of thermal energy, which emits as much thermal energy as it absorbs but which reflects none.

BOURDON TUBE A pressure sensing element that consists of a curved tube having a flattened elliptical cross-section which is closed at one end. A positive pressure difference between the inside and outside of the tube tends to straighten the tube.

BRIDGE CIRCUIT A network in which the value of an unknown component is obtained by balancing one circuit against another. It consists of a detecting device and four resistances connected in series to form a diamond

BRITISH THERMAL UNIT A unit of heat. The amount of heat required to raise the temperature of one pound of water one degree Fahrenheit.

BUFFER An industrial process solution having a definite resistance to change of pH when an acid or base is added to it.

C

CALIBRATION The procedure laid down for determining, correcting, or checking the absolute values corresponding to the graduations on a measuring instrument.

CAPACITANCE A measure in units of

quantity that is determined by the type of quantity contained and the type of reference variable.

CAPACITY A measure of the maximum amount of energy or material that may be stored in a given system.

CASCADE CONTROL In an automatic control system, the resetting of the control point of a secondary controller by the output of a primary controller.

CHARLES LAW Pressure increase in a closed system is proportional to temperature increase given a constant volume.

CHOPPER Device used to interrupt dc to produce a pulsating current.

CLOSED LOOP A combination of control units in which the process variable is measured and compared with the desired value (or set point). If the measured value differs from the desired value, a corrective signal is sent to the final control element to bring the controlled variable to the proper value.

COEFFICIENT OF LINEAR EXPANSION Increase in unit length per degree of temperature rise.

COEFFICIENT OF VOLUMETRIC EXPANSION Increase in unit volume per degree of temperature rise.

COLLECTOR Term used to indicate an end terminal of a junction transistor. Analogous to the anode of a vacuum tube. See JUNCTION TRANSISTOR.

COMMON-BASE AMPLIFIER A transistor amplifier circuit arrangement in which the base is common to both input and output.

COMMON-EMITTER AMPLIFIER A transistor amplifier circuit arrangement in which the emitter is common to both input and output.

COMPENSATED THERMOMETER SYSTEM Thermometer system which has been compensated to nullify temperature variations at the recording point which tend to distort accurate process temperature readings.

COMPENSATION Provision of a supple-mental device to counteract known sources of error.

COMPUTER A machine for carrying out mathematical calculations automatically.

CONDUCTION OF HEAT The transfer of heat from one part of a body to another part in direct contact with it, the heat energy being passed from molecule to molecule.

CONTINUOUS PROCESS Applies to a process where raw material is treated by flowing continuously through a series of operations.

CONTROL AGENT The process energy or material which is manipulated to hold the controlled medium at its desired value. In heating water with steam, the steam is the control agent.

CONTROL ELEMENTS The portion of the feedback control system which is required to produce the manipulated variable from the actuating signal.

CONTROL POINT The value of controlled variable which, under any fixed set of conditions, an automatic controller operates to maintain.

CONTROL SPRING A spring with characteristics predetermined so that its torque is equal and opposite to that of the instrument for any deflection of the pointer within the scale range.

CONTROL SYSTEM An assemblage of control apparatus coordinated to execute a planned set of control functions.

CONTROLLED MEDIUM The process, energy or material which is to be adjusted to a definite value.

D

DERIVATIVE ACTION Same as rate action (*q.v.*).

DESIRED VALUE The value of the controlled variable which it is desired to maintain.

DEVIATION The difference between the instantaneous value of the controlled variable and the set point.

DIAPHRAGM A thin, flexible partitioning used to transmit pressure from one substance to another while keeping them from direct contact.

DIAPHRAGM MOTOR   A pneumatic diaphragm mechanism used to position a valve or other final control element in response to the action of a pneumatic controller or a pneumatic positioning relay.

DIAPHRAGM MOTOR VALVE   A pneumatic-powered valve which regulates fluid flow in response to a pneumatic signal.

DIFFERENTIAL GAP   Applies to two position (ON-OFF) controller action. It is the smallest range of values through which the controlled variable must pass in order to move the controller output from its ON to its OFF position (or vice versa).

DIFFERENTIAL PRESSURE   The difference in pressure between two pressure sources, measured relative to one another.

DIFFERENTIAL PRESSURE CELL   (d/p cell) A device for measuring the difference between two pressures, using diaphragms or bellows. d/p cells are used to measure flow and liquid level.

DIGITAL COMPUTER   A type of computer that makes calculations using digits rather than continuous signals.

DIODE   A two-electrode device containing an anode and a cathode.

DRAIN   Term used to describe a main terminal of a field effect, or unipolar, transistor. See FIELD EFFECT TRANSISTOR.

DRIFT   Gradual departure of instrument output from the correct value.

DYNAMIC RESPONSE   The behavior of an output in response to a changing input.

E

ELECTRIC CONTROLLER   A device or a group of devices which serves to govern the electric power delivered to the apparatus to which it is connected.

ELECTRIC THERMOMETER   An instrument which uses electrical means to measure temperature.

ELECTRIC TRANSDUCER   A transducer in which all the waves concerned are electric.

ELECTRODE   A conducting element that performs one or more of the functions of emitting, collecting, or controlling by an electric field the movements of electrons or ions.

ELECTRONIC   Pertains to the application of that branch of science which deals with small electrical quantities. Applies especially to circuits containing electron tubes and special conductors and semi-conductors.

ELECTRON TUBE   An electron device in which conduction by electrons takes place through a vacuum or gaseous medium within a gas-tight envelope.

EMISSIVITY   The rate at which a substance will radiate thermal energy.

EMITTER   Term used to describe one of the end terminals of a junction, or bipolar, transistor. See JUNCTION TRANSISTOR.

END DEVICE   The final system element that performs the final conversion of measurement to an indication, record or the initiation of control.

END-POINT CONTROL   Quality control through continuous or periodic analysis of the final product of a process (sometimes referred to as stream analysis). In highly automatic operations, the final product is analyzed and corrected continuously and automatically.

ERROR   In automatic control terminology, the difference between the actual controlled variable and set point. The margin by which an automatic controller misses its target value.

ERROR SIGNAL   A measurement of the error by an automatic controller.

F

FEEDBACK   Part of a closed loop system which brings back information about a given condition for comparison with the desired condition.

FEEDBACK CONTROLLER   A mechanism which measures the value of the controlled variable, accepts the value of the command, and, as a result of a comparison, manipulates the controlled system in order to maintain an established relationship between the controlled variable and the command.

FEEDBACK CONTROL SYSTEM   A control system which tends to maintain a prescribed relationship of one system variable to another by comparing functions of these variables and using the difference as a means of control.

FEEDBACK ELEMENTS   The portion of the feedback control system which establishes the relationship between the primary feedback and the controlled variable.

FEEDBACK SIGNAL   A signal that is returned to the input of the system and compared with the reference signal to obtain an actuating signal which returns the controlled variable to the desired value.

FIELD EFFECT TRANSISTOR   A transistor made from a single crystal of silicon (P-type), with two small regions on opposite sides of the crystal composed of N-type material. These two small regions are electrically connected and are called the gate. One end of the main crystal is called the source, the other the drain. Also called a unipolar transistor.

FILAMENT   A cathode of a thermionic tube, usually in the form of a wire or ribbon, to which heat may be supplied by passing current through it.

FINAL CONTROL ELEMENT   Unit of a control loop (such as a valve) which manipulates the control agent.

FLEXIVITY   Term used to indicate the movement of a bimetal strip when heated. The flexivity of a bimetal strip is proportional to temperature, length, and thickness.

FLOATING ACTION   Occurs where there

is a predetermined relation between the deviation and the rate of motion of a final control element.

FLOATING CONTROL   A term that describes a control action in which the rate of motion of the final control element is determined by the deviation of controlled variable from set point.

FLOW DIAGRAM   A graphical representation of a sequence of operations.

FLOW, LAMINAR   (or streamline) Any part of a fluid in which the velocity is smooth and constant.

FLOW, TURBULENT   Any part of a fluid in which the velocity at a given point varies more or less rapidly in magnitude and direction with time.

FORWARD BIAS   State where diode or transistor is so connected in a circuit that it will conduct a current.

FREQUENCY   A measure of the number of times a cycling quantity repeats itself. Expressed as cycles per second.

FREQUENCY RESPONSE   The response of a component, instrument, or control system to input signals at varying frequencies.

FREQUENCY RESPONSE ANALYSIS   A method of systematically analyzing process control problems, based on introducing cyclic inputs to a device or system and measuring the resulting output signals at various frequencies.

FULL SCALE   The maximum value of the rate or range of an instrument.

FULL SCALE CYCLE   A complete transversal of the range of an instrument from minimum reading to a full scale and back to minimum reading.

FULL-WAVE RECTIFIER   A combination of rectifier elements so arranged that the output current is unidirectional.

G

GAGE PRESSURE   The pressure of a liquid or gas measured relative to the ambient atmospheric pressure.

GAIN   Amount of increase in a signal as it passes through any part of a control system. If a signal gets smaller it is said to be attenuated. If it gets larger, it is said to be amplified.

GALVANOMETER   An instrument for indicating or measuring a small electric current or a function of the current by means of a mechanical motion derived from electromagnetic or electrodynamic forces which are set up as a result of the current.

GATE   Term for one of the main terminals of a field effect transistor. See FIELD EFFECT TRANSISTOR.

GRAPHIC PANEL   A control panel which pictorially displays and traces the relative position and function of measuring and control equipment to process equipment. Graphic panels can represent a total plant operation.

GRID   An electrode having one or more openings for the passage of electrons or ions.

GRID CIRCUIT   A circuit which includes the grid-cathode path of an electron tube in a series connection with other elements.

GROUND   An electrically conducting connection, accidental or intentional, to the earth or to some other conducting body at zero potential with respect to the earth.

H

HALF-WAVE RECTIFIER   A rectifier which delivers unidirectional output current only during the half cycle when the applied alternating current voltage is of the polarity at which the rectifier has low resistance. During the opposite half cycle the rectifier passes no current; hence a half-wave rectifier rectifies only one-half of the alternating current wave.

HEAD   Pressure resulting from gravitational forces on liquids. Measured in terms of the depth below a free surface of the liquid which is the reference zero head.

HOLES   Positive charges, the movement of which in the P-type material of transistors constitutes the main current-carrying activity within the transistor.

HUNTING   The undesirable oscillation of an automatic control system so that the controlled variable swings on both sides of the predetermined reference value without seeming to approach it.

HYGROSCOPIC   Descriptive of material which readily absorbs and retains moisture.

HYSTERESIS   The total difference between the response of a unit or system to an increasing signal and the response to a decreasing signal.

I

IMPEDANCE   The complex ratio of a force-like quantity (force, pressure, voltage, temperature, or electric field strength) to a related velocity-like quantity (velocity, volume velocity, current, heat flow, or magnetic field strength).

INCLINED TUBE MANOMETER   A manometer with one arm at an angle, permitting the scale on that arm to be expanded for more precise readings of low pressure.

INDUCTANCE   The property of an electrical circuit which tends to oppose change of current in the circuit.

INDUSTRIAL CONTROL   The methods and means of governing the performance of a device, apparatus, equipment, or system used in industry.

INPUT   Incoming signal to a control unit or system.

INSTRUMENT   Used broadly to connote a device incorporating measuring, indicating, recording, controlling, and/or operating abilities.

INSTRUMENTATION   The instruments that are used in a process system, usually including the control valves. Also refers to the science of applying instruments to manufacturing processes.

INTEGRAL ACTION Same as reset action (q.v.).

INTEGRATOR A device which continually totalizes or adds up the value of a quantity for a given time.

INVERSE DERIVATIVE ACTION Control which produces a corrective operation inversely proportional to the rate at which the process variable deviates from the set point. For instance, if there is a sudden process change, this action causes the final control element to lag behind the process in producing any corrective action.

ION Any electrically charged particle of molecular, atomic, or nuclear size.

ISOTHERMAL Without change in temperature.

J

JUNCTION TRANSISTOR A transistor consisting of three sections, the base, emitter, and collector, joined end to end. The sections can be arranged in an NPN or PNP configuration. The points where the sections join are called junctions. Also called bipolar transistor.

K

KELVIN TEMPERATURE SCALE A thermodynamic absolute temperature scale, having as its zero the absolute zero of temperature (−273.15°C).

L

LAG Refers to delay, and is expressed in seconds or minutes. Lag is caused by conditions such as capacitance, inertia, resistance and dead time, either separately or in combination.

LINEARITY The degree to which the calibration curve of a device matches a straight line. The linearity error is generally the greatest departure from the best straight line that can be drawn through the measured calibration points.

LOAD The amount of energy or material that a device or machine must deliver or handle.

LOGGER An instrument which automatically scans conditions (temperature, pressure, humidity) and records, or logs, findings on a chart, usually with respect to time. A digital logger records numerical values in tubular form by such means as an automatic typewriter.

M

MAGNETIC AMPLIFIER A device similar in construction and appearance to a transformer which is used to perform the amplifying functions of electronic tubes or transistors in some applications.

MAGNETIC FIELD A state of the medium in which moving electrified bodies are subject to forces by virtue of both their electrifications and motion.

MANIPULATED VARIABLE That quantity of condition of the control agent which is varied by the automatic controller so as to affect the value of the measured (controlled) variable. In heating water with steam, the flow of steam is the manipulated variable.

MANOMETER A gage for measuring pressure of gases and vapors.

MANUAL CONTROLLER A controller having all its basic functions performed by devices that are operated by hand.

MASS FLOW MEASUREMENT The measurement of flow in weight units rather than conventional volumetric units.

MEASURED VARIABLE Analogous to controlled variable when used in connection with control applications.

MEASURING JUNCTION The junction of the two dissimilar wires of a thermocouple which is exposed to the temperature to be measured.

MEASURING MEANS Those elements of an automatic controller which are involved in ascertaining and communicating to the controlling means either the value of the controlled variable, the error, or the deviation.

MINIATURIZATION   Method of reducing the size of instruments to minimize panel space requirements. Permits more instruments to be mounted in smaller spaces.

MOTOR OPERATOR   A portion of the controlling means which applies power for operating the final control element.

MULTIPLE ACTION   Motion in which two or more controller actions are combined.

MULTIPLE HELIX BIMETAL THERMOMETER   Thermometer in which the bimetal measuring element is arranged in the form of a helix coil within a helix coil, permitting the use of long bimetal strips within a compact space for greater sensitivity.

MULTIPOSITION ACTION   Movement in which a final control element is moved to one of three or more predetermined positions, each corresponding to a definite range of values of the controlled variable.

N

NEEDLE VALVE   Small valve inserted in the process pipeline which is subject to pulsating pressures. The valve has the effect of dampening or flattening the impulses.

NPN TRANSISTOR   Junction (bipolar) transistor end sections of which are composed of N-type material and center section of which is P-type material. See JUNCTION TRANSISTOR.

N-TYPE MATERIAL   Semiconductor material to which a "donor" impurity is added, resulting in a quantity of loosely bonded or "free" electrons.

NEUTRAL ZONE   A range of measured values in which no control action occurs. Same as dead band.

NOISE   Meaningless stray signals in a control system, similar to radio static. Some types of noise interfere with the correctness of an output signal.

NOZZLE   A duct of changing cross section in which fluid velocity is increased.

O

OFFSET   A sustained deviation of the controlled variable from set point. (This characteristic is inherent in proportional controllers that do not incorporate reset action.) Offset is caused by load changes.

OHMMETER   A direct-reading instrument for measuring electric resistance. It is provided with a scale, usually graduated in either ohms or megohms.

ON-OFF CONTROL ACTION   (Same as two position action.) Occurs when a final control element is moved from one of two fixed positions to the other with a very small change of controlled variable.

OPEN LOOP   A system in which no comparison is made between the actual value and the desired value of a process variable.

OPERATING - PRESSURE RANGE   Stated high and low values of pneumatic pressure required to produce full-range operation when applied to a pneumatic intelligence - transmission system, a pneumatic motor operator, or a pneumatic positioning relay.

OPTIMALIZATION   Theoretical analysis of a system, including all of the characteristics of the process, such as thermal lags, capacity of tanks or towers, length and size of pipes, etc. This analysis is made, usually with the aid of frequency response curves, to obtain the most desirable instrumentation and control.

ORIFICE   A symmetrical aperture, having circular transverse cross sections, the diameter of the smallest of which is large in comparison with the thickness of the plate in which it is cut and which has such sudden approach curvature that contraction is fully developed or only partially suppressed.

OSCILLATOR Circuit used to generate a constantly varying AC voltage or signal.

OUTPUT Outgoing signal of a transmitter or control unit.

OVERSHOOT The amount by which a changing process variable exceeds the desired value as changes occur in a system.

P

PELTIER EFFECT Depending on the direction of current flow, heat is either absorbed or liberated at the junction of two dissimilar metal wires through which a current is passing.

PENTODE A five-electrode electron tube containing an anode, a cathode, a control electrode, and two additional electrodes that are ordinarily grids.

PERIOD Length of time required to complete one cycle of operation.

pH The measure of effective acidity or alkalinity of solutions based on a measurement of the concentration of hydrogen ions. pH values less than 7 are considered acidic, pH values greater than 7 are considered basic.

PHASE SHIFT A time difference between the input and output signal of a control unit or system.

PHOTOELECTRIC CELL A device whose electrical properties undergo a change when it is exposed to light.

PITOT TUBE A cylindrical tube with an open end pointed upstream, used in measuring impact pressure.

PNP TRANSISTOR Junction (bipolar) transistor whose end sections are composed of P-type material and whose center section is composed of N-type material. See JUNCTION TRANSISTOR.

POSITIONING ACTION Movement in which there is a predetermined relation between value of the controlled variable and position of a final control element.

POTENTIOMETER Measures by comparing the difference between known and unknown electrical potentials. In order to measure process control variables by means of a potentiometer, these variables, such as temperature, pressure, flow and liquid level, must first be translated into electrical signals that vary proportionally with changes in the variable.

POWER UNIT A portion of the controlling means which applies power for operating the final control element.

PRESSURE Force per unit area. Measured in pounds per square inch (psi), or by the height of a column of water or mercury which it will support (in feet, inches, or centimeters).

PRESSURE CAPSULE Two diaphragms, metallic or non-metallic, welded or otherwise joined together to form a sealed capsule which will deflect when subjected to pressure.

PRESSURE GAGE An indicating gage having a scale graduated to show pressure.

PRESSURE POTENTIOMETER A pressure transducer in which the electrical output is derived by varying the position of a contact arm along a resistance element.

PRESSURE SENSING ELEMENT The part of a pressure transducer which converts the measured pressure into a mechanical motion.

PRESSURE SPRING THERMOMETER A type of thermometer which employs a bulb connected by tubing to a hollow spring. As the temperature of the liquid within the system rises the spring tends to unwind, moving an indicator. Can be mercury, liquid, gas, or vapor-filled.

PRESSURE TRANSDUCER An instrument which converts a static or dynamic pressure input into a proportional electrical output.

PRIMARY ELEMENT   The portion of the measuring means which first either utilizes or transforms energy from the controlled medium to produce an effect in response to change in the value of the controlled variable. The effect produced by the primary element may be a change of pressure, force, position, electrical potential, or resistance.

PRIMARY MEASURING ELEMENT   A device or instrument which measures a variable. Primary measuring elements are used to convert a measurement to a signal for transmission to a controller, a recorder, or an indicator. Also known as detector, sensor or sensing element.

PROCESS   Comprises the collective functions performed in and by the equipment in which a variable is to be controlled.

PROGRAM CONTROL   A control system in which the set point is automatically varied during definite time intervals in order to make the process variable vary according to some prescribed manner.

PROPORTIONAL ACTION   Produces an output signal proportional to the magnitude of the input signal. In a control system proportional action produces a value correction proportional to the deviation of the controlled variable from set point.

PROPORTIONAL BAND   The amount of deviation of the controlled variable from set point required to move the final control element through the full range (expressed in % of span). An expression of gain of an instrument (the wider the band, the lower the gain).

PROPORTIONAL + DERIVATIVE ACTION   Proportional-position action and derivative action are combined.

PROPORTIONAL + RESET ACTION   Proportional-position action and propor-

tional-speed floating action are combined.

PROPORTIONAL + RESET + RATE ACTION   Proportional-position action, proportional-speed floating action, and rate action are combined.

P-TYPE MATERIAL   Semiconductor material to which an "acceptor" impurity is added, resulting in a quantity of "holes" or positive charges.

PURGE PRESSURE   A large, constant pressure introduced into the process pressure line to increase the pressure level and accentuate low process pressure changes.

PURGING   Elimination of an undesirable gas or material from an enclosure by means of displacing the undesirable material with an acceptable gas or material.

PYROMETER   An instrument for measuring temperature. Usually refers to temperature measuring instruments used to measure "flame temperature" or temperatures above 1000° F.

R

RADIATION PYROMETER   A pyrometer in which the radiant power from the object or source to be measured is used in the measurement of its temperature. The radiant power within wide or narrow wavelength bands filling a definite solid angle impinges upon a suitable detector. The detector is usually a thermocouple or thermopile, a bolometer responsive to the heating effect of the radiant power, or a photo-sensitive device connected to a sensitive electrical instrument.

RANGE   The difference between the maximum and minimum values of physical output over which an instrument is designed to operate normally.

RANGEABILITY   Describes the relationship between the range and the minimum quantity that can be measured.

RATE ACTION   A control action which

produces a corrective signal proportional to the rate at which the controlled variable is changing. Rate action produces a faster corrective action than proportional action alone. Also called derivative action.

RATE TIME   Amount of time (expressed in minutes) by which proportional action is advanced by the addition of rate action.

RATIO CONTROL   Maintains the magnitude of a controlled variable at a fixed ratio to another variable.

REACTANCE   The component of the impedance of an electrical circuit, not due to resistance, which opposes the flow of alternating current. The reactance is the algebraic sum of that due to inductance in the circuit with value in ohms equal to the product 2π, the frequency in cycles, and the inductance in henrys and that due to capacitance in the circuit with a value in ohms equal to the reciprocal of the product 2π, the frequency in cycles, and the capacitance in farads.

RECORDED VALUE   The value recorded by the marking device on the chart, with reference to the division lines marked on the chart.

RECTIFIER   A device which is used for converting an alternating current into a continuous or direct current by permitting the passage of current in only one direction.

REFERENCE JUNCTION   The junction of a thermocouple which is at a known or reference temperature.

RELAY   A device which enables the energy in one circuit (generally of high power) to be controlled by the energy in another.

RELAY-OPERATED CONTROLLER   One in which the energy transmitted through the primary element is either supplemented or amplified for operating the final control element by employing energy from another source.

REPRODUCIBILITY   The ability of an instrument to duplicate with exactness measurements of a given value. Usually expressed as a % of span of the instrument. Also referred to as repeatability.

RESET ACTION   A control action which produces a corrective signal proportional to the length of time the controlled variable has been away from the set point. Takes care of load changes. Also called integral action.

RESET RATE   "Repeats per minute." Expresses the number of times proportional response is repeated or duplicated in one minute.

RESISTANCE   Property that impedes flow or motion of a quantity. As applied to electrical circuits, resistance is a property that impedes the flow of electricity.

RESISTANCE THERMOMETER   An instrument which measures temperature by measuring the varying resistance of a sensing element whose resistance varies with temperature.

RESISTANCE THERMOMETER ELEMENT The temperature-sensitive unit of a resistance-thermometer bulb comprising a material whose electrical resistance changes with temperature, its supporting structure, and means for attaching conductors.

RESISTIVITY   The resistance of a material expressed in ohms per unit length and unit cross section.

RESISTOR   A device which conducts electricity but converts part of the electrical energy into heat.

RHEOSTAT   A resistor which is provided with means for readily adjusting its resistance.

REVERSE BIAS   State where a diode or transistor is so connected in a circuit that no current can flow through the component.

S

SAMPLING ACTION   Occurs when the difference between set point and the value of the controlled variable is measured and correction made at intermittent intervals.

SCANNER   An instrument which automatically checks a number of measuring points for the purpose of collecting information. A monitor is an instrument which automatically *scans* a number of measuring points and indicates which have wandered too far from the desired values.

SCREEN GRID   A grid placed between a control grid and an anode, usually maintained at a fixed positive potential, for the purpose of reducing the electrostatic influence of the anode in the space between the screen grid and the cathode.

SECONDARY CHAMBER   A seat or socket for an industrial thermometer which permits safe, convenient replacement or removal without disturbing the process pipeline.

SECONDARY WINDING   A winding on the output side.

SEEBECK EFFECT   Current will flow through a thermocouple loop formed of two dissimilar wires, provided the two junctions are at different temperatures.

SELF-OPERATED CONTROLLER   One in which all the energy necessary to operate the final control element is derived from the controlled medium through the primary element. This type of automatic controller must have both self-operated measuring means and self-operated controlling means.

SELF-OPERATED MEASURING MEANS   Where all the energy necessary to actuate the controlling means of an automatic controller is derived from the controlled medium through the primary element.

SELF-REGULATION   A property of a process or instrument by which, in the absence of control, equilibrium is reached after a disturbance.

SEMICONDUCTOR   Material such as silicon or germanium which has a greater resistance to current flow than a conductor, but not as great a resistance as an insulator.

SENSING ELEMENT   The part of a transducer mechanism which is in contact with the medium being measured and which responds to changes in the medium.

SENSITIVITY   (1) Ratio of change of output to change of input. (2) The least signal input capable of causing an output signal having desired characteristics.

SEPARABLE SOCKET   See SECONDARY CHAMBER.

SERVO-MECHANISM   A closed loop system in which the error or deviation from a desired or preset norm is automatically corrected to zero, and in which mechanical position is usually the controlled variable.

SET POINT   The position to which the control point setting mechanism is set, which is the same as the desired value of the controlled variable.

SIGNAL   Information conveyed from one point in a transmission or control system to another. Signal changes usually call for action or movement.

SINE WAVE   A wave made up of instantaneous values which are the product of a constant and the sine of an angle having values varying linearly.

SINUSOIDAL VIBRATION   A cyclical motion in which the object moves linearly. The instantaneous position is a sinusoidal function of time.

SLIDEWIRE   An electrical resistor used with a contacting slider which permits resistance adjustment.

SOLENOID MAGNET   An electromagnet having an energizing coil approximately cylindrical in form and an armature whose motion is reciprocal within and along the axis of the coil.

SOURCE   Main terminal of a field effect (unipolar) transistor. See FIELD EFFECT TRANSISTOR.

SPAN   The difference between the top and bottom scale values of an instrument. On instruments starting at zero, the span is equal to the range.

SPECIFIC HEAT   The ratio of the thermal capacity of any substance to the thermal capacity of water is called the specific heat of that substance.

SQUARE ROOT EXTRACTION   The electrical, mechanical, or pneumatic process whereby the square root of a measurement is derived. In flow measurement, for example, the square root of differential pressure equals flow.

STABILITY   Freedom from undesirable deviation; a measure of the controllability of a process.

STANDARD CELL   A cell which serves as a standard of electromotive force.

STEFAN-BOLTZMANN LAW   States that the thermal energy radiated per second per unit area from a black body (ideal radiator) is proportional to its absolute temperature raised to the fourth power.

STRAIN GAGE   An element (wire) which measures a force by using the principle that electrical resistance varies in proportion to tension or compression applied to the element.

STRIP CHART   A recording instrument chart made in the form of a long strip of paper.

SUPPRESSED RANGE   A suppressed range is an instrument range which does not include zero. The degree of suppression is expressed by the ratio of the value at the lower end of the scale to the span.

SYSTEMS ENGINEERING   Control engineering in which a process and all the elements affecting a process and all the possibilities for introducing automatic controls are considered during the design and installation of processing equipment.

T

TELEMETERING   Transmission of measurements over very long distances, usually by electrical means.

TEMPERATURE   The relative hotness or coldness of a body as determined by its ability to transfer heat to its surroundings. There is a temperature difference between two bodies if, when they are placed in thermal contact, heat is transferred from one body to the other. The body which loses heat is said to be at the higher temperature.

TEMPERATURE, CENTIGRADE   A temperature scale in which the freezing point of water is 0° and the boiling point is 100°.

TEMPERATURE, FAHRENHEIT   A temperature scale in which the freezing point of water is 32° and the boiling point is 212°.

TEMPERATURE, KELVIN   A temperature scale based on the laws of thermodynamics and known as a thermodynamic scale. On this scale the ice point and the steam point are separated by 100 degrees. The zero of this scale is the absolute zero, which is approximately 273.6° Kelvin below the ice point.

TEMPERATURE, RANKINE   A temperature scale based on absolute zero of the Fahrenheit scale, in which the freezing and boiling points of water are separated by 180 degrees. The ice point is approximately 459.69° Rankine.

THERMAL CAPACITY   The amount of heat required to raise the temperature of one pound of any substance one degree Fahrenheit.

THERMIONIC TUBE   An electron tube in which one of the electrodes is heated for the purpose of causing electron or ion emission from that electrode.

THERMISTOR   A resistor whose resistance varies with temperature in a definite desired manner. Used in circuits to compensate for temperature variation, to measure temperature, or as a nonlinear circuit element.

THERMOCOUPLE   A pair of dissimilar conductors so joined that an electromotive force is developed by the thermoelectric effects when the two junctions are at different temperatures.

THERMOCOUPLE WELL   Device used for protecting thermocouples by eliminating direct contact of the thermocouple with possibly corrosive substances being measured.

THERMOCOUPLE PROTECTING TUBE   See THERMOCOUPLE WELL.

THERMOMETER TIME CONSTANT   The time required for a thermometer to reach 63.2% of its final reading.

THERMOPILE   A group of thermocouples connected in series. This term is usually applied to a device either to measure radiant power or as a source of electric energy.

THOMPSON EFFECT   If there is a temperature gradient along a current carrying conductor, heat will be liberated or absorbed at any point where current and heat flow in the same direction, depending on the type of metal used as a conductor.

TRANSDUCER   An electro-mechanical device which converts a physical quantity being measured (such as temperature or pressure) to a proportional electrical output.

TRANSISTOR   A tiny semi-conductor amplifying device which performs the same functions as a vacuum tube.

TRIODE   A three-electrode electron tube containing an anode, a cathode, and a control electrode.

TWO-POSITION ACTION   Action in which a final control element is moved from one of two fixed positions to the other. ("Open and shut action," and "ON-OFF action" are synonymous terms.)

V

VARIABLE   A process condition, such as pressure, temperature, flow, or level, which is susceptible to change and which can be measured, altered, and controlled.

VENA CONTRACTA   The smallest cross section of a fluid jet which issues from a freely discharging aperture or is formed within the body of a pipe owing to the presence of a constriction.

VENTURI TUBE   A short tube of varying cross section. The flow through the Venturi tube causes a pressure drop in the smallest section, the amount of the drop being a junction of the velocity of flow.

VOLTAGE DIVIDER   A network consisting of impedance elements connected in series to which a voltage is applied and from which one or more voltages can be obtained across any portion of the network.

VOLTMETER   An instrument having circuits so designed that the magnitude either of voltage or of current can be measured on a scale calibrated in terms of each of these quantities.

W

WHEATSTONE BRIDGE   A four-arm bridge, all arms of which are predominately resistive.

Z

ZERO SHIFT   (zero error) The output error, expressed as a % of span, at zero input.

Appendix 2 _____ Data

DENSITY AND SPECIFIC GRAVITY OF SOME LIQUIDS*

LIQUID	DENSITY (POUNDS PER CUBIC FOOT)	SPECIFIC GRAVITY (GRAMS PER CUBIC CENTIMETER)	TEMP. (°C)
ALCOHOL (ETHYL)	49.4	0.791	20
CARBOLIC ACID	59.2 to 60.2	.950 to .965	15
GASOLINE	41.0 to 43.0	.66 to .69	..
GLYCERIN	78.6	1.260	0
KEROSENE	51.2	.82	..
MERCURY	849.0	13.6	..
MILK	1.028 to 1.035	64.2 to 64.6	..
OILS:			
CASTOR	60.5	.969	15
COCOANUT	57.7	.925	15
COTTON SEED	57.8	.926	16
OLIVE	57.3	.918	15
SEA WATER	63.99	1.025	15
TURPENTINE	54.3	.87	..
WATER	1.00	62.43	4

*Selected from Smithsonian Tables.

TABLE NO. 2

DENSITY AND SPECIFIC GRAVITY OF SOME GASES USED INDUSTRIALLY

GAS	DENSITY (IN POUNDS PER CUBIC FOOT AT 32°F AT 14.7 POUNDS PER SQUARE INCH)	SPECIFIC GRAVITY (AIR = 1 AT 710 mm)
ACETYLENE	0.073	0.91
AIR	.081	1.00
AMMONIA	.048	0.60
BUTANE	.157	2.08
CARBON DIOXIDE	.123	1.53
CARBON MONOXIDE	.078	0.97
CHLORINE	.201	2.48
ETHANE	.084	1.05
GASOLINE VAPORS (OCTANE)	.290	3.86
HELIUM	.011	0.14
HYDROGEN	.005	0.07
HYDROGEN SULFIDE	.096	1.19
ISOBUTANE	.167	2.06
METHANE (NATURAL GAS)	.045	0.55
NEON	.056	0.69
NITROGEN	.078	0.97
NITROGEN PEROXIDE	.128	1.71
OXYGEN	.089	1.11
PROPANE	.126	1.56
SULFUR DIOXIDE	.183	2.26
STEAM AT 180°F	.037	0.46

TABLE NO. 3

COMMON TEMPERATURE MEASURING DEVICES AND THEIR NAMES

— MEASURING INSTRUMENT

	RANGES (°F)
THERMOMETERS	
BIMETALLIC THERMOMETERS	-300 to + 800
MERCURY-IN-GLASS THERMOMETERS	- 38 to + 950
MERCURY-FILLED PRESSURE-SPRING THERMOMETERS	- 38 to + 1000
NITROGEN-FILLED PRESSURE-SPRING THERMOMETERS	-450 to + 1000
VAPOR-FILLED PRESSURE-SPRING THERMOMETERS	-300 to + 600
PLATINUM WIRE RESISTANCE THERMOMETERS	-400 to + 1000
NICKEL WIRE RESISTANCE THERMOMETERS	-250 to + 600
COPPER WIRE RESISTANCE THERMOMETERS	-328 to + 250

	RANGES (°F)
THERMOCOUPLES	
IRON-CONSTANTAN	0 to + 530
	+530 to + 1400
CHROMEL-ALUMEL	0 to + 530
	+530 to + 2300
PLATINUM/RHODIUM-PLATINUM	0 to + 1000
	+ 1000 to + 2700
COPPER-CONSTANTAN	-300 to - 150
	-150 to - 75
	- 75 to + 200
	+ 200 to + 700

	RANGES (°F)
PYROMETERS	
RADIATION PYROMETERS	0 to + 3150
OPTICAL PYROMETERS	+ 1200 to + 5000

TABLE NO. 4

EQUIVALENTS USED IN INSTRUMENTATION COMPUTATION	
1 inch	= 2.540 centimeters
1 foot	= 0.305 meters
1 yard	= 0.914 meters
1 centimeter	= 0.3937 inches
1 meter	= 3.280 feet
	= 1.0936 yards
1 cubic inch	= 16.387 cubic centimeters
1 cubic foot	= 7.481 gallons
1 cubic centimeter	= 0.061 cubic inches
1 cubic meter	= 35.314 cubic feet
1 gallon	= 0.1337 cubic feet
	= 3.785 liters
1 liter	= 0.2641 gallons
1 cubic foot of water	= 62.36 pounds
1 cubic foot of mercury	= 848.719 pounds
1 gallon of water	= 8.377 pounds
1 inch of water	= 0.0361 psi
	= 5.1972 pounds per square foot
	= 0.07348 inches of mercury
	= 0.5775 ounces per square inch
1 foot of water	= 0.4331 psi
	= 62.426 pounds per square foot
	= 0.8817 inches of mercury
	= 6.930 ounches per square inch
1 inch of mercury	= 0.4912 psi
	= 13.62 inches of water
	= 1.1309 feet of water
	= 7.8585 ounces per square inch
1 mm of mercury	= 0.01934 psi
	= 0.5358 inches of water
	= 0.0446 feet of water
	= 0.0394 inches of mercury
1 psi	= 27.707 inches of water
	= 2.309 feet of water
	= 2.036 inches of mercury
1 ounce per square inch	= 0.1272 inches of mercury
	= 1.7317 inches of water

All mercury equivalents based on 0°C or 32°F.

All water equivalents based on 60°F.

TABLE NO. 5

TABLE OF IRON PIPE SIZES

NOMINAL SIZE	PIPE O.D.	INSIDE DIAMETER		
		STANDARD	EXTRA HEAVY	DOUBLE EXTRA HEAVY
1/8	.405	.269	.215	
1/4	.540	.364	.302	
3/8	.675	.493	.423	
1/2	.840	.622	.546	.252
3/4	1.050	.824	.742	.434
1	1.315	1.049	.957	.599
1-1/4	1.660	1.380	1.278	.896
1-1/2	1.900	1.610	1.500	1.100
2	2.375	2.067	1.939	1.503

TABLE NO. 6 — TABLE OF TUBING SIZES

Tube O.D.		Tube I.D. Available				
1/8	Three sizes	.069	.061	.055		
3/16	Two sizes	.1235	.1175			
1/4	Five sizes	.180	.166	.152	.134	.120
5/16	Five sizes	.2425	.2285	.2145	.1965	.1825
3/8	Five sizes	.305	.291	.277	.259	.245
1/2	Eight sizes	.430 .370	.416 .356	.402 .334	.384 .310	
5/8	Eight sizes	.555 .495	.541 .481	.527 .459	.509 .435	
3/4	Seven sizes	.652 .584	.634 .560	.620 .532	.606	
7/8	Seven sizes	.777 .709	.759 .685	.745 .657	.731	
1	Eight sizes	.902 .834	.884 .810	.870 .782	.856 .760	
1 1/4	Eight sizes	1.152 1.084	1.134 1.060	1.120 1.032	1.106 1.010	
1 1/2	Seven sizes	1.370 1.282	1.356 1.260	1.334 1.232	1.310	
1 3/4	Seven sizes	1.620 1.532	1.606 1.510	1.584 1.482	1.560	
2	Seven sizes	1.870 1.782	1.856 1.760	1.834 1.732	1.810	

TABLE NO. 7

ALLOWANCE IN EQUIVALENT LENGTH OF PIPE FOR FRICTION LOSS IN VALVES AND THREADED FITTINGS*

KIND OF FITTING	EQUIVALENT LENGTH OF PIPE IN FEET FOR THE VARIOUS SIZE FITTINGS.						
	3/8"	1/2"	3/4"	1"	1 1/4"	1 1/2"	2"
90° STD. ELL	1.0	2.0	2.5	3.0	4.0	5.0	7.0
45° STD. ELL	.6	1.2	1.5	1.8	2.4	3.0	4.0
90° TEE	1.5	3.0	4.0	5.0	6.0	7.0	10.0
COUPLING	.3	.6	.8	.9	1.2	1.5	2.0
GATE VALVE	.2	.4	.5	.6	.8	1.0	1.3
GLOBE VALVE	8.0	15.0	20.0	25.0	35.0	45.0	55.0
ANGLE VALVE	4.0	8.0	12.0	15.0	18.0	22.0	28.0

*From National Bureau of Standards and National Plumbing Code.

Symbols

EVERY scientific and technical discipline develops a language of its own to convey information and ideas. This distinctive language includes not only the particularized use of words, but also consists of abbreviations and symbolic representations whose meanings are instantly comprehensible to anyone who pursues the specialized discipline in question.

For those who work in the field of instrumentation, the Instrument Society of America has prepared a report, entitled *Tentative Recommended Practice, Instrumentation Flow Plan Symbols, ISA RP5.1*, with the purpose of providing a satisfactory system of symbols and identifications for industrial process instrumentation equipment, designating and identifying such equipment on flow plans and in other requirements, and thus promoting a uniformity of practice to simplify and expedite instrumentation work. The material in this appendix is taken from ISA RP5.1.

Outline of System

General. Instruments and instrumentation items are identified and represented by a system of letters and numbers, together with a number of simple basic pictorial symbols for illustrating the items on flow plans and other drawings.

Identifications. The identification shall consist of a combination of letters used to establish the *general identity* of the item with its purpose and functions. For some requirements this will be sufficient and complete; but usually it will be followed by a number that will serve to establish the *specific identity* of the item. The identifications shall be used for the complete designation of the item in written work, and in combination with the pictorial symbol for representation on flow plans or other drawings.

General Identifications. The general identifications shall consist of letters as listed in Table No. 1, used

TABLE NO. 1
LETTERS OF IDENTIFICATION

DEFINITION, AND PERMISSIBLE POSITIONS
IN ANY COMBINATION

UPPER CASE LETTER	-FIRST LETTER- Process Variable or Actuation	-SECOND LETTER- Type Reading or Other Function	-THIRD LETTER- Additional Function
A	———	Alarm	Alarm
C	Conductivity	Control	Control
D	Density	———	———
E	———	Element (Primary)	———
F	Flow	———	———
G	———	Glass (No Measurement)	———
H	Hand (Actuated)	———	———
I	———	Indicating	———
L	Level	———	———
M	Moisture	———	———
P	Pressure	———	———
R	———	Recording (Recorder)	———
S	Speed	Safety	———
T	Temperature	———	———
V	Viscosity	———	Valve
W	Weight	Well	———

NOTE 1: When required the following may be used optionally as a first letter for other process variables:

    (1) "A" may be used to cover all types of analyzing instruments.

    (2) Readily recognized self-defining chemical symbols such as CO_2, O_2, etc. may be used for these specific analysis instruments.

    (3) The self-defining symbol "pH" may be used for Hydrogen ion concentration.

NOTE 2: Although not a preferred procedure, when considered necessary it is permissible to insert a lower case "r" after "F" to distinguish Flow Ratio. Likewise, lower case "d" may be inserted after "T" or "P" to distinguish Temperature Difference or Pressure Difference.

in combinations as shown in Table No. 2.

Table No. 1 covers the letters that may be employed, the definition or significance of each, and the permissible position or positions in which each may be used when combining.

Table No. 2 covers the permissible combinations of letters of identification and shows the significance of each such complete general identification.

In the use of the letters or their combinations, the following rules and instructions apply:

1. All identifying letters shall in all cases be written in UPPER CASE. The only exceptions are the *optional* use of "d" and "r," and the use of "p" in the combined first letter "pH"; as per footnotes of Tables No. 1 and No. 2.

TABLE NO. 2
COMPLETE GENERAL IDENTIFICATIONS
(COMBINATIONS OF LETTERS)

SECOND AND THIRD LETTERS (TYPE OF DEVICE)

SHADED IMPOSSIBLE COMBINATIONS

CONTROLLING DEVICES   MEASURING DEVICES   ALARM DEVICES

BLANK IMPROBABLE COMBINATIONS

Separate Controllers

PROCESS VARIABLE (Or Actuation)	FIRST LETTER	Recording -RC	Indicating -IC	Blind -C	Self-Actuated (Integral) Regulating Valves -CV	Safety (Relief) Valves -SV	Recording -R	Indicating -I	Glass Devices for Observation Only (No Measurement) -G	Recording -RA	Indicating -IA	Blind -A	Primary Element -E	Wells -W
Temperature	T-	TRC	TIC	TC	TCV	TSV	TR	TI	///	TRA	TIA	TA	TE	TW
Flow	F-	FRC	FIC				FR	FI	FG	FRA	FIA		FE	///
Level	L-	LRC	LIC	LC	LCV		LR	LI	LG	LRA	LIA	LA		///
Pressure	P-	PRC	PIC	PC	PCV	PSV	PR	PI	///	PRA	PIA	PA	PE	///
Density	D-	DRC	DIC	DC			DR	DI	///	DRA	DIA			///
Hand	H-		HIC	HC	HCV		///	///	///	///	///		///	///
Moisture	M-	MRC	MIC	MC			MR	MI	///	MRA	MIA	MA	ME	///
Conductivity	C-	CRC	CIC				CR	CI	///	CRA	CIA	CA	CE	///
Speed	S-	SRC	SIC	SC	SCV	SSV	SR	SI		SRA	SIA	SA		///
Viscosity	V-	VRC	VIC				VR	VI	VG	VRA	VIA			///
Weight	W-	WRC	WIC				WR	WI		WRA	WIA		WE	///

NOTE: The optional additional process variables given in footnotes of Table No. 1, when used, shall be combined with second and third letters as per above.

2. The *maximum* number of identifying letters in any combination shall be *three* (3). The only exception is in the use of "pH," or chemical symbols such as CO_2, where the self-defining pair is treated as a single letter.

3. A letter shall have only one definition or significance in its use as a "first" letter in any combination, to define the process variable.

4. A letter shall have only one defi-

nition or significance when used as *either* the "second" or the "third" letter in a combination, to define the type of device.

5. It is particularly important in writing the combinations of letters to adhere to the sequence of arrangement shown by Table No. 2.

6. No hyphens shall be used between letters or combinations of letters.

Specific Identifications. In most cases it will be necessary to supplement the general identification of an item by a numerical system, to establish its specific identity. Any system of item or serial numbers may be used, consistent with the requirements of the user. The numbers may pertain only to those items of the same kind within one process unit; or may be a complete serial number system for a plant or an organization. In any case, the series of consecutive numbers will be suitable for use with the general identifications.

When used in written work, the number shall be placed after the letters, and separated from them by a hyphen. For example, temperature recording controller, item number one (1), is written as TRC-1.

Applying the Identifications. The identifications, wherever possible, shall be used to identify a complete instrumentation application with all its components, rather than to as-sign independent identifications to the various pieces required. The rules and instructions for this principle of applying identifications are as follows:

1. For combination instruments that measure more than one kind of variable, or that provide more than one kind of function, each portion of the combination shall have its own identification. Components pertaining to such a portion shall be identified accordingly, and the instrument or equipment common to both shall utilize *both* identifications. For example, a combination recorder for flow and pressure would be PR-1 and FR-5.

2. Multiple pen or point instruments with all points of same general service, and all providing the same functions, shall have one identification. The separate elements and their components shall be identified by suffix numbers added to the number of the item: e.g., TR-1-1, TR-1-2, etc.

3. For remote transmission instruments both the receiver and the transmitter shall have the same identifications, in agreement with the overall service and function of the item.

4. Each control valve shall have

the same identification as the control instrument by which it is actuated. Where more than one valve is actuated by the same controller, they shall be identified by suffix letters added to the *number* of the item: e.g., TRC-1a, TRC-1b, etc.

5. Where accessories such as valve positioners, air sets, switches, relays, etc., require identification, they shall be assigned the same identification as the instrument to which they connect or with which they are used.

6. Primary measuring elements shall be assigned the same identifications as the instruments to which they connect. Where an element does not connect to any instrument, such isolated item (only) shall be assigned separate Primary Element identification. Where more than one element connects to the same instrument, they shall be identified by suffix numbers after the item number, in agreement with the point numbers of the instrument to which they connect.

Symbols. The symbols to be used to show instrumentation on flow plans and other drawings are illustrated on pages 268 to 274 inclusive. Page 268 covers the basic pictorial symbols required. The remainder of the pages show typical symbols, complete with identifications, covering the different process variables and types of equipment that

are most likely to be encountered. All others shall be drawn by use of the basic pictorial symbols shown on page 268 with the proper identifications. The following notes pertain to the use of the symbols:

1. The circle, generally approximately $7/16$ inches in diameter, is used to depict instruments proper and most other instrumentation items. It is also used as a "flag" to enclose identifications and point out items such as valves which have their own pictorial symbol. Optionally such items may have their identification written alongside the pictorial symbol, and the circle for "flagging" omitted.

2. It is generally unnecessary to repeat the identification for transmitter, control valve, primary element, etc., as they are determined by their connection to the instrument proper. Where such components are shown at a remote distance or on a separate sheet, a note of identification may be added alongside the pictorial or connecting line symbol.

3. A brief explanatory notation may be added alongside a symbol if considered necessary to clarify the function or purpose of an item. A few such notes are easier to apply and use than a great variety of more complicated symbols.

BASIC INSTRUMENTATION SYMBOLS

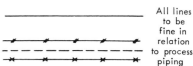

INSTRUMENT PROCESS PIPING (Pressure, Differential, Etc., Connecting Lead Lines: Also Hydraulic Actuating Medium Lines

INSTRUMENT AIR LINES

INSTRUMENT ELECTRICAL LEADS

INSTRUMENT CAPILLARY TUBING

All lines to be fine in relation to process piping

Locally Mounted   Board Mounted

BASIC SYMBOLS FOR INSTRUMENT WITH SINGLE SERVICE AND FUNCTION

Locally Mounted   Board Mounted

BASIC SYMBOLS FOR COMBINATION INSTRUMENT OR DEVICE WITH TWO SERVICES OR FUNCTIONS

Locally Mounted   Board Mounted

BASIC SYMBOLS FOR TRANSMITTER

BASIC SYMBOL FOR DIAPHRAGM MOTOR VALVE

BASIC SYMBOL FOR ELECTRICALLY OPERATED VALVE (SOLENOID OR MOTOR)

BASIC SYMBOL FOR PISTON- OPERATED VALVE (HYDRAULIC OR PNEUMATIC)

3-WAY BODY FOR ANY VALVE

BASIC SYMBOL FOR SAFETY (RELIEF) VALVE

BASIC SYMBOL FOR SELF-ACTUATED (INTEGRAL) REGULATING VALVE

BASIC SYMBOL FOR MANUALLY OPERATED CONTROL VALVE

BASIC SYMBOL SHOWING PNEUMATIC TRANSMISSION INSTRUMENT (ELECTRIC TRANSMISSION SAME EXCEPT FOR TYPE OF CONNECTION)

BASIC SYMBOL SHOWING PNEUMATIC CONNECTION FROM INSTRUMENT TO DIAPHRAGM MOTOR VALVE

TYPICAL INSTRUMENTATION SYMBOLS FOR FLOW

DISPLACEMENT
TYPE FLOW METER

FLOW ELEMENT (PRIMARY)
(When no measuring
instrument is provided)

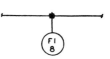

FLOW INDICATOR
DIFFERENTIAL TYPE
LOCALLY MOUNTED

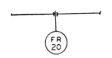

FLOW RECORDER,
DIFFERENTIAL TYPE,
MECHANICAL TRANSMISSION,
LOCALLY MOUNTED

FLOW RECORDER,
OF ROTAMETER
OR OTHER
IN-THE-LINE TYPE

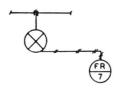

FLOW RECORDER,
PNEUMATIC TRANSMISSION,
TRANSMITTER LOCAL,
RECEIVER MOUNTED ON BOARD

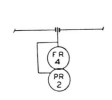

FLOW RECORDER, MECHANICAL
TYPE, WITH DIRECT CONNECTED
PRESSURE RECORDING PEN,
LOCALLY MOUNTED

(Note that in listing such a combination item in specifications, etc., it
would be written as FR-4 and PR-2,
thereby treating each element as
separate entity)

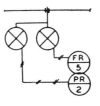

FLOW RECORDER WITH
PRESSURE RECORDING PEN,
BOTH ELEMENTS PNEUMATIC
TRANSMISSION,
TRANSMITTERS LOCAL, AND
RECEIVER BOARD MOUNTED
(Receiver should be written as
FR-5 and PR-2, and each trans-
mitter identified by its own ele-
ment)

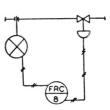

FLOW RECORDING
CONTROLLER,
PNEUMATIC
TRANSMISSION
WITH RECEIVER
MOUNTED ON BOARD
AND LOCAL
TRANSMITTER

TYPICAL INSTRUMENTATION SYMBOLS FOR TEMPERATURE

TEMPERATURE WELL

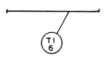

TEMPERATURE INDICATOR
OR THERMOMETER (LOCAL)

TEMPERATURE ELEMENT
WITHOUT CONNECTION
TO INSTRUMENT

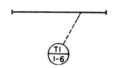

TEMPERATURE INDICATING
POINT CONNECTED TO
MULTIPOINT INDICATOR
ON BOARD

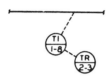

TEMPERATURE INDICATING
AND RECORDING POINT
CONNECTED TO MULTIPOINT
INSTRUMENTS ON BOARD

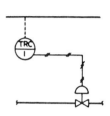

TEMPERATURE RECORDING
CONTROLLER, BOARD
MOUNTED (ELECTRIC
MEASUREMENT)

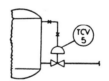

TEMPERATURE CONTROLLER
OF SELF-ACTUATED TYPE

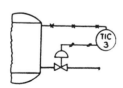

TEMPERATURE INDICATING
CONTROLLER, FILLED
SYSTEM TYPE,
LOCALLY MOUNTED

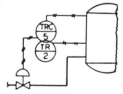

TEMPERATURE RECORDING
CONTROLLER AND TEMPERATURE
RECORDER, COMBINED
INSTRUMENT BOARD MOUNTED

TYPICAL INSTRUMENTATION SYMBOLS FOR LEVEL

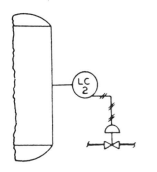

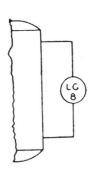

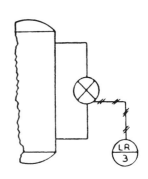

BLIND LEVEL CONTROLLER,
INTERNAL TYPE

GAGE GLASS

LEVEL RECORDER, PNEUMATIC
TRANSMISSION, WITH BOARD
MOUNTED RECEIVER
EXTERNAL TYPE TRANSMITTER

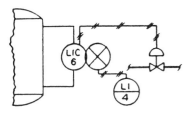

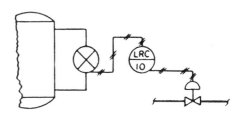

LEVEL INDICATING CONTROLLER
AND TRANSMITTER COMBINED
WITH BOARD MOUNTED LEVEL
INDICATING RECEIVER

LEVEL RECORDING CONTROLLER
EXTERNAL TYPE
PNEUMATIC TRANSMISSION

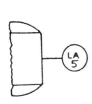

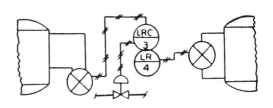

LEVEL ALARM
INTERNAL TYPE

LEVEL RECORDING CONTROLLER AND LEVEL
RECORDER, PNEUMATIC TRANSMISSION
COMBINED RECEIVER BOARD MOUNTED

TYPICAL INSTRUMENTATION SYMBOLS FOR PRESSURE

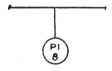

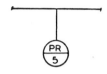

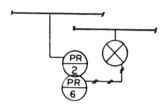

PRESSURE INDICATOR
LOCALLY MOUNTED

PRESSURE RECORDER
BOARD MOUNTED

2-PEN PRESSURE RECORDER,
BOARD MOUNTED, 1-PEN
PNEUMATIC TRANSMISSION

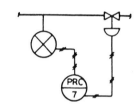

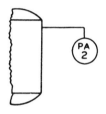

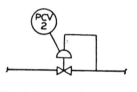

PRESSURE RECORDING
CONTROLLER, PNEUMATIC
TRANSMISSION, WITH
BOARD MOUNTED RECEIVER

PRESSURE
ALARM
LOCAL

SELF-ACTUATED (INTEGRAL)
PRESSURE REGULATING VALVE

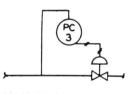

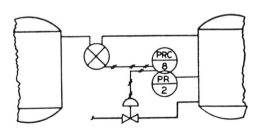

PRESSURE CONTROLLER,
BLIND TYPE
(Show controller directly
above diaphragm if so
mounted)

PRESSURE RECORDING CONTROLLER (DIFFERENTIAL),
PNEUMATIC TRANSMISSION; WITH PRESSURE RECORDER,
COMBINED INSTRUMENT BOARD MOUNTED

TYPICAL INSTRUMENTATION SYMBOLS (MISCELLANEOUS)

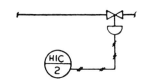

HAND ACTUATED PNEUMATIC
CONTROLLER, BOARD MOUNTED,
WITH INDICATION

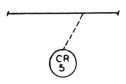

CONDUCTIVITY RECORDER,
LOCALLY MOUNTED

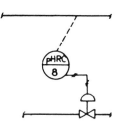

ph RECORDING
CONTROLLER,
BOARD MOUNTED

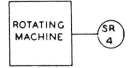

SPEED RECORDER,
LOCALLY MOUNTED

WEIGHT RECORDER,
LOCALLY MOUNTED

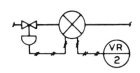

VISCOSITY RECORDER,
PNEUMATIC TRANSMISSION,
BOARD MOUNTED
(Element in sample flow line)

DENSITY CONTROLLER
BLIND, INTERNAL
ELEMENT TYPE

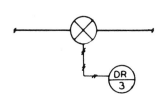

DENSITY RECORDER,
PNEUMATIC TRANSMISSION,
BOARD MOUNTED
(Element in sample flow line)

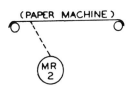

MOISTURE RECORDER,
LOCALLY MOUNTED

TYPICAL INSTRUMENTATION SYMBOLS FOR

COMBINED INSTRUMENTS

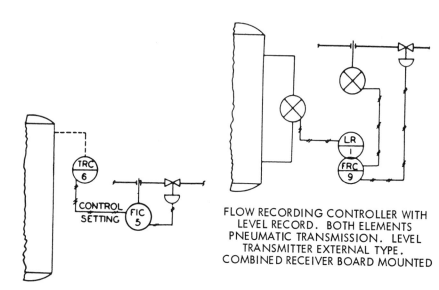

FLOW RECORDING CONTROLLER WITH
LEVEL RECORD. BOTH ELEMENTS
PNEUMATIC TRANSMISSION. LEVEL
TRANSMITTER EXTERNAL TYPE.
COMBINED RECEIVER BOARD MOUNTED

TEMPERATURE RECORDING CONTROLLER,
BOARD MOUNTED, RESETTING LOCALLY
MOUNTED FLOW INDICATING CONTROLLER
(Note that "Control Setting" should be shown
alongside air line to indicate cascade control)

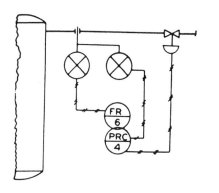

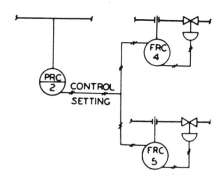

PRESSURE RECORDING CONTROLLER WITH
FLOW RECORD. BOTH ELEMENTS
PENUMATIC TRANSMISSION. COMBINED
RECEIVER BOARD MOUNTED

PRESSURE RECORDING CONTROLLER,
BOARD MOUNTED, RESETTING
LOCALLY MOUNTED FLOW
RECORDING CONTROLLERS

ELECTRICAL SYMBOLS

In addition to the symbols specifically related to instrumentation, the student should also possess a working knowledge of other graphical representations in fields related to instrumentation, particularly the symbols used to convey information about electricity and electronics. A selection of electrical symbols follows.

ADJUSTABLE, CONTINUOUSLY arrow is drawn at about 45 degrees across the symbol	**CONNECTION, MECHANICAL**
ALTERNATING CURRENT SOURCE	**CORE** no symbol indicates air core iron core
BATTERY single cell multicell	**CRYSTAL, PIEZOELECTRIC**
CAPACITOR fixed variable	**FUSE** or
	GROUND used for either ground to earth or chassis
COIL, INDUCTANCE or air core or magnetic core adjustable variable	**INSTRUMENT** * *appropriate letter symbol is placed in circle A—ammeter OHM—ohmmeter G—galvanometer V—voltmeter MA—milliammeter W—wattmeter

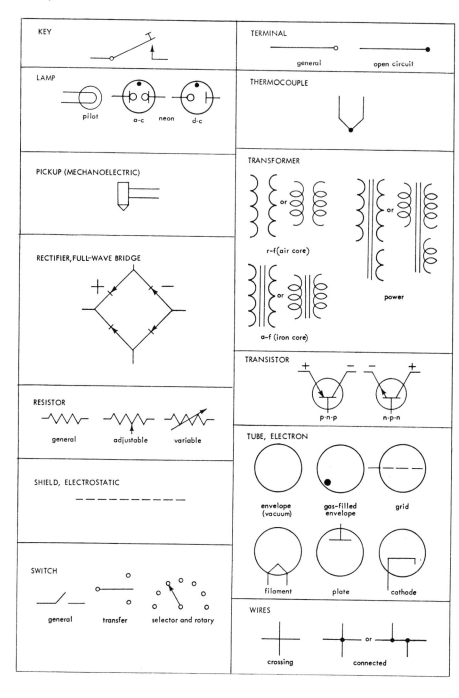

SYMBOL	OBJECT	SYMBOL	OBJECT
○ OR ● (A) TERMINAL STUD (B) PUSH-BUTTON CONTACT		GROUND	
OR FIXED RESISTOR		FIXED CAPACITOR	
OR ADJUSTABLE RESISTOR		FIXED CAPACITOR, SHIELDED	
OR TAPPED RESISTOR		ADJUSTABLE CAPACITOR	
OR VARIABLE RESISTOR		VARIABLE CAPACITOR	
RHEOSTAT		VARIABLE CAPACITOR WITH MOVING PLATE INDICATED	
CONDUCTOR		VARIABLE CAPACITOR, SHIELDED	

Resistor and Capacitor Symbols

SYMBOL	OBJECT	SYMBOL	OBJECT
CONDUCTOR CROSSING		CONDUCTOR CONNECTIONS	
CONTACTS-N.O. (NORMALLY OPEN)		CONTACTS-NC (NORMALLY CLOSED)	
PUSH BUTTON-N.O. (SPRING RETURN)		PUSH BUTTON-NC (SPRING RETURN)	
PUSH BUTTON OPEN AND CLOSED (SPRING RETURN)		NO SYMBOL MULTIPOSITION SWITCH (MASTER-DRUM SELECTOR SWITCH)	
PUSH BUTTON OPEN AND CLOSED (MAINTAIN CONTACT)		DISCONNECT DEVICE (COUPLING OR PLUG TYPE CONTACT)	

Contact and Push-Button Symbols

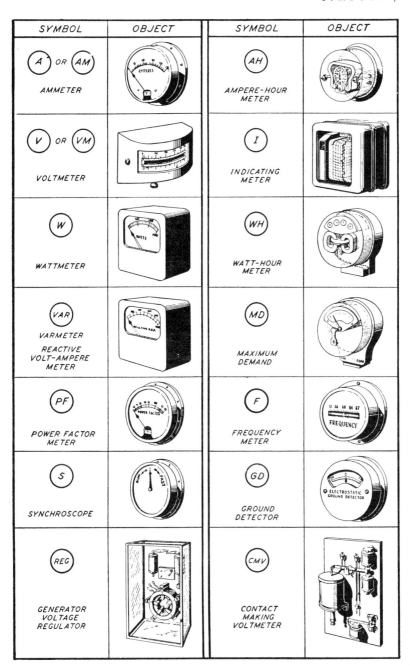

SYMBOL	OBJECT	SYMBOL	OBJECT
(A) OR (AM) AMMETER		(AH) AMPERE-HOUR METER	
(V) OR (VM) VOLTMETER		(I) INDICATING METER	
(W) WATTMETER		(WH) WATT-HOUR METER	
(VAR) VARMETER REACTIVE VOLT-AMPERE METER		(MD) MAXIMUM DEMAND	
(PF) POWER FACTOR METER		(F) FREQUENCY METER	
(S) SYNCHROSCOPE		(GD) GROUND DETECTOR	
(REG) GENERATOR VOLTAGE REGULATOR		(CMV) CONTACT MAKING VOLTMETER	

Electrical Instrument Symbols

Questions

Chapter 1

1. When applied to process instrumentation what does the term "control system" mean?
2. Define the terms:
   Measured variable
   Manipulated variable
3. How is the accuracy of a measuring instrument generally stated?
4. In a controlling instrument, *drift* is the gradual shift in the value of the output signal over an extended period of time, during which the input signal remains unchanged. What characteristic of the controlling instrument is affected by drift?
5. Is it correct to state "the smaller the dead zone of an instrument, the more sensitive it is"?
6. Explain the difference between lag and dead time of either a measuring or controlling instrument.
7. What is meant by the term "dynamic error"?

Chapter 2
TEMPERATURE

1. What is the difference between heat and temperature?
2. State the three methods by which heat is transferred.
3. Name the four principal temperature scales.
4. Convert the following Fahrenheit temperatures to centigrade values: $-40°F$, $+41°F$, $+176°F$, $255°F$.
5. Give the Absolute Zero Temperature values on all four temperature scales.
6. What causes the mercury in a

glass thermometer to rise up the tube when the thermometer bulb is subjected to heat?

7. How would you check to determine whether or not a bimetal thermometer is still accurate after being subjected to too high temperature?

8. Name the three types of pressure spring thermometers and state their useful ranges.

9. What are the two devices used to measure temperature electrically? Which one requires a source of power for its operation?

10. If it was required to measure a temperature at one point and have an indication 500 feet away, how would you do it?

Chapter 3
PRESSURE

1. Express the following pressures in inches of water: .7 psi, 3 psi, 14.7 psi.

2. Express the following pressures in inches of mercury: 14.7 psi, 75 psi, 133 psi.

3. Why is a manometer called a "primary pressure standard?"

4. Which types of elastic deformation pressure elements would you expect to find in gages for the following ranges: a) 0 to 1 psi, b) 0 to 10 psi, c) 0 to 1000 psi.

5. If a pressure of 60 psi is applied to one side of a mercury manometer and a pressure of 80 psi to the other side, what would be the resultant difference in the height of the columns?

6. If there was a possibility that one of the two pressures used in prob-

lem 5 would suddenly drop to 0, should a U-tube manometer be used? If not, what type of differential pressure measuring device would be a better choice?

7. In a bell type manometer, if the fluids whose pressures are being measured contained oil, would oil be a good sealing fluid? If not, why not?

8. Is the weight-balance differential pressure meter a form of manometer?

9. How would you measure differential pressure if only single pressure instruments were available?

10. If it were necessary to measure a differential pressure at one location and have an indication 100 feet away, how would you do it?

Chapter 4
LEVEL

1. What is the difference between a *direct* and an *indirect* level measuring device?

2. How would you measure the level of water in a shallow well?

3. What is the name of the force

which acts upon floats and displacer elements?

4. If a pressure gage mounted at the base of an open water tank indicates a pressure of 5 psi, how many feet of water are there above the pressure gage connection?

5. What is the difference in operation between the air trap and the diaphragm box?

6. In a bubbler system level measuring installation, what air pressure would be required if the maximum level to be measured is 40 feet?

7. When installing a differential pressure type liquid level meter on a pressure tank, where should the high pressure and low pressure sides of the meter be connected?

8. How would you measure the bin level of iron ore which is magnetic and very abrasive?

Chapter 5
FLOW

1. What are the two flow measurements and what is the difference between them?

2. Name the three principal primary flow elements used with differential pressure flowmeters.

3. a) Which of these primary elements is described as concentric, eccentric, or segmental?
   b) Name the three types of flow-metering pressure taps and describe the difference in their installation.

4. What is the relationship between flow rate and differential pressure?

5. Why is a rotameter called a vari-able-area flowmeter?

6. a) Describe the primary elements used for measuring flow rate in open channels.
   b) How is the actual flow measurement made with these elements?

7. How is the average flow rate measured using a positive displacement type flowmeter?

8. What is a compound flowmeter?

9. A flow integrator is a calculator— what calculation does it perform?

10. What is meant by the terms "intermittent flow integrator" and "continuous flow integrator"?

Chapter 6
HUMIDITY

1. State the two terms used to describe humidity measurement. How do these measurements differ?

2. What does a psychrometric chart describe?

3. Define the term "dew point."

4. What is the function of the hy-

groscopic coating used on a dew point element?

5. How does a hygrometer differ from a psychrometer?

6. Describe a sling psychrometer.

7. What are the operating temperature limits of a psychrometer?

8. Name some processes which might require moisture measurement.

9. Is a resistance type moisture meter usually used for measuring the moisture of plaster board suitable for use with plywood without change? If not, why not, and what change must be made?

10. A capacitance type moisture meter registers the difference in the dielectric quality of a material. What does this mean?

Chapter 7
TRANSMISSION

1. What is a transducer ?

2. Name the three required components of a pneumatic transmission system.

3. What is the function of the restriction in the pneumatic transmitter?

4. Describe the function of the sensing and the amplifier section of a typical pneumatic transmitter.

5. List several electrical characteristics which are used for the transmission of such measurements as temperature, pressure, level, and flow.

6. Is a resistance temperature bulb a transducer?

7. Why is an electrical resistance type transmission system limited as to the distance over which it can be used?

8. How does an electrical inductance type transmitter produce varying signals?

9. What is meant by the term "time impulse transmitter?"

10. Which method would you select if you wished to measure a flow rate at one point and transmit it over the following distances: a) 300 feet, b) 300 yards, c) 300 miles?

Chapter 8
CONTROL

1. Describe the four elements essential to a control system.

2. When these four elements are all found in one device what is the resultant controller called?

3. List the four common automatic

actions. Describe their differences.

4. What is meant by the term "feedback" when applied to a controller?

5. In a pneumatic flapper-nozzle

type controller where does the change in the signal to the final element actually take place?

6. What is the name of the adjustment which regulates the amount of departure from set point which causes total motion of the final element?

7. In the pneumatic flapper-nozzle controller described in this text automatic reset action takes place only when the proportional and reset bellows are not in balance. What causes this unbalance?

8. Rate action, when applied to the pneumatic controller, delays the corrective motion of the proportional bellows. What effect does this have on the action of the final element?

9. Define a) load change, b) lag.

10. If a process reacts very quickly to an energy change but there is a possibility of large and prolonged load changes, what control action would you select?

11. What is the meaning of the term "gain control" when referring to an electrical controller?

12. How is automatic reset control accomplished in an electrical control system employing a measurement slidewire and a control slidewire?

13. How would the proportional band adjustment be made on an electric temperature controller which varies the Time ON-Time OFF ratio of electric heaters?

14. The spring force on a diaphragm control valve is adjustable, resulting in changing the air pressure for each valve position. Is this a reset adjustment?

15. What is the principal function of a pneumatic valve positioner?

Chapter 9
ELECTRICITY

1. Define:
   Voltage
   Current
   Resistance

2. List three characteristics of series resistance circuits.

3. List three characteristics of parallel resistance circuits.

4. Draw a sketch of a resistance network using two voltage sources, three resistances in series, and two resistances in parallel with those in series.

5. Electrical resistance refers to the resistance to current flow. What does inductance resist?

6. a) Describe the two types of inductance.
   b) What is the unit of measurement of inductance?

7. Electrical resistance refers to the resistance to current flow. What does capacitance resist?

8. What is the time-constant of a capacitor? How can it be determined?

9. Batteries, photocells and thermocouples produce voltages for di-

rect current systems; what device is used to produce voltage for alternating current systems?

10. What are the positive or negative half cycles of alternating current called?

11. In an alternating current circuit, with a particular inductance the ratio of voltage to current is constant when the voltage is constant. What other electrical characteristic is determined by the voltage/current ratio?

12. Why does the current through a capacitor in an alternating current circuit lead the voltage?

13. What is the term used to describe the sum of inductive reactance and capacitive reactance? Express this relationship by using the proper symbols.

14. Describe the three principal functions of electronic tubes.

15. What are the advantages of a transistor over a triode vacuum tube?

Chapter 10
TEMPERATURE

1. Explain the possible sources of error to which pressure spring thermometers are subject. How are they compensated for in a mercury-filled system?

2. Which responds fastest to a temperature change, a gas-filled, liquid-filled or a vapor pressure thermometer?

3. List the installation conditions which affect the response of pressure spring thermometers.

4. State the two laws of thermoelectricity.

5. What can be done to limit the external resistance in a thermocouple-actuated millivoltme-

ter circuit?

6. Why is it necessary to precisely regulate the circuit voltage in a thermocouple-actuated potentiometer circuit?

7. What is meant by the term "null-balance potentiometer?"

8. Since in modern electronic potentiometers for temperature measurement there are no galvanometers, how is circuit unbalance detected?

9. List the metals used for resistance thermometers and give their useful temperature ranges.

10. Why does a resistance thermometer have three leads?

Chapter 11
PRESSURE

1. a) What is the absolute pressure if the gage pressure at sea level

is 26 psi.

b) What is the reading on the

vacuum scale in inches of mercury if the gage pressure at sea level is −5 psi?

2. If the well area of a well type manometer is 50 square inches (400 times greater than the tube area), what is the actual length of each scale inch?

3. Does the substitution for water of a liquid with a specific gravity of .75 reduce or extend the range of a U-tube manometer? Does it make the instrument more or less sensitive?

4. List the useful ranges of the following elastic deformation pressure sensitive elements: a) slack diaphragm, b) metal bellows, c) Bourdon tube.

5. What is a strain gage? How may one be used to measure pressure?

6. Describe three electrical pressure measuring devices.

7. What might happen to a mercury manometer if one pressure line to the instrument is suddenly ruptured? What devices are usually included in such an instrument to prevent this?

8. What is the function of the hydraulic fluid contained inside the bellows of a typical dry-type differential pressure measuring element?

9. How do the dimensions of the bell type manometer affect the range of the meter?

10. If you wished to measure a differential pressure in a range of 0 to 200 inches of water, when the operating pressure is 2000 psi and there is a possibility of the loss of one of the pressures, what type of instrument would you use?

Chapter 12
FLOW

1. Identify the physical properties of fluids that affect their flow.

2. Describe the difference between laminar and turbulent flow. Which is more common in industrial applications?

3. What is the significance of the efficiency factor in the orifice plate equation?

4. The pressure recovery of the Venturi tube is better than that of the flow nozzle which is better than that of the orifice plate. What does this mean?

5. Describe three installations (other than those mentioned in the text) in which a pitot tube might be the best primary flow element.

6. How are small changes in the viscosity of the flowing fluid overcome in a rotameter?

7. How are small changes in the density of the flowing fluid overcome in a rotameter?

8. What is the nature of the output of a turbine flowmeter?

9. Water and liquid sodium are suitable fluids for use with an electromagnetic flowmeter. What characteristic do these have in

common which make this possible?

10. If it was required to measure the flow of water at a pressure of 1000 psi and transmit this measurement 1000 feet, what equipment would you select?

Chapter 13
ANALYSIS

1. Define a) density, b) specific gravity.

2. List the four methods used for measuring liquid density or specific gravity.

3. How could a U-tube manometer be used for measuring liquid specific gravity.

4. The viscosity of a fluid expresses its resistance to flow.What are the units used to measure viscosity?

5. List the three devices for measuring viscosity in the laboratory and in industry.

6. What is meant by the term "the pH of a solution?"

7. Why is a reference electrode necessary in the measurement of pH?

8. What is the relationship between electrical conductivity and resistance?

9. What is the operating principle of the thermal conductivity cell?

10. How is a thermal conductivity cell used to measure combustion efficiency?

11. What is the function of the column used in chromatography?

12. How is the actual measurement of each ingredient made in a chromatograph?

Chapter 14
CONTROL

1. What characteristics of a process affects its reaction rate?

2. What is the difference between dead time and lag?

3. Three process conditions must exist for two position control to be satisfactory. List them.

4. Give three examples of process load changes.

5. In proportional action control there is a fixed relationship between the position of the final element and the amount of deviation of the measured variable from the set point. Explain this statement in terms of temperature control using a control valve.

6. Why would dead time and transfer lag cause poor control when only proportional action is used?

7. Proportional Band Adjustment is a sensitivity adjustment. Is a wide band more sensitive than a narrow one? Give the reason for your answer.

8. How does the addition of reset

response to a proportional controller eliminate the disturbance caused by a load change?

9. When is it necessary to add rate response to a controller?

10. Describe the order in which the adjustments of a proportional + reset + rate controller should be made. What are the reasons for this procedure?

Chapter 15
APPLICATION

1. Give two examples of products which might be manufactured in a batch process and two which might be manufactured in a continuous process.

2. Safety is an important factor in the selection of all industrial equipment. In temperature control applications, what are some of the possible hazards which might be taken care of by proper selection of controls?

3. What is the function of the pilot on a pilot operated pressure regulator? How does it perform this function?

4. Which of the level detecting devices are applicable to both liquids and solids?

5. What is meant by the term "averaging" liquid as the term is used in liquid level control?

6. Using catalogs, select the equipment necessary for a pneumatic ratio flow control system.

7. Make a sketch of a typical cascade control system in which a temperature controller and a level controller are interconnected. Use electrical components, where possible.

8. Select a process which exists in the home and show how it could be regulated by industrial instruments. By a sketch show how you would do this.

Index